RESOURCES FOR TEACHERS ON THE BILL OF RIGHTS

Edited by

JOHN J. PATRICK

and

ROBERT S. LEMING

 ERIC Clearinghouse for Social Studies/Social Science Education

Funded in part by the Commission on the Bicentennial of the United States Constitution.

Supported by the Bill of Rights Education Collaborative, a joint project of the American Historical Association and the American Political Science Association with funding from The Pew Charitable Trusts.

1991

Ordering Information

This publication is available from:

ERIC Clearinghouse for Social Studies/Social Science Education
Indiana University
2805 East Tenth Street
Bloomington, Indiana 47408-2698
(812) 855-3838

ISBN 0-941339-12-2

**Funded in part by the Commission on the
Bicentennial of the United States Constitution.**

The major funding for development and printing of this publication was provided by the Commission on the Bicentennial of the United States Constitution through grant no. 90-CB-CX-0031. The opinions, findings and conclusions, or recommendations expressed in this publication are those of the authors and do not necessarily reflect the views of the Commission on the Bicentennial of the United States Constitution, an agency of the federal government.

Support for printing and distribution of this publication was provided by the Bill of Rights Education Collaborative, a joint project of the American Historical Association and the American Political Science Association with funding from The Pew Charitable Trusts.

Funding for the development of this publication was provided by the Office of Educational Research and Improvement, U.S. Department of Education, under contract no. RI88062009. The opinions expressed do not necessarily reflect the positions or policies of OERI or ED.

ERIC, Educational Resources Information Center, is an Information System sponsored by the Office of Educational Research and Improvement, within the U.S. Department of Education.

Contents

About the Editors

John J. Patrick is the Director of the Social Studies Development Center and the Director of the ERIC Clearinghouse for Social Studies/Social Science Education at Indiana University. He is also a Professor in Indiana University's School of Education.

Robert S. Leming is the Director of the Indiana Program for Law-Related Education at the Social Studies Development Center of Indiana University.

Acknowledgments

The Editorial Board for the project provided sound advice and constructive criticism in the development of this publication. William G. Baker, a lawyer and law educator from New Castle, Indiana, served as chairperson of the Editorial Board. Baker was assisted by Mary Fortney, Social Studies Consultant, Indiana Department of Education; Rosemarie Kuntz, teacher of government, Perry Meridian High School, Indianapolis; and Connie Yeaton, elementary school teacher, Bartholomew County School Corporation, Indiana.

Vickie Schlene and Carla Homstad provided editorial services that contributed significantly to development of this publication. Barbara Frye served ably as project secretary and typist.

The editors are pleased to recognize the following persons for permitting use in this volume of lessons on the Bill of Rights previously published in books of lessons for teachers: Charles N. Quigley, Center for Civic Education; Carolyn Pereira, Constitutional Rights Foundation; Sheilah Mann, Project '87 of the American Political Science Association and the American Historical Association; and Karen Trusty Braeckel, Newspapers in Education Program of the Indianapolis Newspapers, Inc. These reprinted lessons are presented in Part IV of this volume. Complete credits and acknowledgments of authors are provided in Part IV.

The editors gratefully acknowledge the support of (1) the Commission on the Bicentennial of the United States Constitution and (2) the Bill of Rights Education Collaborative, a joint project of the American Historical Association and the American Political Science Association with funding from The Pew Charitable Trusts.

Funded in part by the Commission on the Bicentennial of the United States Constitution.

Supported by the Bill of Rights Education Collaborative, a joint project of the American Historical Association and the American Political Science Association with funding from The Pew Charitable Trusts.

Introduction

"[A] bill of rights is what the people are entitled to against every government on earth, general or particular, and what no just government should refuse, or rest on inference." Thomas Jefferson wrote these words to James Madison, in a letter from Paris, France (December 20, 1787). He urged Madison to support the addition of provisions about individual rights to the federal Constitution of 1787. He stressed that a federal Bill of Rights would provide "clearly and without the aid of sophisms for freedom of religion, freedom of the press, protection against standing armies, restriction against monopolies, the eternal and unremitting force of the habeas corpus laws, and trials by jury in all matters of fact triable by the laws of the land. . . ."

Jefferson's letter and the tide of public opinion in the United States combined with political events to convince Madison to become a staunch advocate for a federal Bill of Rights, which Madison proposed to the First Federal Congress in June 1789. By the end of September 1789, two-thirds of both Houses of Congress had approved twelve amendments to the Constitution to be submitted to the states for ratification. By the end of 1791, the required three-fourths of the states had ratified ten of these proposed amendments, and they were added to the Constitution. The people now had their federal Bill of Rights, legal guarantees against the power of government to deprive individuals of certain rights, such as freedom of speech, freedom of the press, religious liberty, and right to trial by jury in criminal and civil cases.

The Bill of Rights is an instrument against tyranny by a few rulers of the people. However, in a government of, by, and for the people, a democracy, there is supposed to be rule by representatives of a majority of the people. What if the people's representatives decide to deprive unpopular individuals of certain rights, such as religious liberty or freedom of speech? The result would be tyranny and injustice, even if practiced in the name of the majority of the people.

The federal Bill of Rights, and the Constitution to which it was added, were designed to limit the power of the people's representatives in government and thereby protect the civil liberties and rights of everyone. Thus, a paradoxical relationship between majorities and minorities was established. This is the generic question posed by the majority rule-minority rights paradox of a constitutional democracy: At what point, and under what conditions, should the power of the democratic majority in government be limited by the higher law of the Constitution to secure the rights of individuals in the minority? Alternative responses to this basic question have raised critical constitutional issues throughout the history of the United States about when and how to limit the power of the people's government in order to protect the inherent rights and liberties of each person.

The Supreme Court is called upon to resolve the critical issues raised by the inevitable conflicts in a constitutional government that conjoins the contradictory ideals of majority rule with protection of minority rights. In making its case-by-case decisions, the Court never decides ultimately in favor of the abstract majority or minority. Rather, particular instances of majority rule about minority rights are either voided as unconstitutional or upheld as legitimate decisions.

In a letter to Thomas Jefferson (October 17, 1788), James Madison warned that the danger of majoritarian tyranny was a peculiar malady of popular government. He wrote: "Wherever the real power in a Government lies, there is the danger of oppression. In our Governments the real power lies in the majority of the Community, and the invasion of private rights is *chiefly* to be apprehended, not from acts of Government contrary to the sense of its constituents, but from acts in which the government is the mere instrument of the major number of the constituents."

From the time of Madison and Jefferson to the present, citizens of our American constitutional democracy have confronted the challenges of the majority rule-minority rights paradox. They have deliberated, debated, and decided issues about the constitutional rights of individuals in a civil society. These ongoing controversies have shaped and reshaped the interpretation and application of constitutional rights in the United States from the founding period to the present. This dramatic story about the development of individual liberties and rights should be at the center of elementary and secondary school courses on American history. The principles and issues of civil liberties and rights in our contemporary United States should be focal points of the civics and government curriculum in schools.

This volume, *Resources for Teachers on the Bill of Rights,* includes ideas and information that can enhance education about the constitutional rights of individuals in American history and the current system of government in the United States. What are the contents of this volume? How can the contents contribute to improved teaching and learning about Bill of Rights topics and issues? Following this **Introduction,** there are nine additional parts, which present knowledge and materials on the Bill of Rights for teachers in elementary and secondary schools.

Part I, Background Papers, consists of four essays for teachers on the origins, enactment, and development of the federal Bill of Rights. A fifth paper discusses the substance and strategies for teaching Bill of Rights topics and issues in schools. Teachers will find these papers to be useful sources of ideas and facts on various Bill of Rights topics and issues. Thus, these papers can contribute substantially to the ongoing development of curricula and lesson plans of elementary and secondary school teachers.

Part II, A Bill of Rights Chronology, is a timetable of key dates and events in the making of the federal Bill of Rights, 1787-1792. Teachers can use this chronology as a reference tool in planning classroom lessons. Some teachers might also decide to copy and distribute this chronology to students, who can use it as a handy source of information and aid to their studies of the creation of the Bill of Rights.

Part III, Documents, includes eleven key primary sources about the origins, enactment, and substance of the federal Bill of Rights. Teachers can use these primary documents as sources of ideas and information for planning and executing classroom lessons. The primary documents can also be duplicated and distributed to students as assigned readings in preparation for classroom discussions or as sources of data for writing assignments. For example, students might be asked to compare the Virginia Declaration of Rights with the federal Bill of Rights in order to determine the extent to which the federal document reflects the contents of the state document. This comparison of two primary documents could be the basis for a roundtable classroom discussion. Students could also be asked to conclude this exercise by writing an essay about similarities and differences in the contents of the two documents.

Part IV, Lessons on the Bill of Rights, consists of nine exemplary lessons. There are three lessons for use with elementary school students, three lessons for use with junior high/middle school students, and three lessons for use with high school students. Each lesson includes a teaching plan and materials to copy and distribute to students. Each lesson has been tested and evaluated favorably by teachers and their students. They have been published previously and used extensively by teachers and their students throughout the United States. These lessons are reprinted here by permission of the authors and publishers. Users of this volume also have permission to reproduce and distribute these lessons to students in their classes.

Part V, Papers in ERIC on Constitutional Rights, is an annotated bibliography of materials in the world's largest database on education. This database, known by its acronym, ERIC (Educational Resources Information Center), is managed by the Office of Educational Research and Improvement in the U.S. Department of Education. The items in this bibliography can be used by teachers to derive ideas and information about how to teach about constitutional rights. This bibliography includes papers presented at national conferences and conventions of professional associations, reports of curriculum centers and projects, and publications of various education agencies. Information is provided about how to obtain these materials through ERIC.

Part VI, Select Annotated Bibliography of Curriculum Materials, is a guide to teaching and learning resources on the Bill of Rights. These materials include video programs, poster sets, curriculum guides, and books of lesson plans. Information is provided about how to obtain these materials.

Part VII, Periodical Literature on Teaching the Bill of Rights, is an annotated bibliography of articles in journals and magazines. Each item in this bibliography can be found in the *Current Index to Journals in Education.* These articles are a rich source of ideas and data about teaching and learning the Bill of Rights.

Part VIII, Bill of Rights Bookshelf for Teachers, is a select annotated bibliography of scholarly books. The items in this list are excellent sources of knowledge for teachers to use in planning lessons and developing the curriculum.

Part IX, Directory of Key Organizations and Persons, consists of various lists of individuals who can provide services to educators about teaching and learning the Bill of Rights. Addresses and telephone numbers are provided.

The different parts of this volume constitute a rich reservoir of resources, which will serve various needs of elementary and secondary school teachers. Virtually every teacher of history, civics, and government will find something in this publication that will contribute importantly to improvement of his or her planning of lessons and execution of learning activities on Bill of Rights topics and issues.

John J. Patrick
Director, ERIC
Clearinghouse for
Social Studies/Social
Science Education
and Director, Social
Studies Development
Center of Indiana
University

Congress OF THE United States

begun and held at the City of New-York, on

Wednesday the Fourth of March, one thousand seven hundred and eighty nine

THE Conventions of a number of the States, having at the time of their adopting the Constitution, expressed a desire, in order to prevent misconstruction or abuse of its powers, that further declaratory and restrictive clauses should be added: And as extending the ground of public confidence in the Government, will best ensure the beneficent ends of its institution.

RESOLVED by the Senate and House of Representatives of the United States of America, in Congress assembled, two thirds of both Houses concurring, that the following Articles be proposed to the Legislatures of the several States, as amendments to the Constitution of the United States, all, or any of which Articles, when ratified by three fourths of the said Legislatures, to be valid to all intents and purposes, as part of the said Constitution, viz.

ARTICLES in addition to, and amendment of the Constitution of the United States of America, proposed by Congress, and ratified by the Legislatures of the several States, pursuant to the fifth Article of the original Constitution.

Article the first..... After the first enumeration required by the first Article of the Constitution, there shall be one Representative for every thirty thousand, until the number shall amount to one hundred, after which, the proportion shall be so regulated by Congress, that there shall be not less than one hundred Representatives, nor less than one Representative for every forty thousand persons, until the number of Representatives shall amount to two hundred, after which the proportion shall be so regulated by Congress, that there shall not be less than two hundred Representatives, nor more than one Representative for every fifty thousand persons.

Article the second.... No law, varying the compensation for the services of the Senators and Representatives, shall take effect, until an election of Representatives shall have intervened.

Article the third.... Congress shall make no law respecting an establishment of religion, or prohibiting the free exercise thereof; or abridging the freedom of speech, or of the press; or the right of the people peaceably to assemble, and to petition the Government for a redress of grievances.

Article the fourth.... A well regulated militia, being necessary to the security of a free State, the right of the people to keep and bear arms, shall not be infringed.

Article the fifth.... No Soldier shall, in time of peace be quartered in any house, without the consent of the owner, nor in time of war, but in a manner to be prescribed by law.

Article the sixth.... The right of the people to be secure in their persons, houses, papers, and effects, against unreasonable searches and seizures, shall not be violated, and no warrants shall issue, but upon probable cause, supported by oath or affirmation, and particularly describing the place to be searched, and the persons or things to be seized.

Article the seventh.... No person shall be held to answer for a capital, or otherwise infamous crime, unless on a presentment or indictment of a grand jury, except in cases arising in the land or naval forces, or in the Militia, when in actual service in time of War or public danger; nor shall any person be subject for the same offence to be twice put in jeopardy of life or limb; nor shall be compelled in any criminal case to be a witness against himself, nor be deprived of life, liberty, or property, without due process of law; nor shall private property be taken for public use, without just compensation.

Article the eighth.... In all criminal prosecutions, the accused shall enjoy the right to a speedy and public trial, by an impartial jury of the State and district wherein the crime shall have been committed, which district shall have been previously ascertained by law, and to be informed of the nature and cause of the accusation; to be confronted with the witnesses against him; to have compulsory process for obtaining witnesses in his favor, and to have the assistance of counsel for his defence.

Article the ninth.... In suits at common law, where the value in controversy shall exceed twenty dollars, the right of trial by jury shall be preserved, and no fact tried by a jury shall be otherwise re-examined in any court of the United States, than according to the rules of the common law.

Article the tenth.... Excessive bail shall not be required, nor excessive fines imposed, nor cruel and unusual punishments inflicted.

Article the eleventh.... The enumeration in the Constitution, of certain rights, shall not be construed to deny or disparage others retained by the people.

Article the twelfth.... The powers not delegated to the United States by the Constitution, nor prohibited by it to the States, are reserved to the States respectively, or to the people.

ATTEST,

Frederick Augustus Muhlenberg, Speaker of the House of Representatives.

John Adams, Vice-President of the United States, and President of the Senate.

John Beckley, Clerk of the House of Representatives.

Sam. A. Otis, Secretary of the Senate.

The U.S. Bill of Rights, as it was submitted by the federal government to the States for ratification.

Part I
Background Papers

I

Background Papers

Part I includes background papers on the origins, contents, and historical development of the federal Bill of Rights. In addition, there is one background paper on what and how to teach in schools about the Bill of Rights. These papers present ideas and information for teachers that can help them to improve their lesson planning and classroom teaching on Bill of Rights topics and issues. The five background papers, and their authors, are listed below:

1. "The Origins of the United States Bill of Rights" by Donald S. Lutz, Professor of Political Science, University of Houston.
2. "George Mason's 'Objections' and the Bill of Rights" by Robert Allen Rutland, Professor of History, University of Virginia.
3. "James Madison and the Bill of Rights" by Jack N. Rakove, Professor of History, Stanford University.
4. "The Range and Reach of the Bill of Rights" by Russell L. Hansen, Professor of Political Science, Indiana University.
5. "Teaching the Bill of Rights" by John J. Patrick, Professor of Education and Director, Social Studies Development Center, Indiana University.

In Background Paper 1, Donald Lutz discusses antecedents of the American Bill of Rights—the ideas and events in the Anglo-American heritage that shaped constitutional rights during the founding period of the United States. Professor Lutz demonstrates the importance of the American colonial experience in development of the ideas that were included in the federal Bill of Rights. He also distinguishes clearly the differences in American and English conceptions of individual rights.

Background Paper 2, by Robert Rutland, emphasizes the contribution of George Mason to the federal Bill of Rights. Professor Rutland discusses the influence on the Federalists of Mason's "objections" to the Constitution of 1787 during the debate on ratification of the new frame of government.

The subject of Background Paper 3, by Jack Rakove, is the role of James Madison in the enactment of the federal Bill of Rights. Professor Rakove examines Madison's ideas on constitutional rights, especially his concerns about the dangers of majoritarian tyranny in a popular government. He also tells the story of Madison's conversion from an opponent to a supporter of a federal Bill of Rights.

In Background Paper 4, Russell Hansen treats the development of the Bill of Rights from an instrument that only limits federal government power to one that also applies to state and local governments throughout the United States. Professor Hansen analyzes the important twentieth-century Supreme Court decisions that have used the "due process" clause of the 14th Amendment to apply provisions of the federal Bill of Rights to the states. He also raises constitutional and political issues about the nationalization of the federal Bill of Rights.

Background Paper 5, by John Patrick, discusses the pedagogical and curricular applications of the Bill of Rights. Professor Patrick assesses shortcomings in teaching and learning the Bill of Rights in schools. He offers ideas about how to overcome these educational deficiencies to improve teaching and learning about Bill of Rights topics and issues.

Background Paper 1

The Origins of the United States Bill of Rights

Donald S. Lutz

The English Background

As with the Declaration of Independence and the Constitution, the first thing to clarify about the Bill of Rights is that it was neither the sudden, original, spontaneous product of a few minds, nor an updated American version of the Magna Carta. The Bill of Rights, enacted in 1791, had a long historical pedigree, but that pedigree lay substantially more in documents written by those on American shores.

One way of demonstrating the relative influence of the Magna Carta on the American Bill of Rights is a count of overlapping provisions. The Bill of Rights has twenty-seven separate rights listed in its ten amendments. Of these twenty-seven rights, only four can be traced to Magna Carta using the most generous interpretation of the language in that famous document. (See Table 1 at the end of this paper.) Looking at it from the other direction, only four of the sixty-three provisions of Magna Carta ended up in the U.S. Bill of Rights. The lack of overlap is not surprising since Magna Carta and the U.S. Bill of Rights had enormously different functions. The former defined the relationship between a king and his barons, whereas the latter placed limits on all branches of a government *vis a vis* an entire citizenry.

Despite the enormous historical importance of Magna Carta, in content, form, and intent it is only a distant forerunner of the U.S. Bill of Rights. Nor is the overlap with the rest of English common law, although important, that impressive. In addition to the four rights that can be traced to Magna Carta, another right in the U.S. Bill of Rights can be traced to the 1628 English Petition of Right, and two to the 1689 English Bill of Rights.[1] This brings to seven the number of rights among the twenty-seven in the U.S. Bill of Rights that can be traced to a major English common law document, although the highly respected scholar, Bernard Schwartz, is willing to make such a linkage for only five of these seven rights.

Furthermore, as writers on the English common law always point out, Magna Carta had to be continually reconfirmed, at least forty-seven times by one count, because the document was ignored for long periods of time, and its contents were at best honored in the breach.[2] Indeed, despite the written guarantees for certain rights contained in major documents of English common law, at the time of the American revolution these rights were either not protected at all, or were not protected to the level that had become the case in America.[3]

Even in those instances where protection of a right in England approached that in America, there was a fundamental difference in whose actions were limited. Partly for this reason James Madison said that there were too many differences between common law and the U.S. Bill of Rights to warrant comparison.[4]

> [The] truth is, they [the British] have gone no farther than to raise a barrier against the power of the Crown; the power of the Legislature is left altogether too indefinite. Although I know whenever the great rights, the trial by jury, freedom of the press, or liberty of conscience, come in question [in Parliament] the invasion of them is resisted by able advocates, yet their Magna Charta does not contain any one provision for the security of those rights, respecting which the people of America are most alarmed . . . those choicest privileges of the people are unguarded in the British Constitution. But although . . . it may not be thought necessary to provide limits for the legislative

power in that country, yet a different opinion prevails in the United States.

At the very least, then, the attribution of the American Bill of Rights to English common law and its major documents, such as Magna Carta, must be supplemented; and as Table 1 indicates, it is to documents written on American shores that we must turn. (See Table 1 at the end of this paper.)

The Immediate American Background

It is natural to assume that James Madison used the amendments proposed by the state ratifying conventions when he produced his own list of proposed amendments for Congress. After all, eight of these ratifying conventions had together proposed ninety-seven distinct amendments, and it was the opposition to the Constitution represented by these proposed amendments which Madison needed to address. However, as Table 2 illustrates, the forty-two distinct rights contained in Madison's nine proposed amendments, listed in the order he gave them as numbers 1-42 in the table, bear only slight relation to what was proposed by the ratifying conventions. (See Table 2 at the end of this paper.)

Twenty-six of the amendments proposed by the ratifying conventions ended up on Madison's list, but seventy-one did not. Sixteen rights proposed by Madison were not suggested by any ratifying convention. Nor was there a very "dense" connection between Madison's list and the amendments proposed by the ratifying conventions as can be illustrated by using a very crude measure of association.

The data on state ratifying conventions in Table 2 constitute a matrix that is eight cells wide and ninety-seven cells from top to bottom. The more cells that have an X in them for the matrix defined by the top forty-two rows (that is, the more state ratifying conventions that proposed one of the amendments that ended up in Madison's list), the denser the relationship between Madison's list and the convention proposals. Seventeen percent of the cells are filled (fifty-six out of three hundred and thirty-six cells), which does not suggest a very "dense" relationship between the ratifying conventions' proposals and Madison's list of rights. On the other hand, twenty-four percent of the cells in the matrix defined by the last fifty-five rows have an X in them (107 out of 440 cells). These proposals, not included in Madison's list, were therefore more likely to be recommended by a state ratifying convention than those he did include. This suggests that Madison avoided their more preferred suggestions.

The last conclusion can also be supported by looking at the proposed amendments made by the ratifying conventions that most directly addressed the protection of state sovereignty. Numbers thirty-one, thirty-two, and forty-one through fifty-three seem to be the best candidates, and only three of these fourteen proposals made it onto Madison's list. The density for these fourteen proposals is forty-two percent (47 out of 112 cells), which makes them two and a half times as likely to be recommended by a state as those actually picked by Madison, and about twice as likely as the average proposal in the table as a whole (163 out of 776 cells = 21%)—which suggests a strong interest in state sovereignty by the state ratifying conventions, but a disinterest on Madison's part.

Madison apparently wished to avoid the amendments proposed by the ratifying conventions, but he needed to make some connection with state interests to mollify the Anti-Federalists. The tactic he fastened upon was to exploit seams in the Anti-Federalist position on what amendments to make. Americans who argued most vigorously against the proposed Constitution offered three different kinds of amendments that were often intertwined and confused.

One type of amendment was aimed at checking the power of the national government by withholding a specific power. Examples included prohibitions on direct taxes, monopolies, and borrowing money on credit.

A second type of amendment altered an institution in such a way as to pull its teeth. Examples included making senators ineligible for concurrent terms, giving state and national courts concurrent jurisdiction, and requiring a two-thirds vote in both houses for any bill dealing with navigation or commerce.

A third type of amendment was one suitable for a bill of rights as we now understand it. Examples included protection of the rights to speak, write, publish, assemble, and petition (rights that safeguarded the ability of a people to organize politically); as well as prohibitions on self-incrimination, double punishment, excessive bail, and searches without a warrant (rights that defined an impartial legal system). One can see in Madison's selection process a clear inclination toward the third over the first two kinds of amendments.

In effect, then, Madison avoided any alteration in the institutions defined by the Constitution, largely ignored specific prohibitions on national power, and opted instead for a list of rights that would connect clearly with the preferences of state governments, but would not increase state power *vis a vis* the national government defined in the Constitution. The discussion about powers and rights was subtly shifted to one only about rights.

This finesse upset some Anti-Federalists who argued that he had "thrown a tub to a whale" (that is, had created a distraction to deflect public attention from the real issue), but it worked very well for one critical reason—Madison used the bills of rights attached to the state constitutions as his model. The Anti-Federalists had difficulty opposing Madison's use of this model. It was a model of their own making, and it was part of what they were demanding. Madison offered the Anti-Federalists the "paper barriers" he felt were ineffective in existing state constitutions, and the Anti-Federalists had to either accept such amendments as useful or admit the truth of Madison's paper barrier argument.

The immediate background for the United States Bill of Rights was formed by the state bills of rights written between 1776 and 1787. Madison effectively extracted the least common denominator from these state bills of rights, excepting those rights which might reduce the power of the national government. Almost every one of the twenty-seven rights in the U.S. Bill of Rights could be found in two or three state documents, and most of them in five or more.[5]

The state bills of rights typically contained a more extensive listing than did the national version. Maryland's 1776 document listed forty-nine rights in forty-two sections, Massachusetts' document listed forty-nine rights in thirty sections, and New Hampshire listed fifty rights in the thirty-eight sections to its 1784 document.[6] Virginia's (1776) forty-two rights and Pennsylvania's (1776) thirty-five rights came closest to duplicating the content of the national Bill of Rights.[7]

Table 3 shows clearly the strong connection between the state bills of rights and Madison's proposed amendments. If we look at the matrix formed by the forty-two rights on Madison's list and the seven state bills of rights, fifty-nine percent of the cells in the matrix are filled (174 out of 294 cells) compared to the seventeen percent density between Madison's list and the amendments proposed by the state ratifying conventions. If we construct a matrix using the contents of the state bills of rights and the rights on Madison's list that were eventually ratified as the U.S. Bill of Rights, we find that the percentage of the matrix filled rises to seventy-two percent (130 out of 182 cells), compared with a seventeen percent filled matrix (36 out of 208 cells) when comparing the state ratifying convention proposals with the

rights actually ratified as part of the national Bill of Rights. (See Table 3 at the end of this paper.)

A final comparison between Table 2 and Table 3 indicates another connection between the state and national constitutions. The listing for the two tables is the same for the first forty-two rights since these are, in each case, the rights contained in Madison's proposed amendments in the order in which he proposed them. However, the rights listed after number forty-two vary in the two tables depending upon the actual content of the documents being examined.

In Table 3 rights numbers forty-three through fifty-two have a very high density, and they also happen to be addressed in the body of the U.S. Constitution proper, as are fifty-five, sixty-one through sixty-five, and eighty-one. In other words, many provisions commonly found in state bills of rights had already been addressed in the Constitution, and did not need to be included in the national Bill of Rights. Also, only a few of these provisions from the state bills of rights are directly contradicted by anything in the Constitution. The importance of the state constitutions for the national Constitution is thus even stronger than is apparent from an examination of the Bill of Rights alone. On the other hand, if we look at the list of proposals from the ratifying conventions only eight are addressed in the Constitution proper, while at least twenty of the remaining proposals are directly contradicted by provisions in the Constitution. The state constitutions and their respective bills of rights, not the amendments proposed by state ratifying conventions, are the immediate sources from which the U.S. Bill of Rights was derived.

The Colonial Background to the State Bills of Rights

Where did these state bills of rights come from? They came from bills of rights written by American colonists. Because of English preoccupation with internal political disorder from 1640 to 1688, and then with French competition from 1700 to 1760, the colonists were left with a surprisingly high level of political independence. In addition to writing what amounted to functional constitutions between 1620 and 1775, the colonists also wrote many bills of rights, and these colonial documents stood as background to the state bills of rights.[8] Examples are the New York Charter of Liberties and Privileges (1683), the Laws and Liberties of New Hampshire (1682), William Penn's Charter of Liberties (1682), the General Laws and Liberties of Connecticut (1672), the

Maryland Toleration Act (1649), Laws and Liberties of Massachusetts (1647), and the Massachusetts Body of Liberties (1641).[9] This last document—adopted a century and a half before the American national Bill of Rights, and half a century before the English Bill of Rights (1689)—contained all but four of the twenty-seven rights found in the national document.

Where, then, do the rights in the 1641 Massachusetts Body of Liberties and later colonial documents come from? It is interesting that these colonial documents frequently cite the Bible to justify their various provisions. However, there is no more a listing of rights in the Bible than there is in the writings of Locke, Hume, or Montesquieu. Basically, American notions of rights developed from their own political experience as colonists, an experience significantly affected by the peculiar and historically important conditions in which they found themselves.[10]

First of all, these were a religious people. In attempting to lead exemplary lives, they were acutely sensitive to human relationships; and they believed these relationships should be based upon God's laws as expressed in the Bible. There is in the Bible a strong sense of fairness and a respect for all individuals that easily leads to community rules that look like what we now call rights. Furthermore, the religion these people professed emphasized certain things supportive of a rights orientation.

All humans were viewed as having been made in the image and likeness of God, and therefore a certain equality in value should be accorded every person. Those in government were thus not of a different order from those they governed, and did not have inherent prerogatives or rights different from others. A fundamental equality lay in every person's ability to say "yes" or "no" to God's grace on their own. From this came the ability to give or withhold consent for human laws, and in turn the notion that government should rest upon the consent of those governed was a straightforward deduction.

These tendencies were reinforced by the belief in the ability of each individual to read the Bible and have an independent relationship with God. Not only was there no need for priests to interpret the Bible, each person was viewed as having an independent will. Government could not interfere in this fundamental independence. Also, since God's law was accessible to every person's understanding, so should the human law which was supposed to be in conformity with God's law. There was, by implication, no more need for a class of lawyers to interpret earthly law than there was need for a priestly caste

to interpret the divine law in the Bible. The process for making and enforcing human laws was seen as susceptible to codification, which would treat everyone the same and be understandable to all. These codifications were the first American bills of rights.

In addition to religion, the desperate situation of colonists isolated in pockets scattered along a thousand-mile coastline put a high premium on cooperation if all were to survive. The earliest colony, in Virginia, initially tried a military style of organization, but this soon gave way to a system of eliciting cooperation by treating people well. Early bills of rights were an effective and efficient means for producing order, stability, cooperative behavior, and economic progress.

Finally, the status of American colonies as economic enterprises, especially as seen from England, tended to emphasize economic output rather than political control as the primary consideration. That a loose political control from England produced the most economic output only enhanced the sense colonists had of running their own lives. A confluence of circumstances led Americans to require, develop, and expect a set of rights not found in England, and this set of rights was characterized by a breadth, detail, equality, fairness, and effectiveness in limiting all branches of government that distinguished it from English common law.

No one represented the disjunction between English and American rights better than William Penn, who, because of his Quaker religion, suffered through a trial in England that shocks us today. When he founded Pennsylvania Penn granted religious freedom, something lacking in England, as part of a bill of rights grounded in his religion and experiences. He also consulted the existing codes of Massachusetts, Connecticut, Maryland, and Virginia; and possibly because of common religious assumptions, his list of rights largely overlapped these earlier ones. His Frame of Government (1682) contained 55% (15 out of 27) of the rights in the U.S. Bill of Rights, whereas the English Bill of Rights seven years later had only one-third as much overlap (5 out of 27). English common law did form part of the background to our bills of rights, but in America the common law breathed in a powerful air of equality and independence that transformed it into a profoundly different American version.

Contrasting English and American Notions of Liberty

The American view of rights was distinguished from that in Britain by two important conceptual differences. One fundamental difference lay in the respective notions of liberty. In England the concept of liberty had two quite contradictory meanings. One meaning had to do with the general condition of men based upon natural law, or a condition of all Englishmen based upon their common legal and constitutional past. The second meaning had to do with the medieval idea of a hierarchy of liberties which varied according to an individual's or a group's station and purpose in life. Parliament had certain liberties, as did the monarch. The aristocracy had certain liberties, commoners had others. For example, the property rights of aristocratic women were much broader than women not of the aristocracy. Also, certain localities often had special liberties granted by charter. A given town might contain in its charter liberties not found elsewhere, or a shire or locality might retain special liberties as a result of a connection by marriage to the Crown at some time past. A freeman could, by moving to a new locality, alter his liberties.

In this sense liberty was an exemption from normal obligations or punishments. Frequently the distribution of liberties was related to the distribution of property—a holdover from the feudal system of fiefs. In a broader sense this notion viewed liberty as submission to duly constituted authority as opposed to submission to force. It was not, however, submission to government erected by consent. Indeed, under this notion a man was not considered as being deprived of liberty because he was denied self-government. Magna Carta assumed this second notion of liberty, as did much of English common law.

America, however, was without an aristocracy, cut off from the remnants of feudal relationships in England, populated by a people largely holding to dissenting Protestant theology with the implications noted above, and faced with problems of survival that required cooperation rather than contention over relative rights. The American colonies therefore, failed to include this second British notion of liberty in their political development, at least not to any significant degree. The governing boards back in England, many of the British-trained lawyers in America, and certainly the Crown-appointed governors of the colonies still had a strong sense of liberty as an exemption from law, but there was no room or prudential basis for it in America. American bills of rights, then, did not include this second notion of liberty, but worked from the first. The Massachusetts Body of Liberties did not look like the Magna Carta, and the national Bill of Rights did not look like the English Bill of Rights (1689), and the

absence of this conflicting view of liberty was a major reason.

There was another basic difference, and this too stemmed from the religious background and tenuous situation of most colonists. When we look at the earliest colonial documents of political foundation, such as the Mayflower Compact (1620), the Pilgrim Code of Law (1636), and Fundamental Orders of Connecticut (1639), we find that they usually involved the self-creation of a people—in the double sense of forming a new people, and then of laying out the common values, interests, and goals which bind them as a people.[11] These self-defining or self-creating people were in the habit of providing in later documents updated versions of their fundamental, shared values, and it is such lists of shared values that evolved into what we now call bills of rights.

It made sense for a religious people to cite the Bible in a bill of rights. Since the Bible was central to what they shared, the values they held could be justified by identifying where in the Bible these values were enunciated or implied. As the population became more diverse and less religious, the biblical references might disappear, but not the tendency for bills of rights to use admonitory language rather than legally binding terminology. Consider for example the following typical excerpts from state bills of rights:

> XV. That the freedom of the press is one of the great bulwarks of liberty, and therefore ought never to be restrained (North Carolina, 1776).[12]

> VI. That the legislative, executive, and judicial powers of government, ought to be forever separate and distinct from each other (Maryland, 1776).[13]

> IX. All elections ought to be free; and all the inhabitants of this commonwealth, having such qualifications as they shall establish by their frame of government, have an equal right to elect officers, and to be elected, for public employments (Massachusetts, 1780).[14]

> XIV. That a frequent recurrence to fundamental principles, and a firm adherence to justice, moderation, temperance, industry, and frugality are absolutely necessary to preserve the blessings of liberty and keep government free (Pennsylvania, 1776).[15]

These may strike some people as peculiar statements for bills of rights, yet they are all from state bills of rights, and use language that is typical rather than exceptional. One can see clearly from the use of "ought" and "should"—instead of "shall" and "will"—that the language is admonitory; thus, it is not legally enforceable. One can also easily see how these bills of rights are statements of shared values and fundamental principles. We are here a long way from common law.

Contending Views of Rights in 1789

In 1789, on the eve of the writing of America's Bill of Rights, there were the following contending positions in the Anglo-Saxon world on the nature of rights. One was associated with the common law view of liberty derived from medieval society and embodied in Magna Carta. In this view, the Crown was limited by the rights associated with the aristocracy in the feudal hierarchy, and was attached to the distribution of property. Even though this was the stronger of two strains in common law, it was not part of the American notion of rights.

A second position on rights was associated with the other common law view of liberty—that all Englishmen possessed from their common legal and constitutional past a set of rights that protected them from an arbitrary Crown, especially in the operation of the court system. This position had been read into Magna Carta even though it was not there, most notably by Sir Edward Coke. In Coke's view, the common law protected all Englishmen against royal prerogative. Since this view was used primarily by Parliament in its struggle with the Crown, rights were not seen as limiting Parliament. Since Americans lacked an aristocracy upon which to rest the first version of common law, the second version was dominant in the colonies. However, this view gave them no basis for resisting Parliament in its attempts to tax the colonies. Americans were left with either the older version of common law, which the Glorious Revolution in England had rendered anachronistic, or with a different grounding for rights than that found in the common law.

Fortunately, the colonists had available a view of rights that they had been more or less using for a century and a half, and that was undergirded by both theology and rationalist philosophy. In this third position, all human law had to be judged in terms of its conformity with God's will, which served as a higher law. By implication all branches of government, including the legislature, were limited by this higher law. Since there was no group of men with a special ability to determine God's will or the meaning of the Bible, all men had an equal role in determining whether or not a given human law was in conformity with God's will. A straightforward deduction led to all branches of government being beholden to popular consent, and to rights being

defined as the set of guarantees that protected the free and effective operation of popular consent. Bills of rights, according to this view, were lists of common commitments that both protected the operation of popular consent, and codified what popular consent had already identified as commonly held commitments. By 1776, the language used to express this position had become thoroughly secular, as exemplified in the following excerpt from a state constitution:

> IV. That all power being originally inherent in, and consequently derived from the people: therefore all officers of government, whether legislative or executive, are their trustees and servants, and at all times accountable to them (Pennsylvania, 1776).[16]

Also, preambles to state constitutions frequently had statements similar to the following from the 1780 Massachusetts document:

> The body politic is formed by a voluntary association of individuals; it is a social compact, by which the whole people covenants with each citizen, and each citizen with the whole people, that all shall be governed by certain laws for the common good.[17]

At first blush these last two quotations might appear to be taken from John Locke, but such language was used in America long before Locke's *Second Treatise* was published. The communitarian, popular consent approach to rights was initially derived from dissenting Protestant theology as it was applied to the design of political institutions in seventeenth- and eighteenth-century North America. This view emphasized the needs of the community rather than the rights of individuals, but it did see all branches of government as limited in their operation by universally shared and unchanging human rights.

The similarity in language to that used by John Locke, Algernon Sidney, and other English political theorists is a measure of the extent to which religion and rationalism reached similar political conclusions in late eighteenth-century America. The terms and concepts of Sidney, Locke, Bolingbroke, Milton, and a host of others were efficiently blended with that of dissenting Protestantism, as illustrated by the opening articles in the bills of rights of two prominent state constitutions:

> I. That all men are born equally free and independent, and have certain natural, inherent and inalienable rights, amongst which are the enjoying and defending of life and liberty, acquiring, possessing, and protecting property,

and pursuing and obtaining happiness and safety.

II. That all men have a natural and unalienable right to worship Almighty God according to the dictates of their own consciences and understanding (Pennsylvania, 1776).[18]

Article I. All men are born free and equal, and have certain natural, essential, and unalienable rights; among which may be reckoned the right of enjoying and defending their lives and liberties; that of acquiring, possessing, and protecting property; in fine, that of seeking and obtaining their safety and happiness.

II. It is the right as well as the duty of all men in society, publicly, and at stated seasons, to worship the Supreme Being . . . And no subject shall be hurt, molested, or restrained, in his person, liberty, or estate, for worshipping God in the manner and season most agreeable to the dictates of his own conscience (Massachusetts, 1780).[19]

The rationalist version of this third position on rights will be termed Lockian, although the language just cited was probably taken from Algernon Sidney's *Discourses on Government*. The Lockian approach emphasized the rights of the individual rather than the rights of the community, although the difference between the Lockian and covenantal versions was in fact a matter of emphasis, not fundamental difference in this regard. Locke and Sidney also saw all branches of government as limited by rights, a position that was roundly ignored in England during the eighteenth century. What neither the religious nor the rationalist approaches to this position envisioned was having rights legally enforced by the courts rather than by elections, constitutional revision, or armed rebellion. This important step in the development of American bills of rights was in the future, and to a certain extent would rest upon an accident of history.

Drafting the U.S. Bill of Rights

The American view of rights, derived in part from English common law, undergirded by dissenting Protestant theology, and reinforced by rationalist political philosophy, was essentially developed in the local political arena, and codified at the colony-wide level. Independence in 1776 did not alter the situation in this regard. The articulation, codification, and protection of rights proceeded at the state and local levels. It should not surprise us, then, to learn that it was state and local leaders, not national political leaders, who insisted upon a national bill of rights.

The United States Constitution, as originally written, contained a number of rights scattered through the document, but did not have a fully articulated bill of rights. The Federalists, including Madison and Hamilton, felt that a bill of rights at the national level was unnecessary, and perhaps dangerous.[20]

A national bill of rights was unnecessary for two reasons. First, there were extensive bills of rights already in existence at the state level. Second, the political process defined by the national constitution was viewed as so fair, balanced, and limited that it could not impinge upon rights; and if it did, the states could always use their own bills of rights to protect their respective citizens.

A national bill of rights was potentially dangerous—also for two reasons. First, any listing was bound to leave out rights that would in the future be considered important; but their absence from the bill of rights would imply that they were not protected. Second, since bills of rights were statements of commonly held values and commitments, and there were differences in these values and commitments from state to state, a national bill of rights would either have to contain the least common denominator, and thus leave out things considered important by many people, or else local and state diversity would have to be ignored by the imposition of nationwide standards and values that were in fact not held nationwide. In either case, a national bill of rights would be dangerous to rights and liberty in the long run.

These arguments did not convince the opponents to the proposed Constitution, and opposition centered most vociferously upon the lack of a bill of rights. James Madison promised, at a critical point in the national debate, that if the Constitution was ratified, he would personally see that a bill of rights was added. True to his word, Madison did initiate and carry through congressional approval for the Bill of Rights, but it was perhaps the most lukewarm introduction in political history. The *Annals of Congress*, the early version of the *Congressional Record*, show Madison as in effect saying again that a national bill of rights is unnecessary and dangerous, but since he had promised one, here it was.

Madison, mindful of his own words on the dangers of looking to the least common denominator, nevertheless produced a list of nine amendments containing forty-two rights that constituted the core of most state bills of rights. Madison's proposed amendments were given to a select committee in the House of Representatives, with one member from each state on the committee. The House produced a list with seventeen articles, which the Senate reduced to twelve. A conference committee worked out the differences; and on October 2, 1789, a proposed bill of rights was sent to the states for ratification. (See Table 4 at the end of this paper.)

It was assumed at the beginning of congressional action that the bill of rights would either be placed as a list at the beginning of the Constitution, as was the case with state bills of rights, or scattered through the body of the Constitution proper as Madison proposed. However, the Connecticut delegation insisted that the rights be appended at the end of the document as a set of explicit amendments to reflect their true status. Placing them at the beginning or in the body of a document ratified only with great difficulty implied the need to go through the entire ratification process again; whereas treating them as amendments did not require having to change any wording in the Constitution *per se*.

Roger Sherman's proposal to place the rights at the end, rather than scattering them throughout the document as Madison wanted, turned out to be fateful, since listing the rights together at the end gave them a prominence and combined status over time that would otherwise have been lost. Placing the Bill of Rights at the end, rather than at the beginning as the states preferred, had an unnoted yet historically important effect on the language of the proposed rights.

The lists of rights proposed by the various states almost all used the admonitory "ought" and "should" rather than the legally enforceable "shall" and "will" with which we are now familiar. Madison, because he intended placement of the rights in the body of the Constitution, used the constitutionally proper "shall" and "will." Initially the House of Representatives version used admonitory language, but when the House select committee agreed to go along with Sherman's proposal and place the Bill of Rights at the end as amendments, it was necessary to change everything to legalistically enforceable language, since one cannot amend a "shall" with an "ought."

Without this change in language occasioned by placement at the end of the document, rather than the beginning of the Constitution, it is difficult to see how American rights could have developed as they did, or how the Supreme Court could have emerged as the definer and protector of legalistic rights. The change in wording was entirely due to the placement of the Bill of Rights, not to anything in American rights theory as of 1789. Later developments in American theories of rights would be heavily affected and conditioned by what amounts to an historical accident.

It took two and a half years for the necessary three-fourths of the states to ratify ten of the twelve proposed amendments to the Constitution, which together are now known as the Bill of Rights. Massachusetts, Connecticut, and Georgia did not ratify these amendments until the Sesquicentennial celebration of the Constitution in 1939. That the process took so long, that it failed to elicit ratification by all of the states, and that two proposed amendments failed to receive the necessary three-fourths support are all indicative of some controversy in state legislatures. Much of the controversy stemmed, as Madison had predicted, from different expectations from state to state. Some wanted more or different rights, some wanted fewer. Perhaps we should be surprised that anything coherent passed at all.

The Bill of Rights Since 1792

Passage of the national Bill of Rights didn't really change anything at first. The states were still considered the primary protectors of individual rights. It was not until the early twentieth century that the Supreme Court began to use the national Bill of Rights to protect individual rights in a systematic fashion.

One major effect the Bill of Rights had during the nineteenth century was to lead drafters of state constitutions to recast the language of their bills of rights into the legally binding form using "shall" and "will." With their longer lists of rights, and strengthened language, most states were ahead of the national government in rights development, although nowhere did the breadth and depth of protection approach what it is now.

Two broad developments have occurred during the twentieth century. The first has been the expansion of national rights, as interpreted by the Supreme Court, to an unprecedented degree. We have come to take these rights so much for granted that we forget how recently they have been expanded. The second development has been the application of the national Bill of Rights against the states using the "due process" clause of the Fourteenth Amendment. Both developments were made possible by the legally enforceable language inserted in the national Bill of Rights in 1789.

Scholarship and publicity surrounding the second broad development left the impression that rights at the state level were not well protected, and that the national government had forged ahead in rights protection. This was not completely true. The problem was not lagging rights in the states, but diversity in rights among the states. Many or most states already protected rights at a level required by the Supreme Court, but ten to fifteen states clearly lagged behind. The net effect of federal action has been to establish what is now considered a "floor" in American rights. That minimum guarantee is still exceeded by many states.

Active expansion of rights by the Supreme Court, as much as it was needed, had the effect of temporarily eclipsing the development of rights in states. That may be changing. In recent years, there has been a trend toward "rediscovering" an independent constitutional law at the state level with respect to rights, especially in those states where state bills of rights are stronger and broader in definition than the national Bill of Rights.[21] If this flowering at the state level bears fruit, we might be entering a new era with respect to the Bill of Rights—one which produces a healthy competition in rights protection instead of either state or national dominance which has characterized our past.

Taking an historical perspective toward rights in America has a number of implications for how we think about bills of rights, as well as for how we study and teach them. For one thing, the role of the states needs to be more actively considered, as well as the interaction between state and national bills of rights. Changes in the structure, content, and wording of bills of rights reflect changes in how we conceptualize rights, and these theoretical changes need to be more frankly and explicitly faced.

We now rely primarily upon the courts to protect rights, and this is not a bad thing in itself, but it does have the tendency to focus attention upon court cases, and thus upon rights piecemeal, rather than upon bills of rights and the general principles they embody. Certainly we must think deeply about the preferability of using constitutional amendments instead of court interpretation to expand and codify rights. In fact, this is what still tends to happen at the state level, which is one reason why state constitutions so quickly become lengthy and laden with amendments. Many academics view lengthy constitutions as something to be avoided. Another perspective is that long constitutions indicate a people are still taking the constitution seriously enough to amend it through a political process that engages popular consent. Long constitutions may thus be an indication of political health.

There is something to be said for viewing rights as expressions of fundamental commitments by a people, as the grounding for democratic institutions, and thus an essential part of the total political process in a constitutional order. In short, we may be in need of more frequent public debate as we push our frontiers of freedom forward. These are, after all, our rights, and not simply the conclusions of a priestly caste called judges. Judges may be useful guides to our good conscience as a people, but in the end popular consent, and thus popular support, may be a more secure basis for rights.[22]

Notes

1. The author has relied upon the texts found in Richard L. Perry, editor, *Sources of Our Liberties* (New York: Associated College Presses for the American Bar Association, 1959), 11-22, 73-75, and 245-250.

2. See, for example, Richard L. Perry, editor, *Sources of Our Liberties*, 23-4.

3. See Bernard Schwartz, *The Great Rights of Mankind: A History of the Bill of Rights* (New York: Oxford University Press, 1977), 197; also see Irving Brant, *The Bill of Rights: Its Origin and Meaning* (Indianapolis: Bobbs-Merrill Company, Inc., 1965), especially chapters five and six.

4. *Annals of Congress*, Vol. I, 436.

5. The state constitutions and their respective declarations of rights can be found in Francis N. Thorpe, editor, *The Federal and State Constitutions* (Washington, D.C.: U.S. Government Printing Office, 1907), 7 vols.

6. Thorpe, *The Federal and State Constitutions*, 1686-1691 (Maryland), 1889-1893 (Massachusetts), and 2453-2457 (New Hampshire).

7. Thorpe, 3812-3814 (Virginia), and 3082-3084 (Pennsylvania).

8. These documents are widely scattered, but many can be found in Donald S. Lutz, *Documents of Political Foundation Written By Colonial Americans* (Philadelphia: ISHI Press, 1986).

9. See Lutz, *Documents of Political Foundation*, 435-442, 403-410, 359-362, 309-314, 255-302, and 189-194.

10. The argument being made here is fully developed in Donald S. Lutz, *The Origins of American Constitutionalism* (Baton Rouge: Louisiana State University Press, 1988).

11. These documents can be found in Lutz, *Documents of Political Foundation*, 65-66, 105-112, and 135-142.

12. Thorpe, *The Federal and State Constitutions*, 2788.

13. Ibid., 1687.

14. Ibid., 1891.

15. Ibid., 3083.

16. Ibid., 3082.

17. Ibid., 1889.

18. Ibid., 3082.

19. Ibid., 1889.

20. See Alexander Hamilton, John Jay, and James Madison, *The Federalist* (New York: The Modern Library, 1937), 555-561.

21. For a good introduction to the growing literature on this topic see John Kincaid, "State Court Protections of Individual Rights Under State Constitutions: The New Ju-

dicial Federalism," *The Journal of State Government* 61 (Sept./ Oct. 1988): 163-169.

22. For further discussion on this point see Donald S. Lutz, "Protection of Political Participation in Eighteenth Century America, *Albany Law Review* (Spring, 1990): 1-29.

This paper was adapted by the author from an article written originally for publication in *Publius: The Journal of Federalism*.

Table 1
First Statement of Rights in U.S. Bill of Rights*

Bill of Rights Guarantee	First Document Protecting	First American Guarantee	First Constitutional Guarantee
Establishment of religion	Rights of the Colonists	Same (Boston)	N.J. Const. Art. XIX
Free Exercise of religion	Md. Act Concerning religion	Same	Va. Dec. of Rts., S. 16
Free speech	Mass. Body of Liberties S.12	Same	Pa. Dec. of Rts., Art. XII
Free press	Address to Inhabitants of Quebec	Same	Va. Dec. of Rts., S. 12
Assembly	Dec. & Resolves of Cont. Cong.	Same	Pa. Dec. of Rts., Art. XVI
Petition	Bill of Rts. (England, 1689)	Dec. of Rts. & and Grievances (1765), S. XIII	Pa. Dec. of Rts., Art. XVI
Right to bear arms	Bill of Rts. (England, 1689)	Pa. Dec. of Rts., Art. XIII	Same
Quartering soldiers	Petition of Right (England) S. VI	N.Y. Charter of Liberties	Del. Dec. of Rts., S. 21
Searches	Rights of the Colonists	Same (Boston)	Va. Dec. of Rts., S. 10
Seizures	Magna Carta c. 39	Va. Dec. of Rts., s. 10	Same
Grand jury	N.Y. Charter of Liberties	Same	N.C. Dec. of Rts., Art. VIII
Double jeopardy	Mass. Body of Liberties, S.42	Same	N.H. Bill of Rts., Art. XVI
Self-incrimination	Va. Dec. of Rts., S. 8	Same	Same
Due process	Magna Carta c. 39	Md. Act for Lib. of People	Va. Dec. of Rts., S. 8
Just compensation	Mass. Body of Liberties, S. 8	Same	Vt. Dec. of Rts., Art. II
Speedy trial	Va. Dec. of Rts., S. 8	Same	Same
Jury trial	Magna Carta c. 39	Mass. Body of Liberties, S.29	Va. Dec. of Rts., S. 8
Cause & nature of accusation	Va. Dec. of Rts., S. 8	Same	Same
Witnesses	Pa. Charter of Privileges Art. V	Same	N.J. Consti., Art. XVI
Counsel	Mass. Body of Liberties, S.29	Same	N.J. Consti., Art. XVI
Jury trial (civil)	Mass. Body of Liberties, S.29	Same	Va. Dec. of Rts., S. 11
Bail	Mass. Body of Liberties, S.18	Same	Va. Dec. of Rts., S. 9
Fines	Magna Carta Sects. 20-22	Pa. Frame of Gov., S. XVIII	Va. Dec. of Rts., S. 9
Punishment	Mass. Body of Lib., S. 43, 46	Same	Va. Dec. of Rts., S. 9
Rights retained by people	Va. Const, proposed Amendment 17	Same	Ninth Amendment
Reserved powers	Mass. Dec. of Rights, Art. IV	Same	Same

* Based on: Bernard Schwartz, *The Roots of the Bill of Rights*, Volume 5, (New York: Chelsea House Publishers, 1980), p. 1204. Contrary to Schwartz, this author attributes more to English common law documents. Schwartz attributes the first prohibition on the quartering of troops to the 1683 New York Charter of Liberties instead of the 1628 Petition of Right in England; and he attributes the first prohibition against excessive fines to the 1682 Pennsylvania Frame of Government, whereas it is here attributed to Magna Carta. The difficulty in such attributions lies in the English version always being somewhat different in intent and application, as well as usually being less explicit and sweeping in expression.

		PA	MA	MD	SC	NH	VA	NY	NC	Madison
1.	Power derives from people									X
2.	Gov. exercised for common good									X
3.	Life, liberty, prop. & happiness									X
4.	Right of people to change gov.			X						X
5.	No. of representatives	X	X			X	X	X	X	X
6.	Congressional raises	X					X	X	X	X
7.	Religious freedom			X	X	X				X
8.	Rt. of conscience	X				X				X
9.	Free speech	X		X						X
10.	Free to write			X						X
11.	Free press	X		X						X
12.	Assembly									X
13.	Petition and remonstrance									X
14.	Bear arms	X				X				X
15.	Pacifists—no arms									X
16.	No quartering in peacetime			X		X				X
17.	No quartering									X
18.	Double jeopardy									X
19.	No double punishment									X
20.	Self-incrimination	X								X
21.	Due process of law			X						X
22.	Compensate for property taken									X
23.	Excessive bail or fines									X
24.	Cruel & unusual punishment	X								X
25.	Search & seizure trial	X		X						X
26.	Speedy & public trial	X								X
27.	Told nature of crime	X		X						X
28.	Confronted with accusers	X		X						X
29.	Witnesses for defense									X
30.	Right to counsel	X		X						X
31.	Rts. retained by states or people	X					X		X	X
32.	No implied powers for Cong.			X					X	X
33.	No state violate 8, 9, 11, or 26 above									X
34.	Appeal limited by $ amount									X
35.	Jury cannot be bypassed									X
36.	Impartial jury from vicinity	X		X						X
37.	Jury unanimity									X
38.	Rt. to challenge jud. decision									X
39.	Grand jury		X			X				X
40.	Jury trial for civil cases		X	X						X
41.	Separation of powers	X								X
42.	Powers reserved to states	X	X		X	X	X		X	X
43.	Limit national taxing power	X	X	X	X	X	X	X	X	
44.	No limit on state taxes	X								
45.	No federal election regulation	X	X		X	X	X	X	X	
46.	Free elections	X								
47.	No standing army	X		X		X		X	X	
48.	State control of militia	X					X		X	
49.	State sovereignty retained	X							X	
50.	Limits on judicial power	X	X	X			X	X	X	

Table 2 *(Continued)*

	PA	MA	MD	SC	NH	VA	NY	NC	Madison
51. Treaties accord with state law	X		X						
52. Nat. & St. cts. have concurrent juris.			X						
53. No infringing of state consts.	X		X				X		
54. St. cts. used as lower fed. cts.					X		X		
55. Can appeal Sup. Ct. decisions							X		
56. Defend oneself in court	X				X		X		
57. Civil control of military	X								
58. Liberty to fish, fowl & hunt	X								
59. Advisory council for president	X								
60. Independent judiciary	X								
61. State cts. used is less than x$		X							
62. Trial in state crime occurs		X							
63. Judges hold no other office		X							
64. 4 yr. limit on military service						X		X	
65. Limit on martial law			X			X			
66. No monopolies		X			X		X	X	
67. Citizens of 2 states—no juris.		X			X				
68. No titles of nobility		X			X		X		
69. Keep a congressional record						X	X	X	
70. Publish info. on nat. use of money						X		X	
71. 2/3 Senate ratify commerce treaties						X		X	
72. 2/3 both houses naviga. commerce						X		X	
73. Limit on regulation of D.C.						X	X	X	
74. Pres. term—8 out of 16 yrs.						X		X	
75. Pres. limited to two terms							X		
76. Add st. judges to impeach							X		
77. Senate doesn't impeach senators						X		X	
78. Limit use of militia out of st.			X				X		
79. Judicial salaries not changed						X		X	
80. Requirements for being president							X		
81. 2/3 of both houses to borrow money							X		
82. 2/3 of Congress to declare war							X		
83. Habeas corpus							X		
84. Congress sessions to be open							X		
85. No consecutive terms—Senate							X		
86. St. legis. fill vacant Sen. seat							X		
87. Limit on lower courts							X		
88. No duties to a particular state								X	
89. No interfere in paper money								X	
90. No foreign troops								X	
91. State law used on military bases							X		
92. No multiple office-holding			X			X	X	X	
93. Limit on bankruptcy laws							X		
94. No pres. pardon for treason							X		
95. Pres. not field commander			X				X		
96. Official form for president's acts							X		
97. No poll tax			X						

* The first forty-two rights are arranged in the order used by Madison in his original version sent to the House of Representatives. Going from left to right, the states are arranged in the order their ratifying conventions produced a list of recommended amendments, from earliest to latest. The proposed amendments for each state are taken from Merrill Jensen, John P. Kaminski, Gaspare J. Saladino, et al., eds., *The Documentary History of the Ratification of the Constitution* Madison, Wisconsin, 1976 -); and Madison's forty-two proposed rights are based upon an examination of the original document in the National Archives.

Table 3
Madison's List of Proposed Amendments
Compared with Provisions in the Existing
State Bills of Rights*

		VA	PA	DE	MD	NC	MA	NH	Madison
1.	Power derived from people	X	X	X	X	X	X	X	X
2.	Gov. exercised for common good	X	X	X	X		X	X	X
3.	Life, liberty, prop. & happiness	X	X	X	X		X	X	X
4.	Right of people to change gov.	X	X		X		X	X	X
5.	No. of representatives								X
6.	Congressional raises								X
7.	Free exercise of religion			X	X	X	X	X	X
8.	Freedom of conscience	X	X	X	X	X	X	X	X
9.	Free speech		X						X
10.	Free to write								X
11.	Free press	X	X	X	X	X	X	X	X
12.	Right to assemble	X			X	X			X
13.	Petition and remonstrance	X	X	X	X	X			X
14.	Bear arms		X	X		X	X		X
15.	Pacifists—no arms								X
16.	No quartering in peacetime				X	X		X	X
17.	No quartering without warrant				X	X	X	X	X
18.	Double jeopardy							X	X
19.	No double punishment								X
20.	Self-incrimination	X	X	X	X	X	X	X	X
21.	Due process of law	X	X	X	X	X	X	X	X
22.	Compensate for property taken				X	X	X	X	X
23.	Excessive bail	X		X	X	X	X		X
24.	Cruel & unusual punishment	X		X	X	X	X		X
25.	Search & seizure	X	X	X	X	X	X	X	X
26.	Speedy & public trial	X	X	X	X	X	X	X	X
27.	Told nature of crime	X	X	X	X	X	X	X	X
28.	Confronted with accusers	X	X	X	X	X	X	X	X
29.	Witnesses for defense	X	X	X	X		X	X	X
30.	Right to counsel		X	X	X		X	X	X
31.	Rts. retained by people						X		X
32.	No implied powers for Cong.								X
33.	No state violate 8, 11, or 26 above								X
34.	Appeal limited by $ amount								X
35.	Jury cannot be bypassed								X
36.	Impartial jury from vicinity	X	X	X	X				X
37.	Jury unanimity								X
38.	Rt. of challenge								X
39.	Grand jury					X			X
40.	Jury trial for lawsuits	X							X
41.	Separation of powers	X			X	X	X	X	X
42.	Powers reserved to states or people						X	X	X
43.	No taxation without consent	X	X	X	X	X	X	X	

Table 3 *(Continued)*

		VA	PA	DE	MD	NC	MA	NH	Madison
44.	Free elections	X	X	X	X	X	X	X	
45.	Frequent elections	X	X	X	X	X	X		
46.	No standing army	X	X	X	X	X	X	X	
47.	Civil control of military	X	X	X	X	X	X	X	
48.	No martial law (suspending law)	X		X	X	X	X		
49.	No compulsion to bear arms	X	X					X	
50.	No ex post facto laws			X	X	X	X	X	
51.	No bills of attainder				X		X		
52.	Habeas corpus	X	X						
53.	Justice not sold			X	X		X	X	
54.	Location of trial convenient				X		X	X	
55.	Independent judiciary			X	X		X		
56.	Recurrence to fundamentals	X	X			X	X		
57.	Stake in community to vote	X			X				
58.	Equality						X	X	
59.	Majority rule	X							
60.	Frequent meeting of legislature			X	X		X		
61.	Free speech in legislature				X		X		
62.	Convenient location of legislature				X				
63.	Public office not hereditary	X					X	X	
64.	No title of nobility				X				
65.	No emoluments or privileges					X			
66.	No taxing of paupers				X				
67.	No monopolies				X	X			
68.	Collective property right					X			
69.	No sanguinary laws				X			X	
70.	Right to common law				X				
71.	Right to migrate	X							
72.	No poll tax				X				
73.	No infringing of state consts.	X							
74.	No religious test				X				
75.	Support of public worship					X	X		
76.	Attend religious instruction						X		
77.	Uniform support of religion						X	X	
78.	Support of public teachers						X		
79.	Time to prepare legal defense				X				
80.	Rotation in executive office	X							
81.	No multiple office-holding	X							
82.	Proportional punishment							X	
83.	Qualified jurors							X	

* The first 42 rights are those Madison compiled and sent to the House of Representatives. The order is that used in his list. The rest of the rights are those found in the state bills of rights, but not in Madison's proposed amendments. Madison's list is taken from the original document in the National Archives. The rights in the state bills of rights are based on the documents as collected in Francis N. Thorpe, ed. *The Federal and State Constitutions, Colonial Charters, and Other Organic Laws of the United States* (Washington, D.C.: Government Printing Office, 1907), 7 vols.

Table 4
Madison's Proposed Amendments Compared with Later Versions*

		Madison Version	House Version	Senate Version	Sent to States	Ratified
1.	Power derived from people	X				
2.	Gov. exercised for common good	X				
3.	Life, liberty, prop. & happiness	X				
4.	Right of people to change gov.	X				
5.	No. of representatives	X	X		X	
6.	Congressional raises	X	X	X	X	
7.	Religious freedom	X	X		X	X
8.	Rt. of conscience	X	X			
9.	Free speech	X	X		X	X
10.	Freedom of written expression	X				
11.	Free press	X	X		X	X
12.	Assembly	X	X		X	X
13.	Petition and remonstrance	X	X		X	X
14.	Bear arms	X	X	X	X	X
15.	Pacifists—no arms	X	X			
16.	No quartering in peacetime	X	X	X	X	X
17.	No quartering without warrant	X	X	X	X	X
18.	Double jeopardy	X	X	X	X	X
19.	No double punishment	X				
20.	Self-incrimination	X	X	X	X	X
21.	Due process of law	X	X	X	X	X
22.	Compensate for property taken	X	X	X	X	X
23.	Excessive bail or fines	X	X		X	X
24.	Cruel & unusual punishment	X	X		X	X
25.	Search & seizure	X	X	X	X	X
26.	Speedy & public trial	X	X		X	X
27.	Told nature of crime	X	X		X	X
28.	Confronted with accusers	X	X		X	X
29.	Witnesses for defense	X	X		X	X
30.	Right to counsel	X	X		X	X
31.	Rts. retained by people	X	X	X	X	X
32.	No implied powers for Cong.	X				
33.	No state violate 8, 9, 11, or 26 above	X	X			
34.	Appeal limited by $ amount	X	X			
35.	Jury cannot be bypassed	X	X	X	X	X
36.	Impartial jury from vicinity	X		X	X	X
37.	Jury unanimity	X	X			
38.	Rt. to challenge jud. decision	X	X			
39.	Grand jury	X	X	X	X	X
40.	Jury trial for civil cases	X	X	X	X	X
41.	Separation of powers	X	X			
42.	Powers reserved to states	X	X	X	X	X

* The rights are arranged in the order used by Madison in his June 8, 1789 version sent to the Committee of Eleven of the House of Representatives (the committee was composed of one member from each of the eleven states that had ratified the Constitution by that date). This table is based upon an examination of the original documents in the National Archives.

Background Paper 2

George Mason's "Objections" and the Bill of Rights

Robert Allen Rutland

In 1787 George Mason was a political figure to be reckoned with, spoken of in the same breath with Virginians Washington, Jefferson, Madison, Patrick Henry, and Richard Henry Lee. He was, as they said then, "a man of parts"; Jefferson described him as "of the first order of greatness." The chief author of the Virginia Declaration of Rights in 1776, Mason had been either a legislator or a confidant in the Revolutionary councils of the Old Dominion from 1774 onward. Now, from May to September in 1787, Mason was a key member of his state's delegation to the Federal Convention, a frequent and persuasive speaker, and the man who played a vital role in such matters as presidential impeachment and fiscal responsibility.

But Mason did not approve of the outcome of the Constitutional Convention. He made significant last-minute motions on the convention floor, and one which his colleagues rejected returned to haunt them: Mason belatedly called for the addition of a bill of rights to the Constitution. Mason's call was shaped into a motion by Elbridge Gerry. They must have witnessed the roll call of states with chagrin as the resolution "to prepare a Bill of Rights" was defeated unanimously.

Then and later the Federalists were short-tempered when the subject of a bill of rights arose. Delegate Robert Sherman was their spokesman when he helped derail Mason's motion. Stating that he too was "for securing the rights of the people where requisite," Sherman continued, that "the State Declarations of Rights are not repealed by this Constitution; and being in force are sufficient." Moreover, Sherman contended, "the Legislature may be safely trusted." James Madison sided with Sherman and five days later, thirty-nine of Masons colleagues (one

by proxy) signed the Constitution. Mason, Gerry, and Edmund Randolph (who also declined to sign), watched the convention approve the Constitution, according to Dr. Franklin's motion, "by the unanimous consent of *the States* present."

Franklin's tactic placed the trio of naysayers on the defensive, an awkward position for one like Mason who had been so hopeful at the start of the enterprise. Mason had come to Philadelphia that spring convinced that "the Eyes of the United States are turn'd upon this Assembly, & their Expectations raised to a very anxious Degree." "May God grant we may be able to gratify them," Mason prayed in June 1787. Along with James Wilson and James Madison, Mason had engaged articulately in debates on behalf of enlarging participation. Mason's arguments for popular election of the lower house in Congress, his insistence on the right to impeach a corrupt president, and his approval of presidential elections by a direct vote of the citizenry all fitted his philosophical commitment to a broad-based republic. A slaveowner and man of means, Mason had also denounced the slave trade.

At the same time, Mason sought to keep the Union from swallowing the states, and thus he supported selection of senators by the state legislatures and vowed "he never would agree to abolish the State govts. or render them absolutely insignificant." Mason also adamantly sought protection for southern shipping interests in the form of a two-thirds majority for commercial legislation. Within his own guidelines, Mason steadily argued for a government that trusted the people over the privileged. Fellow delegate William Pierce said of Mason: "He is able and convincing in debate, steady and firm in his principles, and undoubtedly one of the best politicians in America."

After nearly four months of give and take, compromise and bullying, the delegates had survived and so had their Constitution; but in Mason's view the convention still gave too little attention to citizens' rights. Mason distrusted the final draft as a protector of the individual citizen or of the southern planting economy. During that last week, Mason recorded his misgivings about the Constitution on the back of the printed report of the Committee of Style, beginning simply: "There is no Declaration of Rights." From that preamble, Mason proceeded to list what he called his "Objections to this Constitution of Government."

His original list of objections claimed that the Constitution upset the English common law, made Congress into a kind of oligarchy, allowed the federal courts to destroy state ones, and left the presidency rudderless without a "Constitutional Council." Mason feared that without the latter, a natural cabinet "will grow out of the principal officers of the great departments; the worst and most dangerous of all ingredients for such a Council in a free country." The created office of the Vice President, Mason thought, was disastrous and unnecessary, since the incumbent "for want of other employment is made president of the Senate, thereby dangerously blending the executive and legislative powers."

As for the presidential powers, Mason thought the chief executive might misuse his "unrestrained power of granting pardons for treason" and might "screen from punishment those whom he had secretly instigated to commit the crime, and thereby prevent a discovery of his own guilt." The president's treaty-making powers, combined with senatorial approval, made such pacts the supreme law of the land without any scrutiny by the people's branch of government—the House of Representatives. And by allowing a congressional majority to pass laws restricting American commerce "the five Southern states, whose product and circumstances are totally different from that of the eight Northern and Eastern States, may be ruined."

Mason also lambasted the vague construction of the Constitution and foresaw the "general welfare" clause as a catchall term bound to be abused. Although Mason specifically called for declarations of freedom of the press and trial by jury, he lamented the ban on *ex post facto* laws in the state legislatures since "there never was nor can be a legislature but must and will make such laws, when necessity and the public safety require them."

Gloomy to the end, Mason predicted that without an immediate ban on slave trading the nation would be "weaker, more vulnerable, and less capable of defense," and under the Constitution would "set out [as] a moderate aristocracy" then degenerate into either a monarchy or "tyrannical aristocracy." "It will," he predicted, "most probably vibrate some years between the two, and then terminate in the one or the other."

First as a handwritten text and then as a printed pamphlet, Mason's "Objections" made the rounds in Philadelphia's political circles during the last two weeks of September. From the opening phrase of his "Objections" to the bill of rights that James Madison offered in Congress two years later, the line is so direct that we can say Mason forced Madison's hand. Federalist supporters of the Constitution could never overcome the protest created by Mason's phrase: "There is no Declaration of Rights." Months later, Hamilton was still trying "to kill that snake" in *Federalist* No. 84. Oliver Ellsworth's "Landholder" essays in 1787-88, perhaps more influential than the papers of "Publius," also made a frontal attack on Mason's "Objections," as did Federalist James Iredell in North Carolina in 1788.

But the idea was too powerful. Mason's pamphlet soon circulated along the Atlantic seaboard and by the onset of winter the "Objections" had appeared in newspapers in Virginia and New Jersey. Mason himself paid for a second printing and sent Washington the pamphlet early in October, claiming that "a little Moderation & Temper, in the latter End of the Convention, might have removed" his misgivings.

Mason also mailed one to Jefferson, then at his diplomatic post in Paris, explaining that "These Objections of mine were first printed very incorrectly, without my Approbation, or Privity; which laid me under some kind of Necessity of publishing them afterwards, myself. . . . You will find them conceived in general Terms; as I wished to confine them to a narrow Compass." Mason went on to add to his list objections related to regulating the state militia, to the potential power to abuse the election process, and the power of congressmen to raise their own salaries. "But it wou'd be tedious to enumerate all the Objections," Mason concluded, "and I am sure they cannot escape Mr. Jefferson's Observation."

But whatever his other objections, it was the issue of the bill of rights that struck Jefferson. Not long after Mason's pamphlet reached Jefferson's desk in Paris the American minister was writing to friends at home in outspoken terms. Jefferson told Madison he liked the Constitution but was alarmed by "the omission of a bill of rights," and, to John Adams's son-in-law, Jefferson said bluntly: "Were I in America, I would advocate it [the Constitution] warmly till nine states should have adopted, and then as warmly take the other side to convince the remaining four that they ought not to come into it till the declaration of rights is annexed to it."

In a backhanded way, Jefferson's plan became the model. Alarmed by Anti-Federalist strategy that aimed at a second federal convention, friends of the Constitution wanted to derail any scheme for another national gathering. Although Madison was concerned that a bill of rights would offer little real protection and by enumerating some rights put others in jeopardy, if concessions on the bill-of-rights issue could forestall demands for a second convention, Federalists came to realize they must pay that price. Starting at the Massachusetts ratifying convention in February 1788, Federalists in charge of counting votes abandoned their adamant position and began to talk about "recommendatory" amendments.

By conceding that a bill of rights ought to be considered by the first Congress, Madison and his co-workers whittled away at the Anti-Federalist majority in Virginia. Their concession on a bill of rights made it easier for committed Anti-Federalist delegates to swallow the bitter pill of ratification, and in Virginia the Federalists' gesture also gave proponents of the Constitution a way to defend a vote in opposition to Patrick Henry and Mason, who were still not assuaged. As they saw their majority melting away, Henry and Mason wanted their proposed amendments, including a bill of rights, to be a condition for Virginia's ratification. When the convention rejected that tactic and voted instead, as the Massachusetts delegates had done, for "recommendatory" amendments, the game for the staunchest Anti-Federalists was over. The Constitution was quickly ratified.

But James Madison had learned his lesson. A few months later, when he ran for a seat in that first Congress, Madison had to assure constituents that "it is my sincere opinion that the Constitution ought to be revised." What changes would he seek? Nothing less than a bill of rights containing "the most satisfactory provisions for all essential rights, particularly the rights of Conscience in the fullest latitude, the freedom of the press, trials by jury, security against general warrants &c." It seems unlikely that Madison would have made such an about-face without the storm of protest first raised by Mason's "Objections."

By not signing the Constitution, Mason had gained a principle but lost a friend. Or almost so, for a painful estrangement between Madison and himself did not abate until Madison introduced a bill of rights in Congress in September 1789. Mason quickly praised the provisions in a letter to Congressman Samuel Griffin from Virginia, knowing his letter would be seen by Madison. "I have received much Satisfaction from the Amendments to the federal Constitution, which have lately passed the House of Representatives," Mason wrote, "I hope they will also pass the Senate. With two or three further Amendments . . . I cou'd chearfully put my Hand & Heart to the new Government."

One of the most self-effacing men ever to serve the American people, Mason regretted the tensions that grew out of the ratification struggle. Eventually, he welcomed Madison and Jefferson back to his home at Gunston Hall, and their friendship fell into the old grooves. But Mason's standing as a "founding father" was long under a cloud, owing chiefly to his stance on the Constitution. His patriotic service in preparing the Fairfax Resolves in 1774, his cardinal role at the Virginia Convention of 1776, his authorship of that state bill of rights (until 1829), and his offering of time, talent, and money to the American cause between 1776 and 1781 became only dim memories, hardly mentioned in the standard histories. By the early twentieth century, however, attention to civil liberties began to increase and scholars came to note the original role Mason played when he insisted on constitutional protection for a free press and other civil rights. By 1988, Mason was beginning to reap some of the acclaim he deserved for his simple warning: "There is no Declaration of Rights."

This paper is used here with the permission of Project '87 of the American Historical Association and the American Political Science Association. This paper originally appeared in Issue No. 18 of *this Constitution: A Bicentennial Chronicle* (Spring/Summer 1988): 11-13.

Background Paper 3

James Madison and the Bill of Rights

Jack N. Rakove

James Madison went to the Federal Convention of 1787 convinced that it faced no greater challenge than finding some means of checking "the aggressions of interested majorities on the rights of minorities and of individuals." He left it still fearful that the new Constitution would not effectually "secure individuals against encroachments on their rights." In his best known contribution to American political theory, *The Federalist* No. 10, Madison again voiced his great concern that majorities were enacting laws "adverse to the rights of other citizens," and he went on to define the protection of the individual "faculties" of men as "the first object of government."

These and other statements suggest that Madison should have welcomed the addition of a Bill of Rights to the Constitution. And in fact Madison can rightly be regarded as the principal framer of the Bill of Rights which the First Federal Congress submitted to the states in 1789. Many congressmen felt that he was acting with undue haste in calling for quick action on the subject of amendments. Had Madison not pressed them to consider the amendments he had introduced early in the session, the Bill of Rights might never have been added to the Constitution.

Yet even as he was shepherding the amendments through Congress in August 1789, Madison privately described his efforts as a "nauseous project." His acceptance of the need for a Bill of Rights came grudgingly. When the Constitution was being written in 1787, and even after it was ratified in 1788, Madison dismissed bills of rights as so many "parchment barriers" whose "inefficacy" (he reminded his good friend, Thomas Jefferson) was repeatedly demonstrated "on those occasions when [their] control is most needed." Even after Jefferson's entreaties finally led him to admit that bills of rights might have their uses, it still took a difficult election campaign

against another friend, James Monroe, to get Madison to declare that, if elected to the House of Representatives, he would favor adding to the Constitution "the most satisfactory provisions for all essential rights."

To trace the evolution of James Madison's thinking about the virtues and defects of a bill of rights, then, is to confront the ambiguous mix of principled and political concerns that led to the adoption of the first ten amendments. Today, when disputes about the meaning of the Bill of Rights and its lineal descendant, the Fourteenth Amendment, have become so heated—when, indeed, we often regard the Bill of Rights as the essence of the Constitution—it is all the more important to fix the relation between the Constitution of 1787 and the amendments of 1789. To do this there is no better place to begin than with the concerns that troubled James Madison.

Enumerating Rights

Much of the contemporary debate and controversy about the rights-based decisions that the Supreme Court has made over the past three decades centers on the question of whether the judiciary should protect only those rights that enjoy explicit constitutional or statutory sanction, or whether it can act to establish new rights—as in the case of abortion—on the basis of its understanding of certain general principles of liberty. We cannot know how Madison would decide particular cases today. But one aspect of his analysis of the problem of rights seems highly pertinent to the current debate. Madison's deepest reservations about the wisdom of adopting any bill of rights reflected his awareness of the difficulty of enumerating all the rights that deserved protection against the "infinitude of legislative expedients" that could be deployed to the disadvantage of individuals and minorities. Madison's notion of rights was thus open-ended, but his ideas about which kinds of rights were most vulnerable changed over time. In 1787 he felt that the greatest dangers to liberty concerned the rights of property. The passage of paper money laws in various states revealed the depths of "injustice" to which these populist forces were willing to descend. Worse might be yet to come. At the Federal Convention, Madison told his fellow delegates that he foresaw a day when "power will slide into the hands" of "those who labour under all the hardships of life, and secretly sigh for a more equal distribution of its blessings." And even if the Constitution succeeded in checking the danger from a dispossessed proletariat, Madison thought that almost any act of legislation or taxation would affect rights of property. "What are many of the most important acts of legislation," he asked in *Federalist* 10, "but so many judicial determinations . . . concerning the rights of large bodies of citizens?"

But the development of Madison's ideas of liberty long predated the specific concerns he felt about the economic legislation of the 1780s. His first known comments on political issues of any kind expressed his abhorrence at the persecution of religious dissenters in pre-Revolutionary Virginia; and his first notable action in public life had been to secure an amendment to the Virginia Declaration of Rights, the most influential of the bills of rights that had been attached to the state constitutions written at the time of independence. In 1785 Madison led the fight against a bill to provide public aid for all teachers of the Christian religion in Virginia; the *Memorial and Remonstrance Against Religious Assessments* that he published in conjunction with this campaign treated rights of conscience as a realm of behavior entirely beyond the regulation of civil authority.

Majority Misrule

We thus cannot doubt Madison's commitment to the cause of protecting private rights and civil liberties against improper intrusion by the government. But all orthodox republicans in Revolutionary America shared such beliefs. What carried Madison beyond the conventional thought of his contemporaries was, first, his analysis of the sources of the dangers to individual and minority rights, and second, the solutions and remedies he offered.

Traditional republican theory held that the great danger to liberty lay in the relentless efforts of scheming rulers to aggrandize their power at the expense of ordinary citizens. The great safeguard

against such threats was believed to lie in the virtue and vigilance of the people.

The skeptical Madison sought to overturn this received wisdom. In the weeks preceding the gathering of the Federal Convention in May 1787, Madison collected his thoughts in a memorandum on the "Vices of the Political System of the United States." As he saw it, the "multiplicity," "mutability," and most important, "the injustice" of the laws of the states had called "into question the fundamental principle of republican Government, that the majority who rule in such Governments are the safest Guardians both of public Good and of private rights." The experience of the states demonstrated, Madison concluded, that neither legislative majorities nor the popular majorities whom they represented could be expected to refrain "from unjust violations of the rights and interests of the minority, or of individuals," whenever "an apparent interest or common passion" spurred such majorities to act. Religion, honor, a sense of the public good—all the virtues a good republican might hope to see operate as restraints—seemed ineffective.

It is crucial to note that Madison directed his criticism against the character of lawmaking *within the individual states*; and the logic of his analysis further led him to conclude that the greatest dangers to liberty would continue to arise within the states, rather than from a reconstituted national government. The ill effects of majority rule far more likely would emerge within the small compass of local communities or states, where "factious majorities" could easily form, than in the extended sphere of a national republic that would "be broken into a greater variety of interests, of pursuits, of passions," whose very diversity and fluidity would check each other.

A Proposal for a National Veto

The solutions Madison offered to this problem operated at two levels. He reserved his most radical proposal—an absolute national veto over state laws "in all cases whatsoever"—for the continuing need to protect individual rights against majority misrule within the states. In effect, Madison hoped the national government would serve as a "disinterested and dispassionate umpire in disputes between different passions and interests" within the states.

But Madison was also prepared to concede that the wrong kinds of majorities might still coalesce within the new Congress that the Federal Convention would create. "Experience in all the States had evinced a powerful tendency in the Legislature to absorb all power into its vortex," he reminded the

Convention on July 21. Who could say whether Congress might not prove equally "impetuous"? To protect citizens against the danger of unjust *national* legislation, Madison favored establishing a joint executive-judicial council of revision armed with a veto over acts of Congress; he was also attracted to the idea of an independent and powerful Senate, insulated from both the state legislatures and the electorate, to counteract the excesses of the House of Representatives.

Madison justified all of these proposals in terms of the protection they would extend to individual and minority rights. But he went to the Convention convinced that bills of rights could add little if anything to the defense of civil liberty. None of the existing state bills of rights provided an effective check against legislative or popular excess. The problem was that bills of rights were not self-enforcing. The actual protection of the lofty principles they espoused required the existence of well-constituted governments. But if such governments did exist—or could be created—what need would they have for bills of rights?

Most of the framers of Philadelphia agreed that there was no need for adding a bill of rights to the new Constitution, but they rejected Madison's two pet proposals for a national veto and a Council of Revision. The Convention protected individual liberty only by placing a handful of prohibitions on the legislative authority of the states (notably laws impairing the obligation of contracts) or Congress (habeas corpus, ex post facto, bills of attainder). When George Mason belatedly insisted that the new Constitution required a much longer list of enumerated rights, his arguments were ignored.

The rejection of his pet scheme for a national veto on all state laws greatly disappointed Madison. During the first weeks after the Convention's adjournment, he seems to have feared that the new Constitution was fatally flawed because the new government would still lack the authority to deal with the problem of "vicious" popular and legislative majorities in the *states*. Even though the supremacy clause of the Constitution established a basis for state and federal judges to overturn laws violating individual rights, he doubted whether the judiciary could ever muster the will or political excesses or the ingenuity of ambitious legislators.

When it came to the dangers that liberty might face from the *national* government, however, he was far more optimistic. Though not entirely happy with the system of checks and balances that would shape relations among the three branches, Madison thought it would discourage the enactment of harm-

ful legislation. Moreover, he continued to rely confidently on the theory of the advantages of multiple factions he had derived just prior to the Convention. "In the extended republic of the United States, and among the great variety of interests, parties, and sects which it embraces," he wrote in *The Federalist* No. 51, "a coalition of a majority of the whole society could seldom take place upon any other principles than those of justice and the general good." State laws might still work wholesale injustice; national laws, he believed, would not.

Anti-Federalist Clamor

As Madison threw himself into the campaign to ratify the Constitution, however, he was forced to take seriously the growing clamor for the addition of a bill of rights—especially after Jefferson wrote him to affirm *his* conviction "that a bill of rights is what the people are entitled to against every government on earth, general or particular [i.e., national or local], and what no just government should refuse or rest on inference." Had the issue of amendments been confined to matters of rights alone, Madison might have readily agreed. But fearing that many diehard Anti-Federalists hoped to exploit the call for amendments to propose major changes in the Constitution or even to promote a second convention, Madison balked at accepting Jefferson's correction.

In October 1788—more than a year after the adjournment of the Convention, and a good four months after Virginia became the tenth state to ratify the Constitution—Madison wrote Jefferson to explain why, though now willing to see a bill of rights added to the Constitution, he found no other solid reason to support it than the fact "that it is anxiously desired by others." With other Federalists—notably James Wilson of Pennsylvania—he still thought that a bill of rights was superfluous because the federal government could exercise only those powers that were expressly delegated to it—and those powers did not extend to violating individual liberties. Moreover, Madison confessed his "fear that a positive declaration of some of the most essential rights could not be obtained in the requisite latitude." Better (in other words) not to have any bill of rights than to incorporate in the Constitution weak statements that might actually leave room for the violation of the very liberties they were meant to protect.

Again, however, Madison drew his greatest doubts about the value of a bill of rights from his analysis of the problem of majority tyranny. In a monarchical regime, Madison noted, such declarations might serve as "a signal for rousing and uniting the superior force of the community" against the government. But in a republic, where the greatest dangers to liberty arose not from government but from the people themselves, a bill of rights could hardly serve to rally the majority against itself. The most Madison would concede was that a bill of rights might help to instill in the people greater respect for "the fundamental maxims of the free government," and thus "counteract the impulses of interest and passion." He was willing to entertain, too, the idea that a bill of rights would be useful in case "usurped acts of the government" threatened the liberties of the community—but in his thinking, that problem remained only a speculative possibility.

Like any intellectual, then, Madison valued consistency too highly to renounce ideas to which he was deeply and personally committed. But Madison, for all his originality as a political theorist, was also a working politician. His early disappointment with the Constitution had quickly given way to the belief, as he wrote in *The Federalist* No. 38, that "the errors which may be contained in the Constitution . . . [were] such as will not be ascertained until an actual trial shall have pointed them out." Amendments taking the form of a bill of rights might serve a vital *political* function—even though unnecessary on their merits—if they could be framed in such a way as to reconcile the moderate opponents of the Constitution without opening an avenue to a radical assault on the essential structure of the new government.

This sensitivity to the need to assuage popular opinion was reinforced by Madison's own experience in the first congressional elections of 1788-89, when he faced a difficult fight against James Monroe. With reports abroad that Madison "did not think that a single letter of [the Constitution] would admit of a change," he found it necessary not only to return to Virginia from his seat in the Confederation Congress at New York and to travel around the district debating with Monroe, but more important, to issue public letters affirming his willingness to propose and support amendments guaranteeing such "essential rights" as "the rights of Conscience in the fullest latitude, the freedom of the press, trials by jury, security against general warrants &c." Even then, however, he was careful to note that he had "never seen in the Constitution . . . those serious dangers which have alarmed many respectable Citizens."

Political Exigencies

Madison carried the election by a margin of 336 votes out of 2,280 cast. Four weeks into the first session of Congress, he informed his colleagues of his intention to bring the subject of amendments forward, but another month passed before he was at least able to present a comprehensive set of proposals on June 8, 1789.

Some congressmen thought that Madison was acting from political motives alone. Senator Robert Morris of Pennsylvania scoffed that Madison "got frightened in Virginia 'and wrote a Book'"—a reference to his public letters on amendments. But there was nothing disingenuous about Madison's June 8 speech introducing his plan of amendments. Having reconciled himself to political exigencies, Madison sought to achieve goals consistent with his private beliefs.

In typical scholarly fashion, he had culled from over two hundred amendments proposed by the state ratification conventions a list of nineteen potential changes to the Constitution. Two of his proposals concerned congressional salaries and the population ratio of the House; two can best be described as general statements of principles of government. The remaining amendments fell under the general rubric of "rights."

The most noteworthy aspects of Madison's introductory speech of June 8 is that it faithfully recapitulates the positions he had taken not only in his election campaign against Monroe but also in his correspondence with Jefferson. He took care to deal with the objections that could come from Anti-Federalists and Federalists alike, noting his reasons for originally opposing amendments, explaining why he had changed his mind, yet also leaving his listeners and readers with a clear understanding that he was acting on a mixture of political and principled motives. The central elements of his analysis of the problem of protecting rights in a republican government were all there: the difficulty of enumerating rights, the emphasis on the greater danger from popular majorities than acts of government, the risks of trusting too much to "paper barriers."

Two of his proposals deserve special notice. The first is the forerunner of the Ninth Amendment. In its graceless original wording, it read: "The exceptions here or elsewhere in the constitution, made in favor of particular rights, shall not be so construed as to diminish the just importance of other rights retained by the people; or as to enlarge the powers delegated by the constitution; but either as actual limitations of such powers, or as inserted merely for greater caution." Here Madison sought to prevent the enumeration of specific rights from relegating other rights to an inferior status—a concern that was consistent with both his open-ended notion of rights and his fear that any textually specific statement might inadvertently or otherwise create loopholes permitting the violation of liberties. As finally adopted by Congress and ratified by the states, this amendment came to read: "The enumeration in the Constitution, of certain rights, shall not be construed to deny or disparage others retained by the people."

Among all the provisions of the Bill of Rights, this somewhat mysterious formula has had perhaps the most curious history. Long ignored and disparaged because it did not identify the additional rights it implied should be protected, it was resurrected in the critical 1965 case of *Griswold v. Connecticut*. In his concurring opinion, Justice Arthur Goldberg invoked the Ninth Amendment to support the claim that state prohibition on contraception even for married couples violated a fundamental right of privacy that did not need to be specifically identified to be deserving of constitutional protection. If interpreted in Madisonian terms, this "forgotten" provision is immediately and enormously relevant to the current controversy over the extent to which judges can recognize claims of rights not enumerated in the text of the Constitution itself.

"No State Shall Violate . . ."

The second proposal of particular interest—and arguably the most important to Madison—held that "No state shall violate the equal rights of conscience, or the freedom of press, or the trial by jury in criminal cases." All the other amendments that Madison enumerated elsewhere in his speech imposed limitations on the power of the national government alone. This amendment, by contrast, proposed adding to the prohibitions on state legislative authority already found in Article VI of the Constitution these further restraints in the three critical areas of religion, speech, and criminal law. Here, in effect, Madison belatedly hoped to salvage something of his original intention of creating a national government capable of protecting individual rights within (and against) the individual states, in a manner consistent with his belief that the greatest threats to liberty would continue to arise there, and not at the national level of government.

On this proposal Madison again met defeat. Not until the adoption of the Fourteenth Amendment in 1868 would the Constitution contain provisions that would establish a firm foundation upon which the federal government could finally act as the James Madison of 1787-89 had hoped it would. But after a variety of procedural delays, Congress finally endorsed Madison's remaining provisions for the protection of individual liberty. All of the first ten amendments that we collectively describe as the Bill of Rights appeared, in seminal form, in Madison's speech of June 8. Among the rights he then insisted upon recognizing, Madison included: free exercise of religion; freedom of speech, of the press, and the right of assembly; the right to bear arms; and the protection of fundamental civil liberties against the legal and coercive power of the state through such devices as restrictions on "unreasonable searches and seizures," bail, "the right to a speedy and public trial" with "the assistance of counsel," and the right to "just compensation" for property.

Rethinking

Because the states retained the major share of legislative responsibility for more than another century, the Bill of Rights had little initial impact. Arguably only during the past forty years has it emerged as a central pillar of American constitutionalism—and thus as a central source of political controversy as well, as the current debate over the legitimacy of judicial "activism" in the enforcement and even creation of rights readily attests. But the question of what the prohibitions of the Bill of Rights finally mean can be answered only in part by appealing to the evidence of history.

Madison himself was one of the first to realize how ideas of rights had to be adjusted to meet changing political circumstances. His original breakthroughs in constitutional theory had rested on the conviction that in a republic the greatest dangers to liberty would arise "not from acts of government contrary to the sense of its constituents, but from acts in which the Government is the mere instrument of the major number of the constituents." He had further predicted that the greatest dangers to liberty would continue to arise within the states. Within a decade of the writing of the Constitution, however, the efforts of the Federalist administration of President John Adams to use the Sedition Act of 1798 to quell the opposition press of Madison's Republican party, in seeming defiance of the First Amendment, forced Madison to rethink his position. Now he saw more clearly how the existence of a bill of rights could serve to rally public opinion against improper acts of government; how dangers to liberty could arise at the enlightened level of national government as well as at the more parochial level of the states; and even how the political influence of the states could be used to check the excesses of national power.

Our ideas of rights and liberty have deep historical and philosophical roots which any good faith effort

and its first ten amendments suggests that his views deserve particular attention and even respect. Yet just as his own efforts to understand both what the Constitution meant and how liberty was to be protected continued well after 1789—indeed literally to his death nearly a half century later—neither can ours be continued to recovering only some one meaning frozen at a mythical moment of supreme understanding. Such a moment has never existed and never will.

This paper is used here with the permission of Project '87 of the American Historical Association and the American Political Science Association. This paper orginially appeared in Issue No. 18 of *this Constitution: A Bicentennial Chronicle* (Spring/Summer 1988): 4-10.

Background Paper 4

The Range and Reach of The Bill of Rights

Russell L. Hanson

For most Americans rights are the essence of modern citizenship. We seldom dwell on the responsibilities we owe to other citizens, or on our obligations to local, state, and national government. Instead, we concentrate on the freedom of individual action that rights allow. Thus, we know our rights, or at least we think we do, and we are quick to claim them when our rights are threatened or violated. We even promise to "take our case all the way to the Supreme Court" in order to defend our rights. Of course, few of us have the resources needed to fulfill this expensive promise, but that does not in the least diminish the importance we attach to legal rights in our conception of civic life.

The range of rights we claim is very broad, even if we exclude privileges often mistaken for rights (e.g., the "right" to drive an automobile). At a minimum, it includes those spelled out in Article I, Section 9 of the Constitution of the United States, its Bill of Rights, and subsequent amendments. Article I, Section 9 prohibits bills of attainder and the suspension of writs of *habeas corpus*, "unless when in Cases of Rebellion or Invasion the public Safety may require it." The Bill of Rights enunciates our most widely known and deeply cherished civil liberties and rights. Less frequently mentioned, but just as important, are the guarantees of the Thirteenth, Fourteenth, Fifteenth, Nineteenth, Twenty-fourth and Twenty-sixth Amendments.[1] A full catalog would also include rights mentioned in state constitutions, which in some cases extend beyond rights protected under the Constitution to include such things as the right to an equal education.[2]

Thus, what I call the *range* of constitutionally protected rights is wide, even under a strict construction or interpretation of fundamental law. In the latter part of the twentieth century, this range has been extended even further by broad interpretations as-

sociated with judicial "activists" in state and federal court systems, especially the Supreme Court under Chief Justice Earl Warren. So profound was the impact of the Warren Court that some contemporary observers refer to its accomplishments as a "second revolution" to mark its expansion of rights in the United States.[3]

Expansions of the range of rights by judicial interpretation are not necessarily permanent, however. Precisely because these extensions are the result of judicial rulings, they are subject to change. Re-interpretation may contract the range of rights enjoyed by Americans: witness the recent decisions of the Rehnquist Court on affirmative action.[4] However, reversion to narrower interpretations of rights are unusual, and when they do occur they tend to be partial and limited to rather specific areas of law. That does not make them any less important, especially for those whose rights are curtailed. Still, it seems quite unlikely that current or future Supreme Court justices will undo their predecessors' handiwork and return to a narrower construction of the range of rights we enjoy.

Even more permanent and sweeping are extensions of the *reach* of rights. The reach of rights refers to those against whom rights—however broadly or narrowly defined—may be asserted. Rights that once could not be claimed against individuals now may be pressed successfully: for example, homeowners may not legally discriminate against renters or buyers of a different race, religion, or ethnic background, though they once could. Neither are corporate actors (e.g., businesses or business-related clubs and organizations) any longer permitted to exclude women, blacks, or other minorities from employment or membership. In case after case, the Supreme Court has struck down national, state, and local laws that either mandated segregation or allowed discrimination to go unchecked. Indeed, the Court has now committed all levels of government to enforce the civil rights of those who are victims of unequal treatment.

Hence, Americans now enjoy a broader range of civil rights than ever before, and their rights reach much deeper than previously. Constitutional amendments and judicial findings have established new rights to "equal protection of the laws," whether those laws are federal, state, or local in origin. These new civil rights are national rights; their establishment is simultaneously an expansion of the range of rights and an extension of their range. It is difficult to imagine how it could be otherwise. The very idea of "equal protection" implies that every citizen has the same rights; no one is entitled to more rights than another, just as no one deserves fewer rights than others. Once recognized, civil rights must be uniformly available to all citizens of the nation.[5]

In short, where civil rights are concerned there is no such thing as "dual citizenship." The basic rights we enjoy do not depend on whether we are residents of Massachusetts or Mississippi, at least not in any legal sense. That is the sense in which the civil rights movement produced new rights. However, the nationalization of rights has another, less familiar, aspect that I want to emphasize here. The second aspect applies certain rights of the Constitution against state and local governments; it therefore extends the reach of "old" rights.

This momentous development is often referred to as the "nationalization of the Bill of Rights," a process that has greatly expanded our civil liberties. In the absence of this development, Americans would not enjoy many of the freedoms they now take for granted. For example, consider the rights of the accused, including so-called "Miranda rights," the right to counsel, and the right to a speedy trial by a jury of peers. The Constitution guarantees these rights in federal courts, but more than ninety percent of all criminal trials in the United States are conducted in state court systems. It is only because these rights have been nationalized that they "reach" to the state and local levels.

If these rights had not been incorporated or nationalized, most persons accused of criminal activity could not claim them in their encounters with the criminal justice system. Advocates of "law and order" might applaud this, but how safe would we feel, how secure would our liberty seem, if we could not count on these rights when we need them?

Similarly, most laws and ordinances regulating speech, political assembly, and religious practices are passed by state and local governments, not the government in Washington. Assuming these laws do not contradict the constitution of the states in which they are enacted, there is no protection from them, except via the nationalization of rights. Hence, the application of the Bill of Rights to the states is a crucial development in the history of our nation; ours would be a *very* different society if this had not happened.

As we approach the Bicentennial of the Bill of Rights, it seems especially appropriate to recall how the nationalization of civil liberties came to pass, and why. The story is an interesting one, full of lessons about how rights and liberties achieve legal recognition. Retelling it is a way for us to convey to our students a sense of the history of rights in this country, and an appreciation for the role of law in determining their range and reach.

Retelling the story of the nationalization of the Bill of Rights is also an invitation to political action, since law is not something that is given to us. Law is something we make for ourselves, or cause others to make for us, in order to live justly with one another. Therefore, the structure of rights and liberties embedded in law is ultimately one of our own design. We may accept rights and liberties as they now exist, or we may prefer a different set of freedoms. The choice is ours, and with it, the responsibility to choose wisely.

The Doctrine of Dual Citizenship

The idea that the Bill of Rights protects us from state and local governments is surprisingly recent; only within our lifetime has the nationalization of the Bill of Rights been substantially accomplished. For most of our nation's history, the Supreme Court consistently held that the Bill of Rights merely protected citizens from actions taken by the national government. It ruled that guarantees mentioned in the first eight amendments did *not* apply to state and local governments, except insofar as state constitutions made provision for them. (And, if a state's constitution did provide such rights and liberties, citizens enjoyed them because they were citizens of that state, not because they were protected under the Constitution.)

This was consistent with the thinking of the Anti-Federalists, who were the strongest supporters of the Bill of Rights.[6] The Anti-Federalists relied on bills of rights in state constitutions to protect them against state and local governments. A national Bill of Rights was necessary only because the Constitution established a central government with substantial powers over the lives and livelihoods of American citizens.

Enumerating the rights of citizens against this government was essential, for it would instill in the populace a high regard for rights, and a willingness to claim them in the face of any abuses of power that might occur.

The Anti-Federalists had no notion that the Supreme Court should apply the Bill of Rights against state governments, and indeed they feared the emergence of a court with such sweeping powers of judicial review. They took little comfort from Alexander Hamilton's characterization of the judiciary as the "least dangerous branch" of the new government, and warned against the possibility of judicial tyranny, if the Court took it upon itself to strike down laws enacted by duly elected state legislatures.[7]

Of course, we know that the Supreme Court, under Chief Justice John Marshall, quickly claimed broad powers of judicial review in *Marbury v. Madison* (1803). The Marshall Court used its powers in a series of landmark decisions asserting the supremacy of national over state law, including *Fletcher v. Peck* (1810), *McCulloch v. Maryland* (1819), *Dartmouth College v. Woodward* (1819) and *Ogden v. Saunders* (1827). Every textbook on U.S. history, and every course on constitutional law, recites this familiar litany of cases upholding the supremacy of the Constitution, in apparent confirmation of the worst fears of the Anti-Federalists.

Yet the supremacy of the Constitution, as understood by the Marshall Court, was largely confined to economic matters involving contracts. Where civil rights and liberties were concerned, the Supreme Court declined to use the power of judicial review to overturn actions undertaken by state and local governments. For example, in *Barron v. Baltimore* (1833), Barron sued the mayor and city council for depriving him of property without just compensation. While engaged in street construction, the city of Baltimore diverted the course of several streams flowing into the harbor, and made Barron's wharf inaccessible to vessels with a deep draught. Barron's lawyer urged the Court to apply the just compensation clause of the Fifth Amendment against the state, and through it, the city of Baltimore. Chief Justice Marshall refused, opining that "the fifth amendment must be understood as restraining the power of the general government, not as applicable to the states. In their several constitutions they have imposed such restrictions on their respective governments as their own wisdom suggested; such as they deemed most proper for themselves. It is a subject on which they judge exclusively, and with which

others interfere no farther than they are supposed to have a common interest."

In so saying, a unanimous Court formally recognized a doctrine of dual citizenship that limited the reach of the Bill of Rights to national government. This doctrine prevailed throughout most of the nineteenth century; its influence was so pervasive that very few even attempted to extend the reach of rights protected under the Constitution. Not until passage of the Fourteenth Amendment was this doctrine questioned, and even then its validity was (temporarily) reasserted by the Court!

The Fourteenth Amendment, which was ratified in 1868, recognized that all persons born or naturalized in this country "are citizens of the United States and of the State wherein they reside." The language echoes the doctrine of dual citizenship, but the first section of the amendment went on to insist that "No State shall make or enforce any law which shall abridge the privileges or immunities of citizens of the United States; nor shall any State deprive any person of life, liberty, or property, without due process of law; nor deny to any person within its jurisdiction the equal protection of the laws."

The authors of this amendment, we now know, intended it to apply to the states.[8] However, the Supreme Court did not see it that way at the time. In the *Slaughter-House Cases* (1873), Justice Samuel F. Miller recognized the importance of the new amendment, but refused to abandon the doctrine of dual citizenship.[9] None of the three clauses ("privileges and immunities," "due process," or "equal protection") provided a basis for extending the reach of most of the rights protected in the Constitution of the United States, except where obviously discriminatory laws were at issue.[10] As far as other rights were concerned, only such rights as *habeas corpus* and relatively unimportant guarantees (e.g., the right to use navigable waters) were effectively incorporated by the Fourteenth Amendment's "privileges and immunities" clause—or so a majority of the justices held.

A similarly narrow construction of the "due process" clause was rendered by the Court in *Hurtado v. California* (1884).[11] In that case Justice Stanley Matthews was of the opinion that the Fourteenth Amendment did not require states to indict persons accused of criminal offenses by means of a grand jury; other methods of indictment (e.g., "information" provided by a public official) were acceptable in the eyes of the Court. This decision was based on a procedural interpretation of due process that emphasized the way in which governments conducted their business. If government officials followed established rules for notifying individuals of actions harmful to their interests or rights, etc., the requirements of due process were met, and no question of constitutionality arose.

The procedural understanding of due process began to give way under the pressure of business interests in favor of a notion of substantive due process. This interpretation entertained the possibility that existing procedures themselves might be harmful to liberty and property. A government that followed the rules, and so met the test of procedural due process, might still be acting unconstitutionally, if the rules themselves failed to respect individual rights. This view was of considerable use to businesses combating state legislatures bent on regulating their activities, and was reluctantly endorsed by the Supreme Court in *Chicago, Milwaukee & St. Paul Railway v. Minnesota* (1890), and *Chicago, Burlington & Quincy Railroad Co. v. Chicago* (1897).

The later case in particular has come to be regarded as a breakthrough in the nationalization of rights, insofar as the Supreme Court specifically used the due process clause of the Fourteenth Amendment to apply Fifth Amendment protections of private property against state actions.[12] Thus, with the dawn of the twentieth century, the doctrine of dual citizenship enunciated by Chief Justice Marshall in *Barron v. Baltimore* was held up to judicial scrutiny and found wanting.

Rights Fundamental to Liberty

By the turn of the century, the Supreme Court finally seemed willing to extend the reach of at least some of the protections provided in the Bill of Rights. However, it was not yet clear which rights would be incorporated, and which would not. Nor was it obvious how, or on what grounds, such decisions should be made. A new doctrine was needed to replace the doctrine of dual sovereignty, and it was not long in coming, though it did not bear fruit until 1925.

The ascendance of substantive due process in American law provided the impetus for a new doctrine of rights. At first, substantive due process only protected property rights from state and local governments.[13] The possibility of incorporating other protections in the Bill of Rights by way of the "due process" clause of Fourteenth Amendment was soon tested, however. The tests raised fundamental questions about the reach of rights: if the rights of the accused were so important as to require constitutional protection in the Bill of Rights, shouldn't those same rights be protected against the actions of state

and local governments? Without that protection, wasn't the liberty of individuals substantially curtailed? Didn't justice require the protection of fundamental rights from all governmental intrusions—federal, state, and local alike?

Clearly, these were (and still are) constitutional questions of the highest order. Depending on their judicial philosophies, Supreme Court Justices could answer them affirmatively or negatively. Those who subscribed to the doctrine of dual sovereignty could answer "No" to each question. Those who would answer "Yes" needed a comparable doctrine to support their interpretations, and of course they needed a majority on the Court in order for their views to prevail. Otherwise their opinion would not carry the day.

Paradoxically, the abandonment of dual sovereignty became evident in *Twining v. New Jersey* 211 U.S. 78 (1908), a case in which the Supreme Court ruled that Fifth Amendment protections against compulsory self-incrimination did *not* apply to state courts.[14] The reason it did not apply was that guarantees against self-incrimination were not "fundamental rights." Only those provisions of the Bill of Rights involving truly fundamental rights could be applied against the states, under the due process clause of the Fourteenth Amendment, or so the Court held.

But in denying relief to Twining, the Court admitted that at least some of the protections included in the Bill of Rights could be applied against the states. Furthermore, the Court (in the person of Justice William Moody) proposed a test for determining which provisions of the Bill of Rights touched on basic rights. To make this determination, it was necessary to ask if the right in question involves "a fundamental principle in liberty and justice which inheres in the very idea of free government and is the inalienable right of a citizen of such a government?" If so, the right is fundamental and applies against all levels of government; if not, the right is a restriction only on the actions of officials and agencies of the national government.

To us, the test seems fairly permissive, but the Supreme Court of the time did not understand it that way. It was not until 1925—seventeen years after the *Twining* decision—that the test was "passed" by a challenge based on the First Amendment. In 1925, the Supreme Court upheld the conviction of Benjamin Gitlow, who ran afoul of New York state laws forbidding publication of materials advocating the violent overthrow of the government.[15] Writing for the Court, Justice Edward T. Sanford took the position "that freedom of speech and press—which are protected by the First Amendment from abridgment by Congress—are among the fundamental personal rights and liberties protected by the Fourteenth Amendment from impairment by the States."

The reach of some of our most important civil liberties and rights was dramatically extended by this pronouncement. Gitlow still went to jail, however. A majority of the justices did not believe that freedom of political expression ranged so widely as to include the publication of incendiary manifestoes. Under certain circumstances, they held, the national government may regulate expression, and so, too, may the states. Thus, in *Gitlow* the Court decided that the state governments must respect freedom of expression as much—but no more—than the national government.[16]

The fundamental character of freedom of speech and press was confirmed by the Court in *Stromberg v. California* (1931) and *Near v. Minnesota* (1931).[17] Other provisions of the First Amendment were soon applied to the states as well. *DeJonge v. Oregon* (1937) nationalized the rights of assembly and petition.[18] The free exercise of religion was included in *Cantwell v. Connecticut* (1940), and a New Jersey law establishing religion was struck down in *Everson v. Board of Education of Ewing Township* (1947).[19] In these cases and their progeny, the Court insisted that the First Amendment applied equally to national and state governments, however broadly or narrowly construed those rights were.

Were First Amendment guarantees the only "fundamental" rights included in the Bill of Rights? Or were there others that might be incorporated via the due process clause of the Fourteenth Amendment?

The Supreme Court gave its answer in *Palko v. Connecticut* (1937). Once again the justices refused relief to the convicted person, in this case Frank Palko, who was subsequently electrocuted for committing homicide.[20] In reaching their decision, they proposed another test for determining which rights of the accused were fundamental, and hence applied to the state as well as national governments. In the words of Justice Benjamin Cardozo, fundamental rights are "the very essence of a scheme of ordered liberty," without which justice is impossible; deprivation of these rights is "a hardship so acute and shocking that our polity will not endure it."[21]

The already nationalized First Amendment rights were obviously fundamental under this test, and so was the right to a fair trial with advice of counsel.[22] However, a fair trial did not mean that criminal charges must be decided by a jury, or that defendants enjoyed immunity from compulsory self-incrimination, or protection from double jeopardy. Those Fifth Amendment rights were valuable and important, but not fundamental to Cardozo's scheme of ordered liberty. Hence a majority of justices was unprepared to nationalize the rights of the accused, although in *Wolf v. Colorado* (1949) the Court did make an exception to prohibit unreasonable searches and seizures by state officials.[23]

The Doctrine of Selective Incorporation

By the end of the Second World War, sentiment on the Court was changing, and its catalog of "fundamental" rights had become more extensive than Cardozo's. A doctrinal shift was proposed by Justice Hugo Black in his dissenting opinion in *Adamson v. California* (1947), where he argued that "the language of the first section of the Fourteenth Amendment, taken as a whole, was thought by those responsible for its submission to the people, and by those who opposed submission, sufficiently explicit to guarantee that thereafter no state could deprive its citizens of the privileges and protections of the Bill of Rights."[24] Hence, he urged the total incorporation of these rights, out of deference to the will of the people as expressed in the Fourteenth Amendment, and as a way of minimizing judicial discretion in deciding which rights were in accordance with "fundamental principles of liberty and justice."[25]

Three of Black's brethren—Justices William O. Douglas, Wiley Rutledge, and Frank Murphy—endorsed his doctrine of *total* incorporation, but a majority under the leadership of Felix Frankfurter did not.[26] However, a doctrine of *selective* incorporation was advanced by Chief Justice Earl Warren and Justice William Brennan, who joined the Court in 1953 and 1956, respectively. Advocates of selective incorporation agreed that most, but not all, of the rights mentioned in the first eight Amendments of the Constitution, applied to the states, just as they applied to the national government. This became the dominant view of the Warren Court, which revolutionized criminal procedure in the United States.

Selective incorporation proceeded in piecemeal fashion. In *Mapp v. Ohio* (1961), a majority of the Supreme Court held that state and local law enforcement officials were bound by the Fourth Amendment restrictions on unreasonable searches and seizures, and the so-called "exclusionary rule," which had applied in federal courts since 1914.[27] Fifth Amendment protections against self-incrimination were incorporated by *Malloy v. Hogan* (1964), and double jeopardy was prohibited in *Benton v. Maryland* (1969).[28] Sixth Amendment rights to assistance of counsel were incorporated by *Gideon v. Wainwright*

(1963); the right to confront and cross-examine witnesses was guaranteed in *Pointer v. Texas* (1965), and *Klopfer V. North Carolina* (1967) insured the right to a speedy trial.[29] The right to a trial by jury in criminal cases was incorporated in *Duncan v. Louisiana* (1968).[30] The cruel and unusual punishment clause of the Eighth Amendment was incorporated by *Robinson v. California* (1962).[31]

Thus, by the end of the 1960s most of the so-called rights of the accused applied against all levels of government. Among these rights, only the jury trial in civil cases involving more than $20, and the excessive fines and bail clause of the Eighth Amendment, had not been absorbed or incorporated. Neither had the Third Amendment's restrictions on the quartering of troops, nor the Second Amendment's right to bear arms, been applied to the states.[32]

The situation has not changed since then, and there is little likelihood that these rights will soon be incorporated. The Warren Court, which was strongly inclined toward incorporation, saw no reason to include them, although it had chances to do so. The Berger and Rehnquist Courts have been more conservative than the Warren Court, and less receptive to innovations in these areas. Moreover, there is no movement to overcome this judicial resistance, no organized demand to continue the process of incorporation to its conclusion, no strategy of litigation with that end in mind, as there was during the Civil Rights era.

If anything, public opinion has turned against liberal construction of the rights of the accused, and in favor of more aggressive law enforcement measures (e.g., preventive detention, permissive rules of evidence, and harsher sentences). The War on Drugs has replaced the War on Poverty in the minds of the people, and this was bound to affect the decisions of the Court. After all, the members of the Court are political appointees, as the recent controversy over Robert Bork reminds us. Presidents nominate candidates whose judicial philosophy seems consistent with their own, which in turn is a reflection of what their supporters among "the people" desire from the Court. The Senate, which must confirm nominees, also brings popular opinion to bear on the selection of the membership of the Court. In this way, the Court is made accountable to the people, and its judicial thinking is brought into line with mass sentiment.

Back to the Future

Although a total incorporation of the Bill of Rights now seems quite unlikely, it would be incorrect to assume that the nationalization of rights has run its full course. This would be true only if the Bill of Rights had fully secured liberty and justice for all; that is, if the first eight Amendments to the Constitution exhausted the list of fundamental rights and liberties. While that might be a comforting conclusion, it is certainly not one that enjoys the assent of all Americans. For example, the Bill of Rights is silent on the question of civil rights against unequal treatment. Anti-discrimination cases generally have been brought to the Court under the equal protection clause of the Fourteenth Amendment, which does not incorporate old rights, so much as it establishes new rights. More precisely, it allows the Court to expand the range of rights via judicial interpretation, if a majority of its members are so inclined. The fact that *Brown v. Board of Education* overturned *Plessy v. Ferguson* (1896), a decision rendered almost thirty years *after* ratification of the Fourteenth Amendment, shows that expansive interpretations of equal protection are far from automatic.[33] *University of California v. Bakke* (1978), and more recently *Wards Cove Packing Company v. Atonio* (1989), also remind us of the Court's reluctance to move beyond support for anti-discrimination to vigorous affirmative action.[34]

Neither does the Bill of Rights say anything about such "fundamental" rights as the right to privacy, which is central to current debates about state laws governing abortion and the "right to die." Those who claim the right to privacy in its various manifestations surely do not mean to restrict its application to the national government. In fact, these rights are most especially meant to apply against state governments, since it is state policymakers, not national officials, who are most determined to regulate medical practices central to abortion and the treatment of terminally ill persons.

Thus, as with civil rights, decisions about the range of privacy rights are now inextricably bound up with considerations of their reach. Nowhere is this illustrated better than in the abortion cases. As is well known, *Roe v. Wade* (1973) was prepared by *Griswold v. Connecticut* (1965), where Justice Douglas found a right of privacy not explicitly mentioned anywhere in the Constitution.[35] That right, he argued, was implicit in other rights which "create zones of privacy." Thus, the First Amendment's right of association, the Third Amendment's restriction on the quartering of troops, the Fourth Amendment's proscription of unreasonable searches and seizures, and the Fifth Amendment's protection against compulsory self-incrimination, implied a fundamental right of privacy, which Douglas also said might be among the unenumerated rights "retained" by the people in the Ninth Amendment.[36]

It was this fundamental right of privacy that was the basis for the majority's opinion in *Roe v. Wade*, which held that states may proscribe abortion only in the last trimester of pregnancy, when the fetus is "viable." Since then, a series of decisions has permitted states more latitude in regulating abortion. In some states, minors may be compelled to notify parents before obtaining an abortion; and in others, medical insurance for indigent women does not cover abortions. Of course, the so-called "Hyde Amendment" prohibits the expenditure of federal funds on abortion, making it impossible for women to terminate their pregnancies under Medicaid.[37]

These decisions allow restrictions on abortion, but they do not permit states to outlaw abortion outright. Unless *Roe v. Wade* is overturned, the right of privacy is fundamental and includes "freedom of reproductive choice." That freedom exists within limits, and the limits may differ from state to state, but the existence of the right is legally indisputable. So is its reach; *Roe* specifically enjoins state and local governments from proscribing abortion, and in that sense it recognizes a "national" right.

It remains to be seen if *Webster v. Reproductive Health Services* (1989) points toward an eventual reversal of *Roe v. Wade*; certainly, there are signs that a number of the current members of the Rehnquist Court are interested in revisiting this question. A majority of justices may eventually decide that the right to privacy does not exist, or more likely that it does not guarantee access to abortions. If so, the states will be free to regulate or outlaw abortions as they see fit; they will no longer be restricted by constitutional considerations.

What the justices will not do, however, is return to the doctrine of dual citizenship, and assert that the right to abortion is constitutionally protected from actions of the national government, but does not apply against state governments. The very idea seems so strange as to make it impossible for the Court to adopt this line of reasoning.[38] That is a telling measure of how far the nationalization of rights has proceeded. Now, once a constitutional right is recognized, it applies to all levels of governments; its scope is no longer an issue.

Precisely for that reason, the impact of Supreme Court decisions has never been greater. Opinions that define the range of rights, determine their reach as well. The controlling effects of landmark decisions are felt throughout our judicial system, giving the Supreme Court an enormous role in deciding some of the most important and divisive questions of our time. Knowing this, diverse groups of citizens press their cases upon the justices, hoping for a settlement that would compel national, and especially state, policymakers to embody their preferences in law. The extensive mobilization of resources and the pursuit of detailed litigation strategies by interested parties show how "political" this process of appealing to the Court has become.[39]

The proliferation of claimed rights and a corresponding politicization of the Supreme Court are unavoidable results of this process. Indeed, they are part and parcel of the nationalization of rights in our country. Without rights-conscious citizens willing and able to claim constitutional protection, test cases never would have been heard by the Supreme Court, and its decisions never would have had the effect of nationalizing the Bill of Rights. But citizens were willing to make claims, and the Court has been sympathetic to doctrines of incorporation, at least recently. As a result, the nationalization of rights has become self-sustaining, and is likely to remain so until citizens have decided they have quite enough rights and liberty.

Notes

1. Respectively, these amendments outlaw slavery, insist on due process and equal protection of laws, enfranchise racial minorities, extend suffrage to women, prohibit poll taxes, and lower the voting age to eighteen.

2. In *Brown v. Board of Education of Topeka*, 347 U.S. 483 (1954) the Supreme Court held racially segregated school systems to be unconstitutional, not because they provided unequal educations, but because they were inherently discriminatory. That equal education is not a fundamental right protected under the Constitution was affirmed in *San Antonio Independent School District v. Rodriguez* 411 U.S. 1 (1973). Hence, the importance of rights protected under (some) state constitutions.

3. An excellent review and analysis of this development may be found in Richard C. Cortner, *The Supreme Court and the Second Bill of Rights* (Madison, WI: University of Wisconsin Press, 1981). Cortner does not restrict his attention to the Warren Court, but that Supreme Court necessarily figures quite prominently in his story.

4. For example, see *Wards Cove Packing Company v. Atonio*, 57 U.S.L.W. 4583 (U.S. June 5, 1989).

5. Indeed, non-citizens may also claim them, both on moral and legal grounds. In the following remarks I use the term citizen in a colloquial sense, referring to all residents, regardless of their formal citizenship.

6. Robert A. Rutland's *The Birth of the Bill of Rights, 1776-1791* revised edition (Boston: Northeastern University Press, 1983) expertly recounts the story of the adoption of the Bill of Rights. A fine collection of relevant documents from the period is contained in volume 1 of Philip B. Kur-

land and Ralph Lerner, *The Founders' Constitution* (Chicago: University of Chicago Press, 1987). Volume 5 of the same collection places each of the first ten amendments in historical context.

7. For Hamilton's description of the national judiciary, see *Federalist* No. 78. A good statement of Anti-Federalist views may be found in the essays of Brutus (e.g., No. XV). The essays of Brutus are re-printed in Herbert Storing, ed., *The Anti- Federalist* (Chicago: University of Chicago Press, 1985).

8. Michael Kent Curtis, *No State Shall Abridge: The Fourteenth Amendment and the Bill of Rights* (Duke, NC: Duke University Press, 1987). Raoul Berger's *The Fourteenth Amendment and the Bill of Rights* (Norman: University of Oklahoma Press, 1989) offers a spirited criticism of Curtis' interpretation of the historical record of the genesis of this crucial amendment, a record that does not permit a definitive reading.

9. *Slaughter-House Cases*, 16 Wall 36, 21 L.Ed. 394 (1873). A corrupt Reconstruction government in Louisiana conferred a monopoly upon a New Orleans butchering operation, preventing about one thousand existing firms and individuals from continuing their trade. They claimed that their "privileges and immunities" had been abridged, but the Court held otherwise. Ironically, when the monopoly was suspended by a later legislature, it pressed a "due process" claim upon the Supreme Court, and lost.

10. Wrote Miller: "It is quite clear, then, that there is a citizenship of the United States, and a citizenship of a state, which are distinct from each other, and which depend upon different characteristics or circumstances in its individuals."

11. *Hurtado v. California* 110 U.S. 516 (1884) was brought by Joseph Hurtado, who was convicted of murder and sentenced to hang. His indictment was based on the presentation of information by a prosecuting officer, a method still used in many states for noncapital crimes and civil cases.

12. Richard C. Cortner, "The Nationalization of the Bill of Rights: An Overview," *this Constitution* (Spring/Summer 1988): 14-19.

13. The key decision was *Lochner v. New York* 198 U.S. 45 (1905), in which the Court held unconstitutional a state law restricting the length of bakery employees' work week, on the grounds that it interfered with the freedom of contracts.

14. Albert C. Twining, President of Monmouth Safe & Trust Company, and his treasurer, David C. Cornell, were accused of deceiving a bank examiner. They did not testify in their own defense, and the presiding judge instructed the jury to construe this as a sign of guilt, if it chose.

15. *Gitlow v. New York* 268 U.S. 652 (1925).

16. I shall return to this important point again, when I consider the interaction of changes in the range and reach of rights. Clearly, once rights have been substantially nationalized, any expansion or contraction of their range will almost immediately affect our entire judicial system. This marks a departure from most of our history, when national

and state court systems were unintegrated, except through the slow diffusion of legal reasoning—which is of course much different from the controlling effects of precedent.

17. *Stromberg v. California* 283 U.S. 359 (1931) was an appeal brought by Yette Stromberg, a member of the Young Communist League who led a group of summer camp students in a pledge of allegiance to a red flag. She was convicted of violating a state law prohibiting the display of such flags. *Near v. Minnesota* 283 U.S. 697 (1931) involved scandal-sheet publisher Jay Near, who was convicted of violating the Minnesota Gag Law, which permitted prior restraint on publication by government officials.

18. *DeJonge v. Oregon* 299 U.S. 353 (1937) overturned the conviction of Dirk DeJonge, a member of the Communist Party, whose attendance at a peaceful meeting of the party broke a state law.

19. *Cantwell v. Connecticut* 310 U.S. 296 (1940) involved a father and two sons who were Jehovah's Witnesses. Their prosyletizing in a Roman Catholic neighborhood brought them into conflict with state laws governing solicitation, and inciting a breach of peace (because some of their materials were anti- Catholic). In *Everson v. Board of Education of Ewing Township* 330 U.S. 1 (1947), the "establishment" of religion originated in a state subsidy for transporting students to and from parochial schools.

20. Palko had been tried for killing two policemen. He was charged with murder in the first degree, convicted by a jury of murder in the second degree, and sentenced to life in prison. The state of Connecticut appealed, and won a new trial in which Palko was convicted of first-degree murder, a capital offense. Palko appealed, claiming protection under the double-jeopardy clause of the Fifth Amendment. Cf. *Palko v. Connecticut* 302 U.S. 319 (1937).

21. The founders' views of the relation between liberty and order are ably represented in John J. Patrick, *Liberty and Order in Constitutional Government: Ideas and Issues in the Federalist Papers* (Richmond, VA: The Virginia Jefferson Association, 1989).

22. At least where capital offenses were concerned. Consult the Court's decision on the notorious case of the "Scottsboro" boys, seven illiterate black men who were accused of raping two white girls. The young men were not provided with adequate counsel, which the justices held to be fundamental to a fair trial. Cf. *Powell v. Alabama* 287 U.S. 45 (1932).

23. In *Wolf v. Colorado* 339 U.S. 25 (1949), the Court forbade unreasonable searches and seizures, but declined to force states to "exclude" illegally obtained evidence from trials. This anomaly was not finally removed until 1961.

24. The case involved Adamson, who was charged with first-degree murder, and who at trial invoked Fifth Amendment protections against self-incrimination.

25. Black was not the first to espouse the doctrine of total incorporation. That honor belonged to Justice John Marshall Harlan the elder, who argued alone and in vain for total incorporation in his dissents in *Hurtado* and *Twining*. Joseph P. Bradley's dissent in the *Slaughter-House Cases* was the first opinion to consider the use of the Fourteenth

Amendment as a vehicle for incorporation, total or otherwise.

26. Actually, Rutledge and Murphy were prepared to go further, incorporating not only the Bill of Rights, but other rights as well. Abraham refers to this doctrine as "total incorporation plus," and I shall return to it later. Cf. chapter three in Henry J. Abraham, *Freedom and the Court: Civil Rights and Liberties in the United States*, 5th edition (New York: Oxford University Press, 1988).

27. *Mapp v. Ohio* 367 U.S. 643 (1961). Dolree Mapp and her daughter were convicted of illegal possession of obscene materials. The conviction was overturned, because Cleveland police had obtained the evidence without benefit of a search warrant. The Court held that illegally obtained evidence could not be used in court, applying the "exclusionary rule" articulated in *Weeks v. United States* 232 U.S. 383 (1914).

28. *Malloy v. Hogan* 378 U.S. 1 (1964) concerned Walter Malloy, a convicted gambler who refused to cooperate in a court-ordered investigation of gambling, claiming that his testimony might be self-incriminating. *Benton v. Maryland* 395 U.S. 784 (1969) overturned the conviction of John Benton, who had originally been tried and convicted of burglary, but acquitted of larceny. The results of the first trial were set aside after the Maryland law requiring prospective jurors to swear belief in the existence of God was declared unconstitutional. In Benton's second trial, he was convicted of both larceny and burglary, whereupon he appealed to the Supreme Court, claiming "double jeopardy" on the larceny charge.

29. *Gideon v. Wainwright* 372 U.S. 335 (1963) involved Clarence Gideon, who was sentenced to five years in prison after being convicted of breaking and entering a pool hall with intent to commit a misdemeanor. Key testimony was given by a man later discovered to be the perpetrator of the crime. Gideon was denied public counsel, as the charge did not involve a capital offense. Though he was unable to win acquittal at trial, he proved to be an adept "jailhouse lawyer," presenting his petition *in forma pauperis*. The Court decided that any criminal charges involving a possible jail sentence entitled defendants to public counsel, if they could not afford a private lawyer. *Pointer v. Texas* 380 U.S. 400 (1965) was a case in which Pointer was accused of robbery, but his "victim" moved to California, and did not testify at trial. His accusations were introduced from a transcript of the preliminary hearing, denying Pointer the opportunity to confront and cross-examine his accuser. *Klopfer v. North Carolina* 386 U.S. 213 (1967) concerned a zoology professor who had participated in a sit-in, and was subsequently tried on charges of criminal trespass. Klopfer's first trial ended in a hung jury, but the state reserved its right to retry him at any time, though it had not done so more than two years later. He claimed this was a violation of his right to a speedy trial, and the Court agreed.

30. Gary Duncan, a black youth, was sentenced to sixty days in prison and a $150 fine for slapping the elbow of a white boy. He was not allowed a jury trial, which in Louisiana was reserved for capital offenses or cases in which a sentence of hard labor was possible [*Duncan v. Louisiana* 391 U.S. 145 (1968)].

31. Walter Robinson was convicted of substance abuse on the basis of "tracks" on his arms; he was not accused of the sale or possession of illegal drugs. The justices ruled that narcotic addiction was an illness, not a crime; Robinson should have been hospitalized, not incarcerated [*Robinson v. California* 370 U.S. 660 (1962)].

32. In fact, in *Quilici v. Village of Morton Grove* 532 F. Supp. 1169 (1981) a federal Court of Appeals ruled that state and local governments *may* regulate the sale and possession of guns. In the eyes of the Supreme Court, there is no *individual* right to bear arms, since the Second Amendment refers to militias. However, the political strength of the "gun lobby" has been sufficient to prevent most governments from using the powers at their disposal to regulate arms. No case involving Third Amendment claims has ever reached the Supreme Court, and only one has ever been filed in the lower courts; it was dismissed for lack of basis.

33. *Swann v. Charlotte-Mecklenburg Board of Education* 402 U.S. 1 (1971) upheld the use of court-ordered busing to desegregate schools within a single system, but *Milliken v. Bradley* 418 U.S. 717 (1974) refused to countenance "cross-district busing."

34. In *University of California Regents v. Bakke* 438 U.S. 265 (1978) the Court opposed the use of affirmative action in the form of quota systems. *Wards Cove Packing Company v. Atonio*, 57 U.S.L.W. 4583 (U.S. June 5, 1989), backed away from a string of decisions beginning with *Griggs v. Duke Power Company* 401 U.S. 424 (1971), which placed the burden of proof on employers to show that their hiring practices were not discriminatory.

35. *Griswold v. Connecticut* 381 U.S. (1965). The Court declared unconstitutional a state law prohibiting birth control. Estelle T. Griswold, the Executive Director of Planned Parenthood, and Dr. C. Lee Buxton were convicted as accessories to a crime, after counseling married couples on methods of birth control.

36. There are also those who draw on the liberty interests implied in the Fourteenth Amendment to ground privacy rights, but that is not an argument about incorporation. It is an argument about the range and reach of the Fourteenth Amendment itself, not the meaning of the Bill of Rights *per se*. Hence, I shall not consider this argument here.

37. The constitutionality of the Hyde Amendment was upheld in *Harris v. McRae* 448 U.S. 297 (1980). *Maher v. Roe* 432 U.S. 464 (1977) permitted states to deny use of their funds to provide abortions to women covered under public medical insurance programs.

38. On the other hand, in a July, 1985 statement to the American Bar Association, Attorney General Edwin Meese asserted, "The Bill of Rights was designed to apply only

to the national government. Nowhere else has the principle of federalism been dealt so politically violent and constitutionally suspect a blow as by the theory of incorporation." Meese's views won little sympathy, proving the powerful hold of the doctrine of incorporation.

39. See Frank Sorauf, "Winning in the Courts: Interest Groups and Constitutional Change," *this Constitution* (Fall, 1984): 4-10.

Background Paper 5

Teaching the Bill of Rights

John J. Patrick

The two-hundredth anniversary of the federal Bill of Rights in 1991 is the culmination of a multi-year bicentennial celebration of the U.S. Constitution. It is also a special occasion for renewal and improvement of teaching and learning the principles and values embodied in the U.S. Bill of Rights.

The great importance of the Bill of Rights in the civic life of Americans justifies great emphasis on this document in the curriculum of schools. Effective teaching and learning about the Bill of Rights are required to prepare young Americans for citizenship in their constitutional democracy. As we approach the Bill of Rights Bicentennial, civic educators should examine the status of this document in the curricula and classrooms of schools, and they should identify needs and means to improve teaching and learning about it. They should think about answers to questions such as these:

1. What is the status of the Bill of Rights in social studies programs of elementary and secondary schools?
2. What are major deficiencies in students' knowledge and attitudes about the Bill of Rights?
3. How can teaching and learning about the Bill of Rights be improved?

Status of the Bill of Rights in the Social Studies Curriculum

The Bill of Rights seems to have a prominent place in the curricula of schools, as indicated by curriculum guides and standard textbooks in American history, government, and civics. Constitutional rights and liberties are emphasized in statements of goals for education in the social studies published by local school districts, state-level departments of educa-

tion, and the National Assessment of Educational Progress.[1]

Most Americans have studied the Bill of Rights at least four times in school—(1) in a fifth-grade American studies course, (2) in a junior high/middle school American history course, (3) in a high school American history course, and (4) in a high school American government or civics course. In addition, a growing number of students have learned about Bill of Rights topics and issues through special units or elective courses in law-related education. These formal courses of study expose students to principles and values of the Bill of Rights, their origin and development, and their relevance to citizenship and government in the United States.

Despite these ample opportunities for education on the Bill of Rights, many Americans have failed to learn or retain important knowledge, values, and attitudes about constitutional rights and liberties, as revealed by various studies of the past twenty-five years.[2]

Deficiencies in Knowledge and Attitudes on the Bill of Rights

There are four major categories of deficiencies in the civic learning of Americans about their Bill of Rights:

1. Ignorance of the substance and meaning of the Bill of Rights.
2. Civic intolerance in application of constitutional liberties and rights.
3. Misunderstanding of the federal judiciary's role in regard to Bill of Rights issues.
4. Inability to analyze and appraise Bill of Rights issues.

1. *There is widespread ignorance about the substance and meaning of the Bill of Rights.* A recent nationwide survey by the Hearst Corporation found that a majority of American adults do not know that the Bill of Rights is "the first 10 amendments to the original Constitution."[3] This finding is consistent with surveys in the 1940s and 1950s, which revealed that most Americans could not make a correct statement about any part of their Bill of Rights.[4]

By contrast, a 1987 study by the Center for Civic Education (CCE) showed that most high school students "did know that the Bill of Rights is the first ten amendments to the Constitution and that its purpose is to list and guarantee individual rights."[5] The CCE study also revealed that a majority of high school students in its sample were misinformed about specific constitutional rights and ignorant of the meaning, history, and application of key concepts, such as due process of law, freedom of expression, and freedom of religion. Results of the National Assessment of Educational Progress have also shown glaring gaps in secondary school students' knowledge of the Constitution in general and civil rights and liberties in particular.[6]

One notable exception to the prevailing ignorance of constitutional rights is the category of rights of an accused person, which most adolescents and adults appear to know quite well. Perhaps this reflects their attentiveness to popular prime-time television dramas more than effective teaching and learning in schools.[7]

2. *Public attitudes about the Bill of Rights are generally positive, but support for certain liberties and rights tends to markedly decline when they are applied to cases involving unpopular minority groups or individuals.* Numerous studies from the 1950s to the 1980s have supported this finding.[8] The Purdue Youth Opinion Polls of the 1950s found a large proportion of American high school students to be "authoritarian" in their attitudes toward the Bill of Rights, because they tended to oppose application of certain civil rights and liberties to blacks, communists, atheists, and other unpopular minority groups or individuals.[9]

Adolescents of the 1980s were given the same statements about the Bill of Rights used in the 1950s Purdue polls. An even greater proportion of these 1980s teen-agers displayed authoritarian attitudes about certain constitutional rights than students did in the 1950s. For example, a larger percentage of the 1980s students were willing to allow a police search without a warrant, to deny legal counsel to criminals, and to accept restrictions on religious freedom.[10]

It seems that many Americans lack understanding of a central concept of constitutional democracy: majority rule with minority rights. In a democracy the majority rules; but if the blessings of liberty are to be enjoyed fully by all members of the society, then the rights of individuals in the minority must be protected against the possibility of tyranny, including tyranny of the majority. Thus, the United States Constitution sets limits upon the power of the majority, acting through its representatives in the government, to oppress individuals and minority groups. The Bill of Rights is a set of constitutional limitations upon the power of majorities to deprive minorities of civil liberties and rights.

3. *High school students and adults tend to misunderstand the federal judiciary's role in dealing with disputes about the meaning and application of constitutional rights.* In the Center for Civic Education study, students had misconceptions about judicial review and an independent federal judiciary as bulwarks of constitutional rights against threats of tyranny, whether attempted by majorities or minorities. Most of these students were unaware of the potential conflict between judicial review and majority rule, which may be occasioned by the Supreme Court's responsibility in particular cases for upholding the higher law of the Constitution against the tide of popular opinion.[11]

The Hearst Report also found that about half of the adult respondents misconceived the role and powers of the Supreme Court in our constitutional system of separated powers and checks and balances.[12] Michael Kammen's history of the Constitution in American culture documents the longstanding public ambivalence to and misunderstanding of the Supreme Court's role in protecting individual rights against the potential tyranny of majority rule.[13]

4. *Most high school seniors seem unprepared to define, analyze, and evaluate Bill of Rights issues.* Lack of knowledge is an obvious obstacle to deliberation, discourse, and critical thinking about constitutional issues. If students cannot recognize and comprehend their rights in the U.S. Constitution, then they certainly will not be able to cogently reflect upon them. In their report on the 1986 NAEP study of students' knowledge of history, Ravitch and Finn concluded: "[M]any of the most profound issues of contemporary society . . . have their origins and their defining events in the evolving drama of the Constitution. Yet our youngsters do not know enough about that drama, either in general or in specific terms, to reflect on or think critically about its meaning."[14]

Improvement of Education on the Bill of Rights

Research about teaching strategies and civic learning suggests that understanding of Bill of Rights concepts and issues, and positive attitudes about the paradoxical ideals of a constitutional democracy, such as majority rule with minority rights, can be achieved by most secondary school students. Tested teaching strategies involve (1) systematic and detailed coverage of Bill of Rights topics and issues in standard school courses in history, government/civics, and law-related education; (2) analysis and discussion of case studies on Bill of Rights issues; (3) analysis and discussion of primary documents associated with Bill of Rights topics and issues; and (4) active learning about Bill of Rights topics and issues in an open classroom climate.

1. *Provide systematic and detailed coverage of the subject matter.* Unless they systematically and substantially study Bill of Rights topics and issues, students will not learn them. This simple statement of truth is too often ignored in social studies textbooks and classrooms. The standard textbooks certainly mention ideas, issues, and legal decisions associated with the Bill of Rights, but the mere mentioning of ideas and facts is not sufficient to effective teaching and learning of them. Rather, the ideas in the Bill of Rights, such as freedom of speech and press, freedom of religion, due process of law, and so forth, must be woven deeply into the fabric of courses in the social studies at all levels of schooling.

A review of findings of NAEP studies concluded that,

> [S]tudents who reported "a lot" of study of U.S. history and civics topics [including Bill of Rights topics] also had higher proficiency in those subjects. Yet it appears that many students are not given the opportunity to begin studying these subject areas until later in their school careers. With a solid start in elementary school, students would have the opportunity for more depth and breadth of study.[15]

2. *Teach Bill of Rights issues, and skills in analyzing and making judgments about them, through case studies that vividly portray individuals in conflict over these issues.* The case study teaching strategy has been used successfully in various curriculum development projects from the 1960s through the 1980s.[16] In particular, projects in law-related education have emphasized lessons based on issues in case studies and have documented the instructional effectiveness of this strategy.[17]

Students tend to respond positively to lessons involving cases on constitutional issues in the lives of citizens. Landmark Supreme Court decisions in the development of constitutional rights should be emphasized in the curriculum. Successful use of case studies on Bill of Rights issues involves the following procedures: (a) a review of background information to set a context for analysis of the issue(s) and the Court's decision in the case; (b) statement and clarification of the question(s) and issue(s) in the case; (c) examination and evaluation of the Court's decision in the case; (d) examination and evaluation of dissenting opinions in the case; and (e) assessment of the significance of the Court's decision in the constitutional history of the United States.

3. *Require students to analyze, appraise, and discuss the contents of primary documents associated with Bill of Rights topics and issues.* Students are more likely to achieve higher levels of cognition about Bill of Rights topics and issues if they are taught to find and use evidence in primary documents to answer questions and participate in classroom discussions. Close reading and analysis of primary sources develop skills in interpretive and critical reading and thinking. Application of data derived from this kind of inquiry to articulation of positions in essays and classroom discussions develops essential skills in thinking, writing, and speaking. The use of primary sources in the teaching of history provides students with a grand opportunity to understand history as a dynamic interpretive enterprise, and to overcome the unfortunate, but all too common, view of this subject as static and sterile.[18]

Core documents of the founding period in United States history ought to be primary texts for study of civil liberties and rights. In addition, students need to gain an understanding of how constitutional rights have evolved since the ratification of the federal Bill of Rights in 1791. Toward this end, students should analyze amendments to the Constitution, subsequent to the Bill of Rights, pertaining to civil liberties and rights and examples from the documentary evidence about the arguments that preceded adoption of these amendments. Furthermore, they should examine key parts of the majority and dissenting opinions in landmark decisions of the Supreme Court to learn something of the development of constitutional rights in U.S. history through judicial interpretation.

4. *Establish and maintain an open and supportive classroom environment in which to actively learn about Bill of Rights topics and issues.* If students feel free and secure about investigating and expressing ideas on controversial topics, even if their ideas are unusual

or unpopular, they are more likely to develop positive attitudes about Bill of Rights ideals and to learn high-level cognitive skills needed for responsible citizenship in a constitutional democracy.[19] Active civic learning in an open classroom climate may also be associated with greater achievement of knowledge about our constitutional government. For example, few respondents in the recent national assessment in civics "reported that they had participated many times" in open classroom discussion of constitutional issues, simulated congressional hearings, and mock trials. However, those who had done so (12 percent) "tended to perform better in the assessment than their peers who had occasionally or never participated in these activities."[20]

A summary of findings from NAEP studies across twenty years indicates a strong relationship between active intellectual involvement of learners and higher achievement in the NAEP studies of civics, history, and geography. Students who were regularly required to use multiple resources, including primary documents and case studies, tended to perform better on the NAEP instruments than students who did not have these learning experiences. Students who participated in various types of student-centered learning activities, such as peer tutoring, small-group problem solving, and simulations, tended to achieve more in the NAEP studies than did students who were simply passive recipients of information.[21]

A Concluding Challenge for Teachers

Judge Learned Hand expressed an insight about constitutional rights that should forever guide the work of civic educators. He said: "Liberty lies in the hearts of men and women; when it dies there, no constitution, no law, no court can save it; no constitution, no law, nor court can even do much to help it."[22]

Judge Hand knew, as we civic educators must also know, that constitutional rights and liberties are at risk among people who neither know nor value them, because these precious freedoms are not self-enforcing. Rather, preservation and enforcement of the Bill of Rights depends upon the civic education of each successive generation of Americans. These rights will prevail in the society only if they are embedded in the intellects and spirits of a significant number of people who will publicly speak and act to sustain them.

Civic educators face the critical cyclical challenge of renewing reasoned commitment to the Bill of Rights among each generation of Americans. The great importance of this challenge warrants great

emphasis on the Bill of Rights in the curricula of schools. The Bicentennial of the Bill of Rights in 1991 is the time to revitalize teaching and learning about this fundamental document.

Notes

1. National Assessment of Educational Progress, *Civics, United States Government & Politics Objectives* (Princeton, NJ: Educational Testing Service, 1987); History-Social Science Curriculum Framework and Criteria Committee, *History-Social Science Framework for California Public Schools* (Sacramento: California State Department of Education, 1988).

2. Michael Kammen, *A Machine That Would Go of Itself: The Constitution in American Culture* (New York: Alfred A. Knopf, 1986).

3. Hearst Report, *The American Public's Knowledge of the U.S. Constitution* (New York: The Hearst Corporation, 1987), 13.

4. Kammen, 340-343.

5. Charles N. Quigley et al., *Preliminary Report on High School Students' Knowledge and Understanding of the History and Principles of the U.S. Constitution and Bill of Rights* (Calabasas, CA: Center for Civic Education, 1987), 3.

6. National Assessment of Educational Progress, *The Civics Report Card* (Princeton, NJ: Educational Testing Service, 1990); Diane Ravitch and Chester E. Finn, Jr. *What Do Our 17-Year-Olds Know? A Report of the First National Assessment of History and Literature* (New York: Harper and Row, 1987).

7. Hearst Report, 29-31; National Assessment of Educational Progress, 1990, 65.

8. Herbert McCloskey and Alida Brill, *Dimensions of Tolerance: What Americans Believe about Civil Liberties* (New York: Russell Sage Foundation, 1983).

9. H. H. Remmers and Richard D. Franklin, "Sweet Land of Liberty," in *Anti-Democratic Attitudes in American Schools,* edited by H. H. Remmers (Evanston, IL: Northwestern University Press, 1963), 61-72.

10. Stanley M. Elam, "Anti-Democratic Attitudes of High School Students in the Orwell Year," *Phi Delta Kappan* 65 (January 1984), 327-332.

11. Quigley et al., 5.

12. Hearst Report, 23-26.

13. Kammen, 357-380.

14. Ravitch and Finn, 58.

15. Ina V. S. Mullis, Eugene H. Owen, and Gary W. Phillips, *America's Challenge: Accelerating Academic Achievement, A Summary of Findings from 20 Years of NAEP* (Princeton, NJ: Educational Testing Service, 1990), 71.

16. Examples of successful use of case study materials are provided in these three volumes: Donald W. Oliver and James A. Shaver, *Teaching Public Issues in High School* (Boston: Houghton Mifflin, 1967); John J. Patrick and Richard C. Remy, *Lessons on the Constitution* (Washington, DC: Project '87 of the American Historical Association and the American Political Science Association, 1985); and Isadore Starr, *The Idea of Liberty: First Amendment Freedoms* (St. Paul, MN: West Publishing Company, 1978).

17. Mary Jane Turner and Lynn Parisi, *Law in the Class-room: Activities and Resources* (Boulder, CO: Social Science Education Consortium, 1984).

18. Matthew T. Downey and Linda S. Levstik, "Teaching and Learning History: The Research Base," *Social Education* 52 (September 1988), 336-342.

19. James S. Leming, "Research on Social Studies Curriculum and Instruction: Interventions and Outcomes in the Socio-Moral Domain," in *Review of Research in Social Studies Education*, 1976-1983, edited by William B. Stanley (Washington, DC: National Council for the Social Studies, 1985), 162-163.

20. National Assessment of Educational Progress, 1990, 83-85.

21. Mullis, Owen, and Phillips, 71-72.

22. Learned Hand, *The Spirit of Liberty* (New York: Alfred A. Knopf, 1960), 189-190.

Part II
A Bill of Rights Chronology, 1787-1792

II

A Bill of Rights Chronology, 1787-1792

Main events associated with the origin, development, and ratification of the federal Bill of Rights are listed below. The list begins with the Federal Convention's rejection of George Mason's proposal for a bill of rights. It concludes with the ratification of Amendments I-X of the United States Constitution.

September 12, 1787: Near the end of the Federal Convention, George Mason, delegate from Virginia, proposed that a bill of rights should be included in the Constitution. This proposal was rejected.

September 13, 1787: George Mason drafted "Objections to the Constitution of Government Formed by the Convention" which later was circulated as a printed pamphlet and newspaper editorial; Mason's primary "objection" was: "There is no Declaration of Rights" in the Constitution.

September 17, 1787: Thirty-nine delegates representing 12 states at the Federal Convention signed the completed Constitution of the United States of America; because of his "objections" to the document, George Mason refused to sign it.

September 20, 1787: The Confederation Congress of the United States received the proposed Constitution.

September 27, 1787: Congress voted to send the Constitution to the legislature of each state: Congress asked each state to convene a special ratifying convention, which would either approve or reject the proposed Constitution.

December 7, 1787: Delaware was the first state to ratify the Constitution; the vote was 30-0.

December 12, 1787: Pennsylvania ratified the Constitution by a 46-23 vote.

December 18, 1787: New Jersey ratified the Constitution by a 38-0 vote.

December 20, 1787: In a letter to James Madison, Thomas Jefferson argued that a bill of rights should be added to the U.S. Constitution.

January 2, 1788: Georgia was the fourth state to ratify the Constitution, the vote was 26-0.

January 9, 1788: Connecticut ratified the Constitution by a 128-40 vote.

February 6, 1788: Massachusetts ratified the Constitution by a vote of 187-168; constitutional amendments were proposed to protect the rights of persons and powers of the states.

April 28, 1788: Maryland was the seventh state to ratify the Constitution; the vote was 63-11.

May 23, 1788: South Carolina ratified the Constitution by a vote of 149-73; amendments were proposed.

June 21, 1788: New Hampshire was the ninth state to ratify the Constitution; the vote was 57-47; amendments were proposed.

June 25, 1788: Virginia ratified the Constitution by a vote of 89-79.

June 27, 1788: The Virginia Ratifying Convention proposed amendments to the Constitution; the amendments, including a bill of rights, were advanced initially by Anti-Federalist leaders (for example, George Mason and Patrick Henry); Federalist leaders (James Madison, for example) pledged to add a bill of rights to the Constitution.

July 2, 1788: Cyrus Griffin, the president of Congress, recognized that the Constitution had been ratified by the requisite nine states, a committee was appointed to prepare for the change in government.

July 26, 1788: New York was the eleventh state to ratify the Constitution; the vote was 30-27; amendments were proposed.

August 2, 1788: North Carolina refused to ratify the Constitution without the addition of a bill of rights.

September 30, 1788: Pennsylvania selected two U.S. Senators, the first state to do so. Elections of Senators and Representatives continued through August 31, 1790, when Rhode Island concluded its elections.

October 10, 1788: Congress under the Articles of Confederation completed its last day of business; it was disbanded to make way for a new government under the Constitution of 1787.

October 17, 1788: In a letter to Thomas Jefferson, James Madison discussed the value of a bill of rights in the U.S. Constitution.

February 4, 1789: Presidential electors voted; George Washington was elected President of the United States and John Adams was elected Vice President.

March 4, 1789: The first Congress convened in New York City, with eight Senators and thirteen Representatives in attendance, and the remainder traveling to New York.

April 1, 1789: The House of Representatives acted to organize for business; Frederick A. Muhlenberg of Pennsylvania was elected Speaker of the House.

April 6, 1789: The Senate acted to organize for business; John Langdon of New Hampshire was chosen to be the temporary presiding officer.

April 30, 1789: George Washington was inaugurated as the first President of the United Sates under the Constitution.

June 8, 1789: James Madison, Representative from Virginia, presented a bill of rights to the House of Representatives; he proposed that these rights should become part of the Constitution.

September 24, 1789: Congress enacted the Federal Judiciary Act, which provided for a Chief Justice and five associate Justices of the U.S. Supreme Court and which established three federal circuit courts and thirteen federal district courts.

September 25, 1789: Two-thirds of the members of both Houses of Congress, the House of Representatives and the Senate, approved twelve amendments to the Constitution, a Bill of Rights.

October 2, 1789: President George Washington sent twelve proposed constitutional amendments to the states for their approval. According to Article V of the Constitution, three-fourths of the states had to ratify these proposed amendments in order to add them to the Constitution.

November 20, 1789: New Jersey became the first state to ratify ten of the twelve amendments, which amendments would become the Bill of Rights. Two proposed amendments were rejected: one pertaining to re-apportionment of the House of Representatives and the second prohibiting pay raises for members of Congress until "an election of Representatives shall have intervened."

November 21, 1789: North Carolina became the twelfth state to ratify the Constitution; the vote was 194-77.

December 19, 1789: Maryland ratified the Bill of Rights.

December 22, 1789: North Carolina ratified the Bill of Rights.

January 19, 1790: South Carolina ratified the Bill of Rights.

January 25, 1790: New Hampshire ratified the Bill of Rights.

January 28, 1790: Delaware ratified the Bill of Rights.

February 27, 1790: New York ratified the Bill of Rights.

March 10, 1790: Pennsylvania ratified the Bill of Rights.

May 29, 1790: Rhode Island ratified the Constitution; the vote was 34-32.

June 11, 1790: Rhode Island ratified the Bill of Rights.

January 10, 1791: Vermont ratified the Constitution.

November 3, 1791: Vermont ratified the Bill of Rights.

December 15, 1791: Virginia ratified the Bill of Rights; these ten amendments became part of the Constitution of the United States of America.

March 1, 1792: Thomas Jefferson, U.S. Secretary of State, notified the states that ten amendments to the Constitution—the federal Bill of Rights—had been ratified by three-fourths of the state legislatures and were, therefore, part of the Constitution of the United States of America.

Part III
Documents

III

Documents

This section includes documents associated with the origin and enactment of the federal Bill of Rights. Documents in this section are listed below.

Teachers should use these documents as sources of ideas and information for development of lesson plans and curricula. The documents might also be duplicated and distributed to students, and used as sources for reading and writing assignments and as bases for classroom discussions. Brief commentaries about these documents are presented here.

Document 1, Virginia Declaration of Rights (1776), is the first example of constitutional rights enacted during the founding period of the United States. George Mason was the primary author of this document, which greatly influenced the declaration of rights of other newly independent American states and the federal Bill of Rights.

Document 2, Declaration of Independence (1776), was written primarily by Thomas Jefferson of Virginia and adopted by the Continental Congress about a month after George Mason drafted the Virginia Declaration of Rights. The Declaration of Independence was not written as a Declaration of Rights. Rather, it is a justification for the establishment of the thirteen United States of America. The document does, however, generally proclaim the "unalienable rights" of humankind in its memorable second paragraph.

Document 3, Virginia Statute of Religious Liberty, was drafted by Thomas Jefferson in 1779 and enacted by the Virginia state government in 1786. This law provided for freedom of conscience and expression of religious belief by individuals in Virginia. The state government was prohibited from abridging this right of religious liberty. This idea was incorporated subsequently into the federal Bill of Rights.

Document 4, Articles of Compact, the Ordinance of 1787, constituted the first Bill of Rights enacted by the government of the United States. It was passed on July 13, 1787 by the Confederation Congress (acting under the Articles of Confederation). These six articles, at the end of the Northwest Ordinance, proclaimed certain inviolable rights of the inhabitants of the territory north and west of the Ohio River. Most of these individual rights were later incorporated into the federal Bill of Rights.

Document 5, George Mason's Objections to the Constitution, was written and circulated throughout the United States during the autumn of 1787. Mason represented Virginia at the Constitutional Convention, but he refused to sign the document and campaigned against ratification of it. This document is

Mason's argument against the Constitution of 1787. His primary objection was the lack of a federal Bill of Rights.

Document 6, Letter from Jefferson to Madison, was written on December 20, 1787 in Paris, where Thomas Jefferson was serving as ambassador from the United States to the government of France. In this letter, Jefferson criticizes the Constitution of 1787 because it lacked a bill of rights. His arguments probably influenced James Madison to become an advocate for addition of a bill of rights to the Constitution.

Document 7, Letter from Madison to Jefferson, was written on October 17, 1788 and sent from New York City to Paris, France. Madison explained his views about the functions of a bill of rights in a republican system of government. He also revealed his conversion to the cause of adding a bill of rights to the federal Constitution.

Document 8, Articles on Rights in the Constitution of 1787, includes examples of constitutional rights of individuals in various articles. This document demonstrates that several important civil liberties and rights were included in the main body of the Constitution.

Document 9, Madison's Speech to the House of Representatives, June 8, 1789, was a fulfillment of his pledge to propose a bill of rights for the U.S. Constitution. In this speech, Madison, a Representative from Virginia, included all the provisions that were adopted in 1791 as the federal Bill of Rights. Madison also provided an exemplary rationale for adding certain rights for individuals to the U.S. Constitution. Finally, he recognized the fundamental role of the federal judicial system in securing these constitutional rights.

Document 10, The Federal Bill of Rights, consists of Amendments I-X of the U.S. Constitution. These ten amendments were ratified by the requisite number of states by the end of 1791.

Document 11, Subsequent Constitutional Amendments that Pertain to Rights, were enacted and ratified during the period from the end of the Civil War until 1971, when Amendment XXVI was ratified. These constitutional amendments reveal how the civil liberties and rights of individuals have been expanded through substantive changes in the U.S. Constitution.

Document 1

Virginia Declaration of Rights, 1776

A Declaration of Rights made by the Representatives of the good people of Virginia, assembled in full and free Convention; which rights do pertain to them and their posterity, as the basis and foundation of Government.

1. That all men are by nature equally free and independent, and have certain inherent rights, of which, when they enter into a state of society, they cannot, by any compact, deprive or divest their posterity; namely, the enjoyment of life and liberty, with the means of acquiring and possessing property, and persuing and obtaining happiness and safety.

2. That all power is vested in, and consequently derived from, the People; that magistrates are their trustees and servants, and at all times amenable to them.

3. That Government is, or ought to be, instituted for the common benefit, protection, and security of the people, nation, or community; of all the various modes and forms of Government that is best which is capable of producing the greatest degree of happiness and safety, and is most effectually secured against the danger of mal-administration; and that, whenever any Government shall be found inadequate or contrary to these purposes, a majority of the community hath an indubitable, unalienable, and indefeasible right, to reform, alter, or abolish it, in such manner as shall be judged most conducive to the publick weal.

4. That no man, or set of men, are entitled to exclusive or separate emoluments and privileges from the community, but in consideration of publick services which, not being descendible, neither ought the offices of Magistrate, Legislator, or Judge, to be hereditary.

5. That the Legislative and Executive powers of the State should be separate and distinct from the Judicative; and, that the members of the two first may be restrained from oppression, by feeling and participating the burdens of the people, they should, at fixed periods, be reduced to a private station, return into that body from which they were originally taken, and the vacancies be supplied by frequent, certain, and regular elections, in which all, or any part of the former members, to be again eligible, or ineligible, as the law shall direct.

6. That elections of members to serve as Representatives of the people, in Assembly, ought to be free; and that all men, having sufficient evidence of permanent common interest with, and attachment to, the community, have the right of suffrage, and cannot be taxed or deprived of their property for publick uses without their own consent or that of their Representative so elected, nor bound by any law to which they have not, in like manner, assented, for the publick good.

7. That all power of suspending laws, or the execution of laws, by any authority, without consent of the Representatives of the people, is injurious to their rights, and ought not to be exercised.

8. That in all capital or criminal prosecutions a man hath a right to demand the cause and nature of his accusation, to be confronted with the accusers and witnesses, to call for evidence in his favour, and to a speedy trial by an impartial jury of his vicinage, without whose unanimous consent he cannot be found guilty, nor can he be compelled to give evidence against himself; that no man be deprived of his liberty except by the law of the land, or the judgment of his peers.

9. That excessive bail ought not to be required, nor excessive fines imposed nor cruel and unusual punishments inflicted.

10. That general warrants, whereby any officer or messenger may be commanded to search suspected places without evidence of a fact committed, or to seize any person or persons not named, or whose offence is not particularly described and supported by evidence, are grievous and oppressive, and ought not to be granted.

11. That in controversies respecting property, and in suits between man and man, the ancient trial by

Jury is preferable to any other, and ought to be held sacred.

12. That the freedom of the Press is one of the greatest bulwarks of liberty, and can never be restrained but by despotick Governments.

13. That a well-regulated Militia, composed by the body of the people, trained to arms, is the proper, natural, and safe defence of a free State; that Standing Armies, in time of peace, should be avoided as dangerous to liberty; and that, in all cases, the military should be under strict subordination to, and governed by, the civil power.

14. That the people have a right to uniform Government; and, therefore, that no Government separate from, or independent of, the Government of Virginia, ought to be erected or established within the limits thereof.

15. That no free Government, or the blessing of liberty, can be preserved to any people but by a firm adherence to justice, moderation, temperance, frugality, and virtue, and by frequent recurrence to fundamental principles.

16. That Religion, or the duty which we owe to our Creator, and the manner of discharging it, can be directed only by reason and conviction, not by force or violence; and, therefore, all men are equally entitled to the free exercise of religion, according to the dictates of conscience; and that it is the mutual duty of all to practise Christian forbearance, love, and charity, towards each other.

Document 2

Declaration of Independence, 1776

The Unanimous Declaration of the Thirteen United States of America

When, in the course of human events, it becomes necessary for one people to dissolve the political bands which have connected them with another, and to assume, among the powers of the earth, the separate and equal station to which the laws of nature and of nature's God entitled them, a decent respect to the opinions of mankind requires that they should declare the causes which impel them to the separation.

We hold these truths to be self-evident: that all men are created equal; that they are endowed, by their Creator, with certain unalienable rights; that among these are life, liberty, and the pursuit of happiness. That to secure these rights governments are instituted among men, deriving their just powers from the consent of the governed; that whenever any form of government becomes destructive of these ends, it is the right of the people to alter or to abolish it, and to institute a new government, laying its foundation on such principles, and organizing its powers in such form, as to them shall seem most likely to effect their safety and happiness. Prudence, indeed, will dictate, that governments long established, shall not be changed for light and transient causes; and accordingly all experience hath shown, that mankind are more disposed to suffer, while evils are sufferable, than to right themselves by abolishing the forms to which they are accustomed. But when a long train of abuses and usurpations, pursuing invariably the same object, evinces a design to reduce them under absolute despotism, it is their right, it is their duty, to throw off such government, and to provide new guards for their future security. Such has been the patient sufferance of these colonies; and such is now the necessity which constrains them to alter their former systems of government. The history of the present King of Great Britain is a his-tory of repeated injuries and usurpations, all having in direct object the establishment of an absolute tyranny over these states. To prove this, let facts be submitted to a candid world.

He has refused his assent to laws the most wholesome and necessary for the public good.

He has forbidden his governors to pass laws of immediate and pressing importance, unless suspended in their operation till his assent should be obtained; and when so suspended, he has utterly neglected to attend to them.

He has refused to pass other laws for the accommodation of large districts of people, unless those people would relinquish the right of representation in the legislature; a right inestimable to them, and formidable to tyrants only. He has called together legislative bodies at places unusual, uncomfortable, and distant from the depository of their public records, for the sole purpose of fatiguing them into compliance with his measures.

He has dissolved representative houses repeatedly, for opposing, with manly firmness, his invasions on the rights of the people.

He has refused for a long time, after such dissolutions, to cause others to be elected; whereby the legislative powers, incapable of annihilation, have returned to the people at large for their exercise; the state remaining, in the mean time, exposed to all the dangers of invasions from without, and convulsions within.

He has endeavored to prevent the population of these States; for that purpose obstructing the laws for naturalization of foreigners; refusing to pass others to encourage their migrations hither, and raising the conditions of new appropriations of lands.

He has obstructed the administration of justice, by refusing his assent to laws for establishing judiciary powers.

He has made judges dependent on his will alone, for the tenure of their offices, and the amount and payment of their salaries.

He has erected a multitude of new offices, and sent hither swarms of officers, to harass our people, and eat out their substance.

He has kept among us, in times of peace, standing armies, without the consent of our legislatures.

He has affected to render the military independent of, and superior to the civil power.

He has combined with others to subject us to a jurisdiction foreign to our constitution, and unacknowledged by our laws; giving his assent to their acts of pretended legislation:

For quartering large bodies of armed troops among us;

For protecting them, by a mock trial, from punishment for any murders which they should commit on the inhabitants of these States;

For cutting off our trade with all parts of the world;

For imposing taxes on us without our consent;

For depriving us, in many cases, of the benefits of trial by jury;

For transporting us beyond seas to be tried for pretended offences;

For abolishing the free system of English laws in a neighbouring province, establishing therein an arbitrary government, and enlarging its boundaries, so as to render it at once an example and fit instrument for introducing the same absolute rule into these colonies;

For taking away our charters, abolishing our most valuable laws, and altering fundamentally the forms of our governments;

For suspending our own legislatures, and declaring themselves invested with power to legislate for us in all cases whatsoever.

He has abdicated government here, by declaring us out of his protection, and waging war against us.

He has plundered our seas, ravaged our coasts, burnt our towns, and destroyed the lives of our people.

He is at this time transporting large armies of foreign mercenaries to complete the works of death, desolation, and tyranny, already begun with circumstances of cruelty and perfidy, scarcely paralleled in the most barbarous ages, and totally unworthy the head of a civilized nation.

He has constrained our fellow-citizens, taken captive on the high seas, to bear arms against their country, to become the executioners of their friends and brethren, or to fall themselves by their hands.

He has excited domestic insurrections amongst us, and has endeavoured to bring on the inhabitants of our frontiers the merciless Indian savages, whose known rule of warfare is an undistinguished destruction of all ages, sexes, and conditions.

In every state of these oppressions we have petitioned for redress in the most humble terms. Our repeated petitions have been answered only by repeated injury. A prince, whose character is thus marked by every act which may define a tyrant, is unfit to be the ruler of a free people.

Nor have we been wanting in attentions to our British brethren. We have warned them, from time to time, of attempts by their legislature to extend an unwarrantable jurisdiction over us. We have reminded them of the circumstances of our emigration and settlement here. We have appealed to their native justice and magnanimity, and we have conjured them by the ties of our common kindred to disavow these usurpations, which would inevitably interrupt our connexions and correspondence. They too have been deaf to the voice of justice and of consanguinity. We must, therefore, acquiesce in the necessity which denounces our separation, and hold them, as we hold the rest of mankind, enemies in war, in peace friends.

We, therefore, the representatives of the United States of America, in General Congress assembled, appealing to the Supreme Judge of the world for the rectitude of our intentions, do, in the name, and by authority of the good people of these colonies, solemnly publish and declare. That these United Colonies are, and of right ought to be, free and independent States; that they are absolved from all allegiance, to the British crown, and that all political connexion between them and the state of Great Britain is, and ought to be, totally dissolved; and that, as free and independent States, they have full power to levy war, conclude peace, contract alliances, establish commerce, and to do all other acts and things which independent States may of right do. And for the support of this Declaration, with a firm reliance on the protection of Divine Providence, we mutually pledge to each other our lives, our fortunes, and our sacred honour.

John Hancock

New Hampshire—Josiah Bartlett, William Whipple, Matthew Thornton.

Massachusetts—Samuel Adams, John Adams, Robert Treat Paine, Elbridge Gerry.

Rhode Island,&c.—Stephen Hopkins, William Ellery.

Connecticut—Roger Sherman, Samuel Huntington, William Williams, Oliver Wolcott.

New York—William Floyd, Philip Livingston, Francis Lewis, Lewis Morris.

New Jersey—Richard Stockton, John Witherspoon, Francis Hopkinson, John Hart, Abraham Clark.

Pennsylvania—Robert Morris, Benjamin Rush, Benjamin Franklin, John Morton, George Clymer, James Smith, George Taylor, James Wilson, George Ross.

Delaware—Caesar Rodney, George Read, Thomas M'Kean.

Maryland—Samuel Chase, William Paca, Thomas Stone, Charles Carroll of Carrollton.

Virginia—George Wythe, Richard Henry Lee, Thomas Jefferson, Benjamin Harrison, Thomas Nelson, Jun., Francis Lightfoot Lee, Carter Braxton.

North Carolina—William Hooper, Joseph Hewes, John Penn.

South Carolina—Edward Rutledge, Thomas Hayward, Jun., Thomas Lynch, Jun., Arthur Middleton.

Georgia—Button Gwinnett, Lyman Hall, George Walton.

Document 3

Virginia Statute of Religious Liberty

An Act for Establishing Religious Freedom

I. Whereas Almighty God hath created the mind free; that all attempts to influence it by temporal punishments or burthens, or by civil incapacitations, tend only to beget habits of hypocrisy and meanness, and are a departure from the plan of the Holy author of our religion, who being Lord both of body and mind, yet chose not to propagate it by coercions on either, as was in his Almighty power to do; that the impious presumption of legislators and rulers, civil as well as ecclesiastical, who being themselves but fallible and uninspired men, have assumed dominion over the faith of others, setting up their own opinions and modes of thinking as the only true and infallible, and as such endeavouring to impose them on others, hath established and maintained false religions over the greatest part of the world, and through all time; that to compel a man to furnish contributions of money for the propagation of opinions which he disbelieves, is sinful and tyrannical; that even the forcing him to support this or that teacher of his own religious persuasion, is depriving him of the comfortable liberty of giving his contributions to the particular pastor whose morals he would make his pattern, and whose powers he feels most persuasive to righteousness, and is withdrawing from the ministry those temporary rewards, which proceeding from an approbation of their personal conduct, are an additional incitement to earnest and unremitting labours for the instruction of mankind; that our civil rights have no dependence on our religious opinions, any more than our opinions in physics or geometry; that therefore the proscribing any citizen as unworthy the public confidence by laying upon him an incapacity of being called to offices of trust and emolument, unless he profess or renounce this or that religious opinion, is depriving him injuriously of those privileges and advantages to which in common with his fellow-citizens he has a natural right, that it tends only to corrupt the principles of that religion it is meant to encourage, by bribing with a monopoly of worldly honours and emoluments, those who will externally profess and conform to it; that though indeed these are criminal who do not withstand such temptation, yet neither are those innocent who lay the bait in their way; that to suffer the civil magistrate to intrude his powers into the field of opinion, and to restrain the profession or propagation of principles on supposition of their ill tendency, is a dangerous fallacy, which at once destroys all religious liberty, because he being of course judge of that tendency will make his opinions the rule of judgments, and approve or condemn the sentiments of others only as they shall square with or differ from his own; that it is time enough for the rightful purposes of civil government, for its officers to interfere when principles break out into overt acts against peace and good order; and finally, that truth is great and will prevail if left to herself, that she is the proper and sufficient antagonist to error, and has nothing to fear from the conflict, unless by human interposition disarmed of her natural weapons, free argument and debate, errors ceasing to be dangerous when it is permitted freely to contradict them.

II. Be it enacted by the General Assembly, that no man shall be compelled to frequent or support any religious worship, place or ministry whatsoever, nor shall be enforced, restrained, molested, or burthened in his body or goods, nor shall otherwise suffer on account of his religious opinions or belief; but that all men shall be free to profess and by argument to maintain, their opinion in matters of religion, and that the same shall in no wise diminish, enlarge or affect their civil capacities.

III.   And though we well know that this assembly, elected by the people for the ordinary purposes of legislation only, have no power to restain the acts of succeeding assemblies, constituted with powers equal to our own, and that therefore to declare the act to be irrevocable would be of no effect in law; yet as we are free to declare, and do declare, that the rights hereby asserted are of the natural rights of mankind, and that if any act shall hereafter be passed to repeal the present, or to narrow its operation, such act will be an infringement of natural right.

Document 4

Articles of Compact
in
The Northwest Ordinance, 1787

. . . And for extending the fundamental principles of civil and religious liberty, which form the basis whereon these republics, their laws and constitutions, are erected; to fix and establish those principles as the basis of all laws, constitutions, and governments, which forever hereafter shall be formed in the said territory; to provide, also, for the establishment of States, and permanent government therein, and for their admission to share in the Federal councils on an equal footing with the original States, at as early periods as may be consistent with the general interest,

It is hereby ordained and declared, by the authority aforesaid, That the following Articles shall be considered as Articles of compact, between the Original States and the people and States in the said territory and forever remain unalterable unless by common consent, to wit:

Article the First. No person, demeaning himself in a peaceable and orderly manner, shall ever be molested on account of his mode of worship, or religious sentiments, in the said territory.

Article the Second. The inhabitants of the said territory shall always be entitled to the benefits of the writ of habeas corpus, and of the trial by Jury; of a proportionate representation of the people in the legislature, and of judicial proceedings according to the course of the common law; all persons shall be bailable, unless for capital offences, where the proof shall be evident, or the presumption great; all fines shall be moderate, and no cruel or unusual punishment shall be inflicted; no man shall be deprived of his liberty or property but by the judgment of his peers, or the law of the land; and should the public exigencies make it necessary for the common preservation to take any person's property, or to demand his particular services, full compensation shall be made for the same; and in the just preservation

of rights and property it is understood and declared; that no law ought ever to be made or have force in the said territory, that shall in any manner whatever interfere with, or affect private contracts or engagements, bona fide and without fraud previously formed.

Article the Third. Religion, Morality, and knowledge being necessary to good government and the happiness of mankind, Schools and the means of education shall forever be encouraged. The utmost good faith shall always be observed towards the Indians, their lands and property shall never be taken from them without their consent; and in their property, rights, and liberty, they never shall be invaded or disturbed, unless in just and lawful wars authorised by Congress; but laws founded in justice and humanity shall from time to time be made, for preventing wrongs being done to them, and for preserving peace and friendship with them.

Article the Fourth. The said territory, and the States which may be formed therein, shall forever remain a part of this Confederacy of the United States of America, subject to the Articles of Confederation, and to such alterations therein as shall be constitutionally made; and to all the Acts and Ordinances of the United States in Congress Assembled, conformable thereto. The Inhabitants and Settlers in the said territory, shall be subject to pay a part of the Federal debts, contracted or to be contracted, and a proportional part of the expenses of government to be apportioned on them by Congress, according to the same common rule and measure by which apportionments thereof shall be made on the other States, and the taxes for paying their proportion shall be laid and levied by the authority and direction of the legislatures of the district, or districts, or new States, as in the original States, within the time agreed upon by the United States in Congress Assembled. The Legislatures of those districts, or new States, shall never interfere with the primary disposal of the Soil by the United States in Congress Assembled, nor with any regulations Congress may find necessary for securing the title in such soil to the bona-fide purchasers. No tax shall be imposed on lands the property of the United States; and in no case shall non-resident proprietors be taxed higher than residents. The navigable Waters leading into the Mississippi and Saint Lawrence, and the carrying places between the same, shall be common highways, and forever free, as well to the Inhabitants of the said territory as to be Citizens of the United States, and those of any other States that may be admitted into the Confederacy, without any tax, impost, or duty therefor.

Article the Fifth. There shall be formed in the said territory, not less than three nor more than five States, and the boundaries of the States, as soon as Virginia shall alter her act of cession and consent to the same, shall become fixed and established as follows, to wit: The Western State, in the said territory, shall be bounded by the Mississippi, the Ohio, and the Wabash Rivers; a direct line drawn from the Wabash and Post Vincents due north, to the territorial line between the United States and Canada, and by the said territorial line to the Lake of the Woods and Mississippi. The middle State shall be bounded by the said direct line, the Wabash from Post Vincents to the Ohio, by the Ohio; by a direct line drawn due North from the mouth of the Great Miami to the said territorial line, and by the said territorial line. The eastern State shall be bounded by the last-mentioned direct line, the Ohio, Pennsylvania, and the said territorial line: Provided, however, and it is further understood and declared, that the boundaries of these three States shall be subject so far to be altered, that, if Congress shall hereafter find it expedient, they shall have authority to form one or two States in that part of the said territory which lies north of an east and west line drawn through the southerly bend or extreme of Lake Michigan; and whenever any of the said States shall have sixty thousand free Inhabitants therein, such States shall be admitted by its Delegates into the Congress of the United States, on an equal footing with the original States, in all respects whatever; and shall be at liberty to form a permanent constitution and State government, Provided The constitution and government so to be formed, shall be republican, and in conformity to the principles contained in these Articles; and so far as it can be consistent with the general interest of the Confederacy, such admission shall be allowed at an earlier period, and when there may be a less number of free inhabitants in the State than sixty thousand.

Article the Sixth. There shall be neither slavery nor involuntary servitude in the said territory, otherwise than in the punishment of crimes, whereof the party shall have been duly convicted; provided always, that any person escaping into the same, from whom labor or service is lawfully claimed in any one of the original States, such fugitive may be lawfully reclaimed and conveyed to the person claiming his or her labor or service as aforesaid.

Be it Ordained by the Authority aforesaid, that the Resolutions of the 23d of April 1784 relative to the subject of this ordinance be, and the same are hereby, repealed, and declared null and void.

Done by the United States, in Congress assembled, the 13th day of July, in the year of our Lord 1787, and of their sovereignty and independence the twelfth.

Document 5

George Mason's Objections to the Constitution of Government Formed by the Convention, 1787

There is no Declaration of Rights; and, the Laws of the general Government being paramount to the Laws and Constitutions of the several States, the Declarations of Rights in the separate States are no Security. Nor are the people secured even in the enjoyment of the Benefits of the common Law: which stands here upon no other Foundation than its having been adopted by the respective Acts forming the Constitutions of the several States.

In the House of Representatives there is not the Substance, but the Shadow only of Representation; which can never produce proper information in the Legislature, or inspire Confidence in the People: the Laws will therefore be generally made by Men little concerned in, and unacquainted with their Effects and Consequences.

The Senate have the Power of altering all Money Bills, and of originating Appropriations of Money, and the salaries of the Officers of their own Appointment in Conjunction with the President of the United States; although they are not the Representatives of the People, or amenable to them.

These with their other great powers, (*viz.*, their Power in the Appointment of Ambassadors and all public Officers, in making Treaties, and in trying all Impeachments) their Influence upon and Connection with the supreme Executive from these Causes, their Duration of Office, and their being a constant existing Body almost continually sitting, joined with their being one complete Branch of the Legislature, will destroy any Balance in the Government, and enable them to accomplish what Usurpations they please upon the Rights and Liberties of the People.

The Judiciary of the United States is so constructed and extended as to absorb and destroy the Judiciarys of the several States; thereby rendering Law as tedious, intricate, and expensive, and Justice as unattainable, by a great part of the Community, as in England, and enabling the Rich to oppress and ruin the Poor.

The President of the United States has no constitutional Council (a thing unknown in any safe and regular Government) he will therefore be unsupported by proper Information and Advice; and will generally be directed by Minions and Favorites—or He will become a Tool to the Senate—or a Council of State will grow out of the principal Officers of the great Departments; the worst and most dangerous of all Ingredients for such a Council, in a free Country; for they may be induced to join in any dangerous or oppressive Measures, to shelter themselves, and prevent an Inquiry into their own Misconduct in Office; whereas, had a constitutional Council been formed (as was proposed) of six Members; *viz.*, two from the Eastern, two from the Middle, and two from the Southern States, to be appointed by Vote of the States in the House of Representatives, with the same Duration and Rotation of office as the Senate, the executive would always have had safe and proper Information and Advice, the President of such a Council might have acted as Vice-President of the United States, *pro tempore*, upon any Vacancy or Disability of the chief Magistrate; and long-continued Sessions of the Senate would in a great Measure have been prevented.

From this fatal defect of a constitutional council has arisen the improper Power of the Senate in the Appointment of the public Officers, and the alarming Dependence and Connection between that Branch of the Legislature and the supreme Executive.

Hence also sprung that unnecessary Officer, the Vice-President, who, for want of other Employment, is made President of the Senate; thereby dangerously blending the executive and legislative Powers, besides always giving to some one of the States an unnecessary and unjust Pre-eminence over the others.

The President of the United States has the unrestrained Power of granting Pardon for Treason; which may be sometimes exercised to screen from Punishment those whom he had secretly instigated to commit the Crime, and thereby prevent a Discovery of his own Guilt.

By declaring all Treaties supreme Laws of the Land, the Executive and the Senate have in many cases, an exclusive Power of Legislation; which might have been avoided by proper Distinctions with Respect to Treaties, and requiring the Assent of the House of Representatives, where it could be done with Safety.

By requiring only a Majority to make all commercial and navigation Laws, the five Southern States (whose Produce and Circumstances are totally different from that of the eight Northern and Eastern States) will be ruined; for such rigid and premature Regulations may be made, as will enable the Merchants of the Northern and Eastern States not only to demand an exorbitant Freight, but to monopolize the Purchase of the Commodities at their own Price, for many years; to the great Injury of the landed Interest, and Impoverishment of the People. And the Danger is the greater, as the Gain on one Side will be in Proportion to the Loss on the other. Whereas, requiring two-thirds of the members present in both Houses would have produced mutual moderation, promoted the general Interest, and removed an insuperable Objection to the Adoption of the Government.

Under their own Construction of the general Clause at the End of the enumerated powers the Congress may grant Monopolies in Trade and Commerce, constitute new Crimes, inflict unusual and severe Punishments, and extend their Power as far as they shall think proper; so that the State Legislatures have no Security for the Powers now presumed to remain to them, or the People for their Rights.

There is no Declaration of any kind for preserving the Liberty of the Press, the tryal by Jury in civil causes; nor against the Danger of standing Armyes in time of Peace.

The State Legislatures are restrained from laying export duties on their own Produce. The general Legislature is restrained from prohibiting the further Importation of Slaves for twenty-odd years, though such importations render the United States weaker, more vulnerable, and less capable of Defence.

Both the general Legislature and the State Legislatures are expressly prohibited from making ex post facto Laws; though there never was, or can be a Legislature but must and will make such Laws, when necessity and the public Safety require them; which will hereafter be a Breach of all the Constitutions in the Union, and afford precedents for other Innovations.

This Government will commence in a moderate Aristocracy; it is at present impossible to foresee whether it will, in its Operation, produce a Monarchy, or a corrupt oppressive Aristocracy; it will most probably vibrate some Years between the two, and then terminate in the one or the other.

Document 6

Thomas Jefferson to James Madison

December 20, 1787

. . . The season admitting only of operations in the Cabinet, and these being in a great measure secret, I have little to fill a letter. I will therefore make up the deficiency by adding a few words on the Constitution proposed by our Convention. I like much the general idea of framing a government which should go on of itself peaceably, without needing continued recurrence to the state legislatures. I like the organization of the government into Legislative, Judiciary and Executive. I like the power given the Legislature to levy taxes; and for that reason solely approve the greater house being chosen by the people directly. For tho' I think a house chosen by them will be very illy qualified to legislate for the Union, for foreign nations &c. yet this evil does not weigh against the good of preserving inviolate the fundamental principle that the people are not to be taxed but by representatives chosen immediately by themselves. I am captivated by the compromise of the opposite claims of the great and little states, of the latter to equal, and the former to proportional influence. I am much pleased too with the substitution of the method of voting by persons, instead of that of voting by states: and I like the negative given to the Executive with a third of either house, though I should have liked it better had the Judiciary been associated for that purpose, or invested with a similar and separate power. There are other good things of less moment. I will now add what I do not like. First the omission of a bill of rights providing clearly and without the aid of sophisms for freedom of religion, freedom of the press, protection against standing armies, restriction against monopolies, the eternal and unremitting force of the habeas corpus laws, and trials by jury in all matters of fact triable by the laws of the land and not by the law of Nations. To say, as Mr. Wilson does, that a bill of rights was not necessary because all is reserved in the case of

the general government which is not given, while in the particular ones all is given which is not reserved might do for the Audience to whom it was addressed, but is surely gratis dictim [a statement not supported by fact], opposed by strong inferences from the body of the instrument, as well as from the omission of the clause of our present confederation which had declared that in express terms. It was a hard conclusion to say because there has been no uniformity among the states as to the cases triable by jury, because some have been so incautious as to abandon this mode of trial, therefore the more prudent states shall be reduced to the same level of calamity. It would have been much more just and wise to have concluded the other way that as most of the states had judiciously preserved this palladium, those who had wandered should be brought back to it, and to have established general right instead of general wrong. Let me add that a bill of rights is what the people are entitled to against every government on earth, general or particular, and what no just government should refuse, or rest on inference. The second feature I dislike, and greatly dislike, is the abandonment in every instance of the necessity of rotation in office, and most particularly in the case of the President. Experience concurs with reason in concluding that the first magistrate will always be re-elected if the constitution permits it. He is then an officer for life. This once observed it becomes of so much consequence to certain notions to have a friend or a foe at the head of our affairs that they will interfere with money and with arms. A Galloman or an Angloman will be supported by the nation he befriends. If once elected, and at a second or third election outvoted by one or two votes, he will pretend false votes, foul play, hold possession of the reins of government, be supported by the states voting for him, especially if they are the central ones lying in a compact body themselves and separating their opponents: and they will be aided by one nation of Europe, while the majority are aided by another. The election of a President of America some years hence will be much more interesting to certain nations of Europe than ever the election of a king of Poland was. Reflect on all the instances in history ancient and modern, of elective monarchies, and say if they do not give foundation for my fears, the Roman emperors, the popes, while they were in any importance, the German emperors till they became hereditary in practice, the kings of Poland, the Deys of the Ottoman dependancies. It may be said that if elections are to be attended with these disorders, the seldomer they are renewed the better. But experience shews that the only way to prevent disorder is to render them uninteresting by frequent changes. An incapacity to be elected a second time would have been the only effectual preventative. The power of removing him every fourth year by the vote of the people is a power which will not be exercised. The king of Poland is removeable every day by the Diet, yet he is never removed.— Smaller objections are the Appeal in fact as well as law, and the binding all persons Legislative, Executive and Judiciary by oath to maintain that constitution. I do not pretend to decide what would be the best method of procuring the establishment of the manifold good things in this constitution, and of getting rid of the bad. Whether by adopting it in hopes of future amendment, or, after it had been duly weighed and canvassed by the people, after seeing the parts they generally dislike, and those they generally approve, to say to them 'We see now what you wish. Send together your deputies again, let them frame a constitution for you omitting what you have condemned, and establishing the powers you approve. Even these will be a great addition to the energy of your government.'—At all events I hope you will not be discouraged from other trials, if the present one should fail of its full effect.—I have thus told you freely what I like and dislike: merely as a matter of curiosity for I know your own judgment has been formed on all these points after having heard every thing which could be urged on them. I own I am not a friend to a very energetic government. It is always oppresive. The late rebellion in Massachusetts has given more alarm than I think it should have done. Calculate that one rebellion in 13 states in the course of 11 years, is but one for each state in a century and a half. No country should be so long without one. Nor will any degree of power in the hands of government prevent insurrections. France with all its despotism, and two or three hun-

dred thousand men always in arms has had three insurrections in the three years I have been here in every one of which greater numbers were engaged than in Massachusetts and a great deal more blood was spilt. In Turkey, which Montesquieu supposes more despotic, insurrections are the events of every day. In England, where the hand of power is lighter than here, but heavier than with us they happen every half dozen years. Compare again the ferocious depredations of their insurgents with the order, the moderation and the almost self extinguishment of ours.—After all, it is my principle that the will of the Majority should always prevail. If they approve the proposed Convention in all its parts, I shall concur in it chearfully, in hopes that they will amend it whenever they shall find it work wrong. I think our governments will remain virtuous for many centuries; as long as they are chiefly agricultural; and this will be as long as there shall be vacant lands in any part of America. When they get piled upon one another in large cities, as in Europe, they will become corrupt as in Europe. Above all things I hope the education of the common people will be attended to; convinced that on their good sense we may rely with the most security for the preservation of a due degree of liberty. I have tired you by this time with my disquisitions and will therefore only add assurances of the sincerity of those sentiments of esteem and attachment with which I am Dear Sir your affectionate friend & servant,

TH: Jefferson

P.S. The instability of our laws is really an immense evil. I think it would be well to provide in our constitutions that there shall always be a twelvemonth between the ingrossing a bill and passing it: that it should then be offered to its passage without changing a word: and that if circumstances should be thought to require a speedier passage, it should take two-thirds of both houses instead of a bare majority.

Document 7

James Madison to Thomas Jefferson

October 17, 1788

. . . The little pamphlet herewith enclosed will give you a collective view of the alterations which have been proposed for the new Constitution. Various and numerous as they appear they certainly omit many of the true grounds of opposition. The articles relating to Treaties, to paper money, and to contracts, created more enemies than all the errors in the System positive and negative put together. It is true nevertheless that not a few, particularly in Virginia, have contended for the proposed alterations from the most honorable and patriotic motives; and that among the advocates for the Constitution there are some who wish for further guards to public liberty and individual rights. As far as these may consist of a constitutional declaration of the most essential rights, it is probable they will be added; though there are many who think such addition unnecessary, and not a few who think it misplaced in such a Constitution. There is scarce any point on which the party in opposition is so much divided as to its importance and its propriety. My own opinion has always been in favor of a bill of rights; provided it be so framed as not to imply powers not meant to be included in the enumeration. At the same time I have never thought the omission a material defect, nor been anxious to supply it even by subsequent amendment, for any other reason than that it is anxiously desired by others. I have favored it because I supposed it might be of use, and if properly executed could not be of disservice. I have not viewed it in an important light. 1. Because I conceive that in a certain degree, though not in the extent argued by Mr. Wilson, the rights in question are reserved by the manner in which the federal powers are granted. 2. Because there is great reason to fear that a positive declaration of some of the most essential rights could not be obtained in the requisite latitude. I am sure that the rights of conscience in particular, if sub-

mitted to public definition would be narrowed much more than they are likely ever to be by an assumed power. One of the objections in New England was that the Constitution by prohibiting religious tests opened a door for Jews, Turks and infidels. 3. Because the limited powers of the federal Government and the jealousy of the subordinate Governments, afford a security which has not existed in the case of the State Governments, and exists in no other. 4. Because experience proves the inefficacy of a bill of rights on those occasions when its controul is most needed. Repeated violations of these parchment barriers have been committed by overbearing majorities in every State. In Virginia I have seen the bill of rights violated in every instance where it has been opposed to a popular current. Notwithstanding the explicit provision contained in that instrument for the rights of Conscience it is well known that a religious establishment would have taken place in that State, if the legislative majority had found as they expected, a majority of the people in favor of the measure; and I am persuaded that if a majority of the people were now of one sect, the measure would still take place and on narrower ground than was then proposed, notwithstanding the additional obstacle which the law has since created. Wherever the real power in a Government lies, there is the danger of oppression. In our Governments the real power lies in the majority of the Community, and the invasion of private rights is *chiefly* to be apprehended, not from acts of Government contrary to the sense of its constituents, but from acts in which the Government is the mere instrument of the major number of the constituents. This is a truth of great importance, but not yet sufficiently attended to: and is probably more strongly impressed on my mind by facts, and reflections suggested by them, than on yours which has contemplated abuses of power issuing from a very different quarter. Wherever there is an interest and power to do wrong, wrong will generally be done, and not less readily by a powerful and interested party than by a powerful and interested prince. The difference, so far as it relates to the superiority of republics over monarchies, lies in the less degree of probability that interest may prompt abuses of power in the former than in the latter; and in the security in the former against oppression of more than the smaller part of the Society, whereas in the former it may be extended in a manner to the whole. The difference so far as it relates to the point in question—the efficacy of a bill of rights in controuling abuses of power—lies in this: that a monarchy as the latent force of the nation is superior to that of the Sovereign, and a solemn charter of popular rights must have a great effect, as a standard for trying the validity of public acts, and a signal for rousing and uniting the superior force of the community; whereas in a popular Government, the political and physical power may be considered as vested in the same hands, that is in a majority of the people, and consequently the tyranical will of the sovereign is not to be controuled by the dread of an appeal to any other force within the community. What use then it may be asked can a bill of rights serve in popular Governments? I answer the two following which though less essential than in other Governments, sufficiently recommended the precaution. 1. The political truths declared in that solemn manner acquire by degrees the character of fundamental maxims of free Government, and as they become incorporated with the national sentiment, counteract the impulses of interest and passion. 2. Altho' it be generally true as above stated that the danger of oppression lies in the interested majorities of the people rather than in usurped acts of the Government, yet there may be occasions on which the evil may spring from the latter sources; and on such, a bill of rights will be a good ground for an appeal to the sense of the community. Perhaps too there may be a certain degree of danger, that a succession of artful and ambitious rules, may by gradual and well-timed advances, finally erect an independent Government on the subversion of liberty. Should this danger exist at all, it is prudent to guard against it, especially when the precaution can do no injury. At the same time I must own that I see no tendency in all Governments to an augmentation of power at the expence of liberty. But the remark as usually understood does not appear to me well founded. Power when it has attained a certain degree of energy and independence goes on generally to further degrees of relaxation, until the abuses of liberty beget a sudden transition to an undue degree of power. With this explanation the remark may be true; and in the latter sense only is it in my opinion applicable to the Governments in America. It is a melancholy reflection that liberty should be equally exposed to danger whether the Government have too much or too little power; and that the line which divides these extremes should be so inaccurately defined by experience.

Supposing a bill of rights to be proper the articles which ought to compose it, admit of much discussion. I am inclined to think that absolute restrictions in cases that are doubtful, or where emergencies may overrule them, ought to be avoided. The restrictions however strongly marked on paper will never be regarded when opposed to the decided sense of the public; and after repeated violations in extraordinary cases, they will lose even their ordinary efficacy. Should a Rebellion or insurrection alarm the people as well as the Government, and a suspension of the Hab. Corp. [habeas corpus] be dictated by the alarm, no written prohibitions on earth would prevent the measure. Should an army in time of peace be gradually established in our neighbourhood by Britn: or Spain, declarations on paper would have as little effect in preventing a standing force for the public safety. The best security against these evils is to remove the pretext for them. With regard to Monopolies they are justly classed among the greatest nusances in Government. But is it clear that as encouragements to literary works and ingenious discoveries, they are not too valuable to be wholly renounced? Would it not suffice to reserve in all cases a right to the public to abolish the privilege at a price to be specified in the grant of it? Is there not also infinitely less danger of this abuse in our Governments than in most others? Monopolies are sacrifices of the many to the few. Where the power is in the few it is natural for them to sacrifice the many to their own partialities and corruptions. Where the power, as with us, is in the many not in the few, the danger can not be very great that the few will be thus favored. It is much more to be dreaded that the few will be unnecessarily sacrificed to the many. . . .

Document 8

Articles on Rights in the United States Constitution, 1787

Article I, Section 9

2. The Privilege of the Writ of Habeas Corpus shall not be suspended, unless when in Cases of Rebellion or Invasion the public Safety may require it.

3. No Bill of Attainder or ex-post-facto Law shall be passed.

Article I, Section 10

1. No State shall . . . pass any Bill of Attainder, ex post facto Law, or Law impairing the Obligation of Contracts, or grant any Title of Nobility.

Article III, Section 2

3. The Trial of all Crimes, except in cases of Impeachment; shall be by Jury; and such Trial shall be held in the State where the said Crimes shall have been committed; but when not committed within any State, the Trial shall be at such Place or Places as the Congress may by Law have directed.

Article III, Section 3

1. Treason against the United States shall consist only in levying War against them, or in adhering to their Enemies, giving them Aid and Comfort. No Person shall be convicted of Treason unless on the Testimony of two Witnesses to the same overt Act, or on Confession in open Court.

2. The Congress shall have Power to declare the Punishment of Treason, but no Attainder of Treason shall work Corruption of Blood, or Forfeiture except during the Life of the Person attainted.

Article IV, Section 2

1. The Citizens of each State shall be entitled to all Privileges and Immunities of Citizens in the several States.

Article VI

3. The Senators and Representatives before mentioned, and the Members of the several State Legislatures, and all executive and judicial officers, both of the United States and of the several States, shall be bound by Oath or Affirmation to support this Constitution; but no religious Test shall ever be required as a Qualification to any Office or public Trust under the United States.

Document 9

Madison's Speech to the House of Representatives

June 8, 1789

. . . I will state my reasons why I think it proper to propose amendments, and state the amendments themselves, so far as I think they ought to be proposed. . . .

. . . It appears to me that this House is bound by every motive of prudence, not to let the first session pass over without proposing to the State Legislatures some things to be incorporated into the constitution, that will render it as acceptable to the whole people of the United States, as it has been found acceptable to a majority of them. I wish, among other reasons why something should be done, that those who have been friendly to the adoption of this constitution may have the opportunity of proving to those who were opposed to it that they were as sincerely devoted to liberty and a Republican Government, as those who charged them with wishing the adoption of this constitution in order to lay the foundation of an aristocracy or despotism. It will be a desirable thing to extinguish from the bosom of every member of the community, any apprehensions that there are those among his countrymen who wish to deprive them of the liberty for which they valiantly fought and honorably bled. And if there are amendments desired of such a nature as will not injure the constitution, and they can be ingrafted so as to give satisfaction to the doubting part of our fellow-citizens, the friends of the Federal Government will evince that spirit of deference and concession for which they have hitherto been distinguished.

It cannot be a secret to the gentlemen in this House, that notwithstanding the ratification of this system of Government by eleven of the thirteen United States, in some cases unanimously, in others by large majorities; yet still there is a great number of our constituents who are dissatisfied with it; among whom are many respectable for their talents and patriotism, and respectable for the jealousy they

have for their liberty, which, though mistaken in its object, is honorable in its motive. There is a great body of the people falling under this description, who at present feel much inclined to join their support to the cause of Federalism, if they were satisfied on this one point. We ought not to disregard their inclination, but on principles of amity and moderation, conform to their wishes and expressly declare the great rights of mankind secured under this constitution. The acceptance which our fellow-citizens show under the Government, calls upon us for a like return of moderation. But perhaps there is a stronger motive than this for our going into a consideration of the subject. It is to provide those securities for liberty which are required by a part of the community: I allude in a particular manner to those two States that have not thought fit to throw themselves into the bosom of the Confederacy. It is a desirable thing, on our part as well as theirs, that a re-union should take place as soon as possible. I have no doubt, if we proceed to take those steps which would be prudent and requisite at this juncture, that in a short time we should see that disposition prevailing in those States which have not come in, that we have seen prevailing in those States which have embraced the constitution.

But I will candidly acknowledge, that, over and above all these considerations, I do conceive that the constitution may be amended; that is to say, if all power is subject to abuse, that then it is possible the abuse of the powers of the General Government may be guarded against in a more secure manner than is now done, while no one advantage arising from the exercise of that power shall be damaged or endangered by it. We have in this way something to gain, and, if we proceed with caution, nothing to lose. And in this case it is necessary to proceed with caution; for while we feel all these inducements to go into a revisal of the constitution, we must feel for the constitution itself, and make that revisal a moderate one. I should be unwilling to see a door opened for a reconsideration of the whole structure of the Government—for a re-consideration of the principles and the substance of the powers given; because I doubt, if such a door were opened, we should be very likely to stop at that point which would be safe to the Government itself. But I do wish to see a door opened to consider, so far as to incorporate those provisions for the security of rights, against which I believe no serious objection has been made by any class of our constituents: such as would be likely to meet with the concurrence of two-thirds of both Houses, and the approbation of three-fourths of the State Legislatures. I will not propose a single alteration which I do not wish to see take place, as intrinsically proper in itself, or proper because it is wished for by a respectable number of my fellow-citizens; and therefore I shall not propose a single alteration but is likely to meet the concurrence required by the constitution. There have been objections of various kinds made against the constitution. Some were levelled against its structure because the President was without a council; because the Senate, which is a legislative body, had judicial powers in trials on impeachments; and because the powers of that body were compounded in other respects, in a manner that did not correspond with a particular theory; because it grants more power than is supposed to be necessary for every good purpose, and controls the ordinary powers of the State Governments. I know some respectable characters who opposed this Government on these grounds; but I believe that the great mass of the people who opposed it, disliked it because it did not contain effectual provisions against encroachments on particular rights, and those safeguards which they have been long accustomed to have interposed between them and the magistrate who exercises the sovereign power; nor ought we to consider them safe, while a great number of our fellow-citizens think these securities necessary.

It is a fortunate thing that the objection to the Government has been made on the ground I stated, because it will be practicable, on that ground, to obviate the objection, so far as to satisfy the public mind that their liberties will be perpetual, and this without endangering any part of the constitution, which is considered as essential to the existence of the Government by those who promoted its adoption.

The amendments which have occurred to me, proper to be recommended by Congress to the State Legislatures, are these:

First, That there be prefixed to the constitution a declaration, that all power is originally rested in, and consequently derived from, the people.

That Government is instituted and ought to be exercised for the benefit of the people; which consists in the enjoyment of life and liberty, with the right of acquiring and using property, and generally of pursuing and obtaining happiness and safety.

That the people have an indubitable, unalienable, and indefeasible right to reform or change their Government, whenever it be found adverse or inadequate to the purposes of its institution.

Secondly, That in article 1st, section 2, clause 3, these words be struck out, to wit:

"The number of Representatives shall not exceed one for every thirty thousand, but each State shall have at least one Representative, and until such enumeration shall be made;" and that in place thereof be inserted these words, to wit: "After the first actual enumeration, there shall be one Representative for every thirty thousand, until the number amounts to _____ , after which the proportion shall be so regulated by Congress, that the number shall never be less than _____ , nor more than _____ , but each State shall, after the first enumeration, have at least two Representatives; and prior thereto."

Thirdly, That in article 1st, section 6, clause 1, there be added to the end of the first sentence, these words, to wit: "But no law varying the compensation last ascertained shall operate before the next ensuing election of Representatives."

Fourthly, That in article 1st, section 9, between clauses 3 and 4, be inserted these clauses, to wit: The civil rights of none shall be abridged on account of religious belief or worship, nor shall any national religion be established, nor shall the full and equal rights of conscience be in any manner, or on any pretext, infringed.

The people shall not be deprived or abridged of their right to speak, to write, or to publish their sentiments; and the freedom of the press, as one of the great bulwarks of liberty, shall be inviolable.

The people shall not be restrained from peaceably assembling and consulting for their common good; nor from applying to the Legislature by petitions, or remonstrances, for redress of their grievances.

The right of the people to keep and bear arms shall not be infringed; a well armed and well regulated militia being the best security of a free country; but no person religiously scrupulous of bearing arms shall be compelled to render military service in person.

No soldier shall in time of peace be quartered in any house without the consent of the owner; nor at any time, but in a manner warranted by law.

No person shall be subject, except in cases of impeachment, to more than one punishment or one trial for the same offence; nor shall be compelled to be a witness against himself; nor be deprived of life, liberty, or property, without due process of law; nor be obliged to relinquish his property, where it may be necessary for public use, without a just compensation.

Excessive bail shall not be required, nor excessive fines imposed, nor cruel and unusual punishments inflicted.

The rights of the people to be secured in their persons; their houses, their papers, and their other property, from all unreasonable searches and seizures, shall not be violated by warrants issued without probable cause, supported by oath or affirmation, or not particularly describing the places to be searched, or the persons or things to be seized.

In all criminal prosecutions, the accused shall enjoy the right to a speedy and public trial, to be informed of the cause and nature of the accusation, to be confronted with his accusers, and the witnesses against him; to have a compulsory process for obtaining witnesses in his favor; and to have the assistance of counsel for his defence.

The exceptions here or elsewhere in the constitution, made in favor of particular rights, shall not be so construed as to diminish the just importance of other rights retained by the people, or as to enlarge the powers delegated by the constitution; but either as actual limitations of such powers, or as inserted merely for great caution.

Fifthly, That in article 1st, section 10, between clauses 1 and 2, be inserted this clause, to wit:

> No State shall violate the equal rights of conscience, or the freedom of the press, or the trial by jury in criminal cases.

Sixthly, That, in article 3d, section 2, be annexed to the end of clause 2d, these words, to wit:

> But no appeal to such court shall be allowed where the value in controversy shall not amount to _____ dollars: nor shall any fact triable by jury, according to the course of common law, be otherwise re-examinable than

may consist with the principles of common law.

Seventhly, That in article 3d, section 2, the third clause be struck out, and in its place be inserted the clauses following, to wit:

> The trial of all crimes (except in cases of impeachments, and cases arising in the land or naval forces, or the militia when on actual service, in time of war or public danger) shall be by an impartial jury of freeholders of the vicinage, with the requisite of unanimity for conviction, of the right of challenge, and other accustomed requisites; and in all crimes punishable with loss of life or member, presentment or indictment by a grand jury shall be an essential preliminary, provided that in cases of crimes committed within any county which may be in possession of an enemy, or in which a general insurrection may prevail, the trial may by law be authorized in some other county of the same State, as near as may be to the seat of the offence.
>
> In cases of crimes committed not within any county, the trial may by law be in such county as the laws shall have prescribed. In suits of common law, between man and man, the trial by jury, as one of the best securities to the rights of the people, ought to remain inviolate.

Eighthly, That immediately after article 6th, be inserted, as article 7th, the clauses following, to wit:

> The powers delegated by this constitution are appropriated to the departments to which they are respectively distributed: so that the legislative department shall never exercise the powers vested in the executive or judicial nor the executive exercise the powers vested in the legislative or executive departments.
>
> The powers not delegated by this constitution, nor prohibited by it to the States, are reserved to the States respectively.

Ninthly, That article 7th be numbered as article 8th.

The first of these amendments relates to what may be called a bill of rights. I will own that I never considered this provision so essential to the federal constitution, as to make it improper to ratify it, until such an amendment was added; at the same time, I always conceived, that in a certain form, and to a certain extent, such a provision was neither improper nor altogether useless. . . .

In our Government it is, perhaps, less necessary to guard against the abuse in the executive department than any other; because it is not the stronger branch of the system, but the weaker. It therefore must be levelled against the legislative, for it is the most powerful, and most likely to be abused, because it is under the least control. Hence, so far as a declaration of rights can tend to prevent the exercise of undue power, it cannot be doubted but such declaration is proper. But I confess that I do conceive, that in a Government modified like this of the United States, the great danger lies rather in the abuse of the community than in the legislative body. The prescriptions in favor of liberty ought to be levelled against that quarter where the greatest danger lies, namely, that which possesses the highest prerogative of power. But it is not found in either the executive or legislative departments of Government, but in the body of the people, operating by the majority against the minority.

It may be thought that all paper barriers against the power of the community are too weak to be worthy of attention. I am sensible they are not so strong as to satisfy gentlemen of every description who have seen and examined thoroughly the texture of such a defence; yet, as they have a tendency to impress some degree of respect of them, to establish the public opinion in their favor, and rouse the attention of the whole community, it may be one means to control the majority from those acts to which they might be otherwise inclined.

It has been said, by way of objection to a bill of rights, by many respectable gentlemen out of doors, and I find opposition on the same principles likely to be made by gentlemen on this floor, that they are unnecessary articles of a Republican Government, upon the presumption that the people have those rights in their own hands, and that is the proper place for them to rest. It would be a sufficient answer to say, that this objection lies against such provisions under the State Governments, as well as under the General Government: and there are, I believe, but few gentlemen who are inclined to push their theory so far as to say that a declaration of rights in those cases is either ineffectual or improper. It has been said, that in the Federal Government they are unnecessary, because the powers are enumerated, and it follows, that all that are not granted by the constitution are retained; that the constitution is a call of powers, the great residuum being the rights of the people; and, therefore, a bill of rights cannot be so necessary as if the residuum was thrown into the hands of the Government. I admit that these arguments are not entirely without foundation; but they are not conclusive to the extent which has been supposed. It is true, the powers of the General Government are circumscribed, they are directed to particular objects; but even if Government keeps

within those limits, it has certain discretionary powers with respect to the means, which may admit of abuse to a certain extent, in the same manner as the powers of the State Governments under their constitutions may to an indefinite extent; because in the constitution of the United States, there is a clause granting to Congress the power to make all laws which shall be necessary and proper for carrying into execution all the powers vested in the Government of the United States, or in any department or officer thereof; this enables them to fulfil every purpose for which the Government was established. Now, may not laws be considered necessary and proper by Congress for it is for them to judge of the necessity and propriety to accomplish those special purposes which they may have in contemplation, which laws in themselves are neither necessary nor proper; as well as improper laws could be enacted by the State Legislatures, for fulfilling the more extended objects of those Governments. I will state an instance, which I think in point, and proves that this might be the case. The General Government has a right to pass all laws which shall be necessary to collect its revenue; the means for enforcing the collection are within the direction of the Legislature: may not general warrants be considered necessary for this purpose, as well as for some purposes which it was supposed at the framing of their constitutions the State Governments had in view? If there was reason for restraining the State Governments from exercising this power, there is like reason for restraining the Federal Government.

It may be said, indeed it has been said, that a bill of rights is not necessary, because the establishment of this Government has not repealed those declarations of rights which are added to the several State constitutions; that those rights of the people, which had been established by the most solemn act, could not be annihilated by a subsequent act of that people, who meant, and declared at the head of the instrument, that they ordained and established a new system, for the express purpose of securing to themselves and posterity the liberties they had gained by an arduous conflict.

I admit the force of this observation, but I do not look upon it to be conclusive. In the first place, it is too uncertain ground to leave this provision upon, if a provision is at all necessary to secure rights so important as many of those I have mentioned are conceived to be, by the public in general, as well as those in particular who opposed the adoption of this constitution. Besides, some States have no bills of rights, there are others provided with very defective ones, and there are others whose bills of rights are not only defective, but absolutely improper; instead of securing some in the full extent which republican principles would require, they limit them too much to agree with the common ideas of liberty.

It has been objected also against a bill of rights, that, by enumerating particular exceptions to the grant of power, it would disparage those rights which were not placed in that enumeration; and it might follow, by implication, that those rights which were not singled out, were intended to be assigned into the hands of the General Government, and were consequently insecure. This is one of the most plausible arguments I have ever heard urged against the admission of a bill of rights into this system; but, I conceive, that it may be guarded against. I have attempted it, as gentlemen may see by turning to the last clause of the fourth resolution.

It has been said, that it is unnecessary to load the constitution with this provision, because it was not found effectual in the constitution of the particular States. It is true, there are a few particular States in which some of the most valuable articles have not, at one time or other, been violated; but it does not follow but they may have, to a certain degree, a salutary effect against the abuse of power. If they are incorporated into the constitution, independent tribunals of justice will consider themselves in a peculiar manner the guardians of those rights; they will be an impenetrable bulwark against every assumption of power in the legislative or executive; they will be naturally led to resist every encroachment upon rights expressly stipulated for in the constitution by the declaration of rights. Besides, this security, there is a great probability that such a declaration in the federal system would be enforced; because the State Legislatures will jealously and closely watch the operations of this Government, and be able to resist with more effect every assumption of power, than any other power on earth can do; and the greatest opponents to a Federal Government admit the State Legislatures to be sure guardians of the people's liberty. I conclude, from this view of the subject, that it will be proper in itself, and highly politic, for the tranquility of the public mind, and the stability of the Government, that we should offer something, in the form I have proposed, to be incorporated in the system of Government, as a declaration of the rights of the people.

In the next place, I wish to see that part of the constitution revised which declares that the number of Representatives shall not exceed the proportion of one for every thirty thousand persons, and allows one Representative to every State which rates below that proportion. If we attend to the discussion of this subject, which has taken place in the State conventions, and even in the opinion of the friends to the constitution, an alteration here is proper. It is the sense of the people of America, that the number of Representatives ought to be increased, but particularly that it should not be left in the discretion of the Government to diminish them, below that proportion which certainly is in the power of the Legislature as the constitution now stands; and they may, as the population of the country increases, increase the House of Representatives to a very unwieldly degree. I confess I always thought this part of the constitution defective, though not dangerous; and that it ought to be particularly attended to whenever Congress should go into the consideration of amendments.

There are several minor cases enumerated in my proposition, in which I wish also to see some alteration take place. That article which leaves it in the power of the Legislature to ascertain its own emolument, is one to which I allude. I do not believe this is a power which, in the ordinary course of Government, is likely to be abused. Perhaps of all the powers granted, it is least likely to abuse; but there is a seeming impropriety in leaving any set of men without control to put their hand into the public coffers, to take out money to put in their pockets; there is a seeming indecorum in such power, which leads me to propose a change. We have a guide to this alteration in several of the amendments which the different conventions have proposed. I have gone, therefore, so far as to fix it, that no law, varying the compensation shall operate until there is a change in the Legislature; in which case it cannot be for the particular benefit of those who are concerned in determining the value of the service.

I wish also, in revising the constitution, we may throw into that section, which interdict the abuse of certain powers in the State Legislatures, some other provisions of equal, if not greater importance than those already made. The words, "No State shall pass any bill of attainder, ex post facto law," &c. were wise and proper restrictions in the constitution. I think there is more danger of those powers being abused by the State Governments than by the Government of the United States. The same may be said of other powers which they possess, if not controlled by the general principle, that laws are unconstitutional which infringe the rights of the community. I should therefore wish to extend this interdiction, and add, as I have stated in the 5th resolution, that no State shall violate the equal right of conscience, freedom of the press, or trial by jury in criminal cases; because it is proper that every Government shall be disarmed of powers which trench upon those particular rights. I know, in some of the State constitutions, the power of the Government is controlled by such a declaration; but others are not. I cannot see any reason against obtaining even a double security on those points; and nothing can give a more sincere proof of the attachment of those who opposed this constitution to these great and important rights, than to see them join in obtaining the security I have now proposed; because it must be admitted, on all hands, that the State Governments are as liable to attack the invaluable privileges as the General Government is, and therefore ought to be as cautiously guarded against.

I think it will be proper, with respect to the judiciary powers, to satisfy the public mind of those points which I have mentioned. Great inconvenience has been apprehended to suitors from the distance they would be dragged to obtain justice in the Supreme Court of the United States, upon an appeal on an action for a small debt. To remedy this, declare that no appeal shall be made unless the matter in controversy amounts to a particular sum; this, with the regulations respecting jury trials in criminal cases, and suits at common law, it is to be hoped, will quiet and reconcile the minds of the people to that part of the constitution.

I find, from looking into the amendments proposed by the State conventions, that several are particularly anxious that it should be declared in the constitution, that the powers not therein delegated should be reserved to the several States. Perhaps words which may define this more precisely than the whole of the instrument now does, may be considered as superflous. I admit they may be deemed unnecessary: but there can be no harm in making such a declaration, if gentlemen will allow that the fact is as stated. I am sure I understand it so, and do therefore propose it.

These are the points on which I wish to see a revision of the constitution take place. How far they will accord with the sense of this body, I cannot take upon me absolutely to determine; but I believe every gentleman will readily admit that nothing is in contemplation, so far as I have mentioned, that can endanger the beauty of the Government in any one important feature, even in the eyes of its most sanguine admirers. I have proposed nothing that does not appear to me as proper in itself, or eligible as patronized by a respectable number of our fellow-citizens; and if we can make the constitution better in the opinion of those who are opposed to it, without weakening its frame, or abridging its usefulness, in the judgment of those who are attached to it, we act the part of wise and liberal men to make such alterations as shall produce that effect.

Having done what I conceived was my duty, in bringing before this House the subject of amendments, and also stated such as I wish for and approve, and offered the reasons which occurred to me in their support, I shall content myself, for the present, with moving "that a committee be appointed to consider of and report such amendments as ought to be proposed by Congress to the Legislatures of the States, to become, if ratified by three-fourths thereof, part of the constitution of the United States." By agreeing to this motion, the subject may be going on in the committee, while other important business is proceeding to a conclusion in the House. I should advocate greater despatch in the business of amendments, if I were not convinced of the absolute necessity there is of pursuing the organization of the Government; because I think we should obtain the confidence of our fellow-citizens, in proportion as we fortify the rights of the people against the encroachments of the Government.

Document 10

The Bill of Rights: Amendments I-X of the Constitution

(Ratified and Effective as of December 15, 1791)

[Amendment I]

Congress shall make no law respecting an establishment of religion, or prohibiting the free exercise thereof, or abridging the freedom of speech, or of the press, or the right of the people peaceably to assemble, and to petition the Government for a redress of grievances.

[Amendment II]

A well regulated Militia, being necessary to the security of a free State, the right of the people to keep and bear Arms, shall not be infringed.

[Amendment III]

No Soldier shall, in time of peace be quartered in any house, without the consent of the Owner, nor in time of war, but in a manner to be prescribed by law.

[Amendment IV]

The right of the people to be secure in their persons, houses, papers, and effects, against unreasonable searches and seizures, shall not be violated, and no Warrants shall issue, but upon probable cause, supported by Oath or affirmation, and particularly describing the place to be searched, and the persons or things to be seized.

[Amendment V]

No person shall be held to answer for a capital, or otherwise infamous crime, unless on a presentment or indictment of a Grand Jury, except in cases arising in the land or naval forces, or in the Militia, when in actual service in time of War or public danger; nor shall any person be subject for the same offence to be twice put in jeopardy of life or limb, nor shall be compelled in any criminal case to be a witness against himself, nor be deprived of life, liberty, or property, without due process of law; nor shall private property be taken for public use, without just compensation.

[Amendment VI]

In all criminal prosecutions, the accused shall enjoy the right to a speedy and public trial, by an impartial jury of the State and district wherein the crime shall have been committed; which district shall have been previously ascertained by law, and to be informed of the nature and cause of the accusation; to be confronted with the witnesses against him, to have compulsory process for obtaining Witnesses in his favor, and to have the assistance of Counsel for his defence.

[Amendment VII]

In Suits at common law, where the value in controversy shall exceed twenty dollars, the right of trial by jury shall be preserved, and no fact tried by a jury shall be otherwise re-examined in any Court of the United States, than according to the rules of the common law.

[Amendment VIII]

Excessive bail shall not be required, nor excessive fines imposed, nor cruel and unusual punishments inflicted.

[Amendment IX]

The enumeration in the Constitution, of certain rights, shall not be construed to deny or disparage others retained by the people.

[Amendment X]

The powers not delegated to the United States by the Constitution, nor prohibited by it to the States, are reserved to the States respectively, or to the people.

Document 11

Constitutional Amendments Subsequent to the Bill of Rights that Pertain to Civil Liberties and Rights

[Amendment XIII, Ratified December 6, 1865]

Section 1. Neither slavery nor involuntary servitude, except as a punishment for crime whereof the party shall have been duly convicted, shall exist within the United States, or any place subject to their jurisdiction. . . .

[Amendment XIV, Ratified July 9, 1868]

Section 1. All persons born or naturalized in the United States and subject to the jurisdiction thereof, are citizens of the United States and of the State wherein they reside. No State shall make or enforce any law which shall abridge the privileges or immunities of citizens of the United States; nor shall any State deprive any person of life, liberty, or property, without due process of law; nor deny to any person within its jurisdiction the equal protection of the laws. . . .

[Amendment XV, Ratified February 3, 1870]

Section 1. The right of citizens of the United States to vote shall not be denied or abridged by the United States or by any State on account of race, color, or previous condition of servitude. . . .

[Amendment XIX, Ratified August 18, 1920]

The right of citizens of the United States to vote shall not be denied or abridged by the United States or by any State on account of sex. . . .

[Amendment XXIV, Ratified January 23, 1964]

Section 1. The right of citizens of the United States to vote in any primary or other election for President or Vice President, for electors for President or Vice President, or for Senator or Representative in Congress, shall not be denied or abridged by the United States or any State by reason of failure to pay any poll tax or other tax. . . .

[Amendment XXVI, Ratified July 1, 1971]

Section 1. The right of citizens of the United States, who are eighteen years of age or older, to vote shall not be denied or abridged by the United States or by any State on account of age. . . .

Part IV
Lessons on the Bill of Rights

IV

Lessons on the Bill of Rights

Part Four includes nine lessons on the Bill of Rights for use with elementary and secondary school students. Three lessons (A-1, A-2, and A-3) were designed for high school students in U.S. history and government courses. Three lessons (B-1, B-2, and B-3) were created for junior high/middle school students in U.S. history and civics courses. Three lessons (C-1, C-2, and C-3) were written for elementary school students in grades four and five; the social studies curriculum for these grades usually includes subject matter on citizenship and the Constitution. Each lesson includes a teaching plan and materials for students, which follow the plan for teachers. The nine lessons are listed below.

A. High School Lessons

Lesson A-1: "How Does Procedural Due Process Protect Your Right to Life, Liberty, and Property?" by Charles N. Quigley et al. (This lesson was published in 1986 by the Center for Civic Education, Calabasas, CA in *We the People. . ., A Secondary Level Student Text*; the lesson is reprinted here with permission of the authors and publisher.)

Lesson A-2: "Drugs and the Courts: Applying the Exclusionary Rule" by Stacy Armonda et al. (This lesson was published in 1990 by the Constitutional Rights Foundation, Chicago, IL in *The Drug Question: The Constitution and Public Policy*; the lesson is reprinted here with permission of the authors and publisher.)

Lesson A-3: "Constitutional Rights in a Time of Crisis, 1941-1945" by John J. Patrick and Richard C. Remy. (This lesson was published in 1985 by Project '87 of the American Historical Association and the American Political Science Associ-

ation, Washington, DC in *Lessons on the Constitution*; the lesson is reprinted here with permission of the authors and publisher.)

B. Junior High/Middle School Lessons

Lesson B-1: "Bill of Rights Cases" by Diana Hess. (This lesson was published in 1987 by the Constitutional Rights Foundation, Chicago, IL in *We the People: Law-Related Lessons on Teaching the Constitution*; the lesson is reprinted here with permission of the author and publisher.)

Lesson B-2: "How Does the Constitution Protect Freedom of Expression?" by Charles N. Quigley et al. (This lesson was published in 1988 by the Center for Civic Education, Calabasas, CA in *We the People. . ., A Middle School Student Text*; the lesson is reprinted here with permission of the authors and publisher.

Lesson B-3: "How Does the Constitution Protect Freedom of Religion?" by Charles N. Quigley et al. (This lesson was published in 1988 by the Center for Civic Education, Calabasas, CA in *We the People. . ., A Middle School Student Text*; the lesson is reprinted here with permission of the authors and publisher.)

C. Elementary School Lessons

Lesson C-1: "How Does the Constitution Protect Your Right to Be Treated Fairly by the Government?" by Charles N. Quigley et al. (This lesson was published in 1989 by the Center for Civic Education, Calabasas, CA in *We the People. . ., Student Text for Level I*; the lesson is reprinted here with permission of the authors and publisher.)

Lesson C-2: "The Bill of Rights" by Connie S. Yeaton and Karen Trusty Braeckel. (This lesson was published in 1986 by the Newspaper in Education Program of the Indianapolis Newspapers, Inc. in *A Salute to Our Constitution and the Bill of Rights, Grades 4-6*; the lesson is reprinted here with permission of the authors and publisher.)

Lesson C-3: "How Does the Constitution Protect Your Freedom of Expression?" by Charles N. Quigley et al. (This lesson was published in 1989 by the Center for Civic Education, Calabasas, CA in *We the People. . ., Student Text for Level I*; the lesson is reprinted here with permission of the authors and publisher.)

Lesson A-1 treats the fundamental constitutional principle of procedural due process. The meaning and importance of this principle are examined. Questions are raised for student inquiry about cases involving applications of the Fourth, Fifth, Sixth, and Eighth Amendments to the Constitution.

Lesson A-2 is about the U.S. Supreme Court decision in *California v. Greenwood* (1986). This case involved a Fourth Amendment issue. After studying the facts of this case, students are involved in a decision-making simulation activity about the issue in this case. The lesson is concluded with a writing assignment about the simulation and the decision in this case.

Lesson A-3 presents the constitutional issues associated with internment of Americans of Japanese ancestry during World War II. Students examine the facts, issues, and decisions in three U.S. Supreme Court cases: *Hirabayashi v. United States* (1943); *Korematsu v. United States* (1944); and *Ex parte Endo* (1944).

Lesson B-1 consists of a series of hypothetical situations about Bill of Rights issues. Students are asked to decide whether or not each situation in this set contains a violation of the Bill of Rights.

Lesson B-2 examines the meaning, significance, and applications of freedom of expression. Students are challenged to examine and make judgments about cases involving limitations of freedom of expression.

Lesson B-3 treats religious liberty guaranteed by the First Amendment. Students examine the meaning and applications of the "establishment" and "free exercise" clauses of the First Amendment. Opportunities are provided for students to deliberate, discuss, and decide about religious liberty cases.

Lesson C-1 presents the concept of due process of law to elementary school students. The provisions of the Bill of Rights associated with due process are identified and discussed. The concept of due process is applied to the U.S. Supreme Court case of *Gideon v. Wainwright* (1963).

Lesson C-2, designed for students in grades four-six, emphasizes the concept of free speech and examines issues about this aspect of the Bill of Rights.

Lesson C-3 provides elementary school students with opportunities to examine the meaning of freedom of expression. Cases that raise free speech issues are presented.

Lesson A-1

How does procedural due process protect your rights to life, liberty, and property?

LESSON OVERVIEW

This lesson deals with procedural due process. Both the federal and state governments are required by the Constitution and the Bill of Rights to use fair procedures when gathering information and making decisions regarding the lives, liberty, and property of citizens. Although this lesson focuses on the criminal justice system, the requirements of procedural due process apply in some degree to all of the branches and functions of government.

While many will agree with the idea of the use of fair procedures in the abstract, the application of those procedures to specific cases is more difficult, particularly in situations when an accused person is alleged to have committed heinous crimes. Justice Felix Frankfurter once said that America provides due process guarantees:

> not out of tenderness for the accused, but because we have reached a certain stage of civilization . . . [a civilization which], by respecting the dignity even of the least worthy citizen, raises the stature of all of us.

LESSON OBJECTIVES

At the conclusion of this lesson:

1. Students should be able to explain the relationship between the Framers' inclusion of procedural protections of the individual in the Constitution and the Bill of Rights, and their ideas about the nature of constitutional government.

2. Students should be able to describe procedural due process and identify the specific procedural rights included in the Constitution and the Bill of Rights and their historical antecedents.

3. Students should be able to explain how these rights apply to the criminal justice system.

TEACHING PROCEDURES

A. Reading and Group Activity:
Understanding procedural due process

Introduce the lesson by telling the students that they will be studying procedural due process, that is, the requirement that the government use fair procedures when gathering information or making decisions. In particular, this lesson will deal with procedural due process as it relates to criminal procedures used by law enforcement agencies and the courts. This involves the protection of the individual's rights to life, liberty, and property when suspected, accused, or convicted of a crime. The goal of procedural limitations on government is to make sure individuals' rights are not unfairly violated by an arbitrary government.

Be sure students understand that although the emphasis in this lesson is on criminal issues, fairness is also required of the government in civil cases and other matters as well.

Next, divide the class into seven groups and have each read "The importance of procedural due process" and the first paragraph of "What are your procedural rights and why are they important?" Then assign one of each of the seven sections of this selection to each group. Each group should then read the selection and be prepared to report to the class the protections of rights that it contains, the reasons for the protections, and the historical basis or reasons for the protections if such information is contained in that selection.

After the seven groups have reported, lead a discussion of the importance of procedural due process to the protection of the rights of the individual and its relationship to constitutional government and the concerns of the Founders.

B. Reading and Discussion:
Controversies over due process and review of lesson

Have students read "Controversies over procedural due process." Be sure they understand the conflict it describes between the need to balance the protections of the individual against the needs of society.

C. Concluding Activity

Conclude the lesson by leading a discussion of the questions in "Reviewing and using the lesson."

OPTIONAL ACTIVITIES

For Reinforcement, Extended Learning, and Enrichment

1. Arrange to have the class visit and observe procedures at a local court hearing. If possible, have the judge discuss procedures and other issues with students.

2. Assign *Gideon's Trumpet* by Anthony Lewis. This is a vivid account of the facts surrounding *Gideon v. Wainwright*, 372 U.S. 335 (1963). You may be able to get a tape of the TV movie of the book, starring Henry Fonda.

3. Assign a report on *Mapp v. Ohio*, 367 U.S. 643 (1961) or other cases centering on procedural due process issues.

4. Lead a class discussion on the topic, "Why is the right of habeas corpus sometimes considered the most fundamental of all constitutional rights?"

5. Have students complete the following matching assignment to reinforce their knowledge of procedural rights and the constitutional source of these rights.

Right	**Source**
1. jury trial	
2. notification of charges	a. 4th amendment
3. reasonable bail	b. 5th amendment
4. public trial	c. 6th amendment
5. assistance of counsel	d. 8th amendment
6. right to remain silent	
7. no unreasonable search	
8. confrontation of witnesses	
9. no cruel punishment	
10. one trial per offense	

Key: (1)c (2)c (3)d (4)c (5)c (6)b (7)a (8)c (9)d (10)b

How does procedural due process protect your rights to life, liberty, and property?

As you have learned, the Fifth and Fourteenth Amendments contain protections of your rights under their due process clauses. In the last lesson, you learned that "due process" has been interpreted to mean, in part, that the content of laws must be reasonable and fair. Procedural due process, the subject of this lesson, is the requirement that the procedures used by your federal and state governments be reasonable and fair. The requirements of procedural due process apply in some degree to all of the branches and functions of government. However, in this lesson we will focus specifically on one of their most important applications, that is, to criminal procedures. By showing how these procedural protections might apply to you, we hope to increase your understanding of their importance as part of your rights to life, liberty, and property.

When you have completed this lesson, you should be able to explain the meaning of procedural due process and the reasons for its various protections. Basic ideas and terms included in the lesson which you should be able to explain are listed below.

> **procedural due process**
> **Fourth Amendment**
> **unreasonable search and seizures**
> **Sixth Amendment**
> **notice clause**
> **assistance of counsel**
> **Fifth Amendment**
> **privilege against self-incrimination**
> **writ of habeas corpus**
> **Eighth Amendment**
> **bail**
> **trial by jury**
> **cruel and unusual punishment**
> **double jeopardy**

The importance of procedural due process

The Founders knew that throughout history governments had used their power to enforce criminal laws in ways that had violated the most basic rights of citizens. This was a lesson they had learned from long and painful experience in both England and in the colonies. The criminal law had often been used as a political weapon. This frequently resulted in punishment of the innocent and unfair and inhumane treatment of the guilty. For this reason, they included in the Constitution and the Bill of Rights a number of rights that were specific limitations designed to prevent the possible abuse of power by their government. They were safeguards to protect long-accepted ideas of human freedom, privacy, and dignity from the kinds of attacks they had been subjected to by past governments.

Through the due process clause of the Fourteenth Amendment, most of the procedural protections guaranteed to you by the Constitution and Bill of Rights which originally applied only to the federal government now apply to state governments as well. These protections, taken together, are called procedural due process or due process of law. To understand their importance, let's see how they protect you.

What are your procedural rights and why are they important?

Suppose you are suspected of a crime, arrested, imprisoned while awaiting trial, tried, convicted, and sentenced to prison by a court. What rights are guaranteed to you under the Constitution at each step of that process? How did these rights come to receive the protection of the Constitution? And what is their importance to you and the rest of society? Some of the most important of these rights, their sources, and the reasons they are protected are set forth here.

purpose of this protection is to give you the information necessary to answer the charges and to prepare to defend yourself.

- The Sixth Amendment also guarantees you the right to have a lawyer help you answer the accusation.

It guarantees you the right to the "assistance of counsel" for your defense. If you are like most people, you probably know little about the law, or about the rights you are entitled to while being held in jail, or about court procedures, such as those that deal with examining witnesses. You would be at a great disadvantage trying to answer charges against you even if you were innocent and had been arrested by mistake.

Until about fifty years ago, the right to counsel was interpreted to mean that you were merely free to hire a lawyer to help you if you wanted one. Since that time, the Supreme Court has interpreted the right to counsel to mean that if you are accused of a crime and are too poor to hire a lawyer, the government must provide one at public expense to represent you at all stages of the criminal proceeding.

- The Fifth Amendment guarantees that you have the right to remain silent both at the time of your arrest and throughout your trial.

This right protects you from being forced to give evidence against yourself. It is contained in the "privilege against self-incrimination clause" which says that a person cannot be "compelled in any criminal case to be a witness against himself." The right has its origins in the English common law system dating back at least to the 1500s.

The Framers knew that throughout history it had been common practice to torture people to make them confess to crimes. Even if you were innocent, you might confess to a crime if you were tortured, or given the "third degree." This protection also reflects the belief that even if you were guilty, you should be treated with dignity and not be subjected to cruel and inhumane treatment by your government.

3. You think you have been arrested and are being held in jail unfairly.

Suppose you think that the police have arrested you without having a good reason for doing so, that they are keeping you in jail unfairly, or that they have denied you one of your other basic rights to due process. What can you do?

- Article I, Section 9, of the Constitution guarantees you the right to have a judge hear your story and decide if you are being treated unfairly.

This part of the Constitution guarantees you the protection of the writ of habeas corpus or the "Great Writ of Liberty" as it was known by the Framers. This protection, included in the Magna Carta, has its origins in the English common law and is considered one of the most important safeguards of freedom in the British and American governmental systems. It means that if you are being held in jail, you or someone acting for you, may get an order from a court requiring the police to take you to court so you can argue before a judge that you have been unfairly arrested and should be set free. The police would have to present the evidence they had against you to the judge to justify their actions. If the judge agreed with you, you would be set free. If not, you would be held for trial.

The purpose of the right to habeas corpus is to protect you from being held in jail for a long period of time without being tried and convicted. The Framers knew that it was a common practice for governments to arrest people and put them in jail without ever giving them a fair trial. Today, the writ has also been interpreted to protect you if you have been convicted and are being held in a state or federal prison and can argue that your conviction had been unfairly obtained. It gives you the right to have a judge review your case

cry against searches made by British troops which had been made possible by the detested general warrants known as "writs of assistance." A main purpose of the Fourth Amendment was to place strict limits on the issuing of search warrants by judges.

When the Framers placed the protection against "unreasonable searches and seizures" in the Constitution, they could not know of the technological advances that would allow government agents to engage in search methods such as electronic eavesdropping on conversations.

The Supreme Court has dealt with such changes by interpreting your due process protections to mean that you should be given reasonable protections against government eavesdropping. For example, the Supreme Court has ruled that the police have to get a warrant before they can tap your phone and listen to your conversations.

1. You are suspected of a crime.

Suppose a law-enforcement officer suspects you of having committed a crime. How does the right to due process of law protect you from unfair treatment?

- The Fourth Amendment guarantees that law-enforcement officers cannot search you or your property, arrest you, or take your property unless they can show a good reason for doing so.

This amendment has been interpreted to mean that, except in certain emergencies where they must act quickly, law enforcement officers must get the permission of a judge (in the form of a warrant) to search you or your property, arrest you, or take your property. Further, the judge can only give this permission if the police officer can present reasonable evidence that you may be guilty of a crime, and can describe the evidence being sought. As you can imagine, applying these protections in specific situations can lead to considerable disagreement over such questions as to whether a search or arrest is "reasonable."

The prohibition against unreasonable searches has a long history in English and colonial experience. It dates back to the seventeenth and eighteenth centuries, when judges placed restrictions on the right of police to search people and their homes. The judges had decided this right was necessary when they learned that police had been unreasonable and unfair in searching the homes and meeting places of people with unpopular political and religious beliefs. In the last years of the colonial period, there was public out-

2. You have been arrested and taken to jail. What are your rights?

- The Sixth Amendment guarantees you the right to know why you have been arrested.

It contains the "notice clause" which says that you must be informed of the "nature and cause of the accusation" for which you have been arrested. The main

to see if you have been treated unfairly. It is not guaranteed during times of "rebellion or invasion."

4. You are in jail waiting for your trial.

Suppose after you have been arrested, a judge decides that there is enough evidence that you may be guilty to justify holding you for trial. What rights do you have?

- The Eighth Amendment guarantees the right to be free on reasonable bail while you wait for your trial.

It says that "Excessive bail shall not be required." This idea has a long history in English common law dating back to the Magna Carta. It was a part of the legal tradition that the colonists brought from England. Bail is an amount of money left with the court to guarantee that an accused person will return to court to be tried. It is an attempt to reduce the harm done by imprisonment between arrest and trial. Such imprisonment may punish in advance someone who is eventually found innocent, may cause someone to lose a job or be unable to fulfill family duties, and may make it more difficult to prepare a defense.

The "right to bail" is limited to those who can afford to pay the amount set by the court, which is not considered "excessive" or unreasonable if it is the amount normally charged for a particular offense. If you don't have the money for bail, you may have to remain in jail until your trial. Also, if a judge decides, for example, that you would not show up for your trial or that if you were free you might endanger others, you might be refused the right to be set free on bail.

- The Sixth Amendment guarantees you the right to a speedy and public trial.

This right serves two purposes. First, it protects you from being kept in jail for a long time even though you have not been convicted. Second, it protects you from being tried in secret where members of government might treat you unfairly and no one would ever know about it. The Framers knew that governments had used secret trials to unfairly convict people of crimes for which they probably would not have been convicted in a public trial by a jury of their peers.

5. You are brought to trial. What are your rights in court?

- Article III, Section 2 of the Constitution, and the Sixth Amendment guarantee you the right to a trial by an impartial jury.

The Framers knew that the right to a trial by jury was one of the greatest protections from unfair treatment by the king and his judges that the people of England had developed. In England, the jury was traditionally made up of twelve persons selected from the community at large; they were not members of the government. The purpose of a jury trial is to provide an unprejudiced group to determine the facts and to provide fair judgments about guilt or innocence. Requiring a jury trial is a way of making sure that the criminal justice system is democratic and involves citizens of the community.

- The Sixth Amendment guarantees you the right to be confronted with the witnesses against you.

Suppose a secret informer tells law-enforcement officers that you have committed a crime, but that person is not required to face you and your lawyer in court. You don't know who the person is and have no chance to challenge the accusation. The purpose of this protection is to make sure that you and your lawyer have the chance to face and question anyone who has given evidence against you which may be used to convict you.

- The Sixth Amendment guarantees you the right to compel witnesses in your favor to testify for you.

Suppose you know someone who knows something that might help you with your case, or who even might have evidence to show you are innocent, but the person won't testify for you for one reason or another. As a result, you might be convicted of a crime you didn't commit. This right says that in such situations, the government must do everything it can to bring witnesses who may be in your favor to court to testify for you.

6. You have been convicted of a crime. What rights do you now have?

● The Eighth Amendment guarantees that you may not be subjected to cruel and unusual punishment.

This protection has been interpreted to mean that the punishment shall not be "barbaric." Such punishments as branding or whipping are prohibited. The punishment shall not be "excessive." For example, you cannot be given, as happened in the past, the death sentence for stealing a loaf of bread.

7. You have been tried and found innocent. What rights do you have?

● The Fifth Amendment guarantees you the right to be free from being tried again for the same crime.

The protection against "double jeopardy" is the oldest of the procedural protections that were included in the Constitution. It has its roots in ancient Greek and Roman law, it is in English common law, and it is found in the laws of many nations. It is intended to prevent the government from abusing its power by trying you again and again for the same crime of which you have been found innocent. To allow the government to do this would be to subject you to continued embarrassment, expense, anxiety, and insecurity, and the possibility of eventually being found guilty even though you are innocent. The protection against double jeopardy also protects you, if you have been found guilty, from being punished more than once for the same crime.

Controversies over procedural due process

Controversies over procedural due process have not been over the rightness or wrongness of the basic rights themselves but over how they should be interpreted and applied. The Supreme Court's interpretations of these rights show how it has tried, under changing and often difficult circumstances, to balance your rights as an individual against the responsibility of government to protect all of us from people who break the law and who may endanger our lives, liberty, or property. Since the protection of your individual rights is the main purpose of constitutional government, the problem of balancing these interests is one of the most difficult problems of a limited government.

While controversy remains with regard to the interpretation and extent of particular rights and how they are to be protected, all justices have agreed that fairness in the <u>procedures</u> by which a person is accused and tried for a crime is a cornerstone of our constitutional democracy. The guarantees of procedural fairness or justice are among the most important of your rights contained in the Constitution and Bill of Rights.

Reviewing and using the lesson

1. Make a chart listing Amendments 4, 5, 6, and 8 to the Constitution, which contain guarantees of procedural due process. For each amendment state the right(s) of procedural due process that it protects.

2. What is the right to <u>habeas corpus</u>? Explain why it is one of the most important protections of individual freedom.

3. Are the guarantees of procedural due process outlined in this lesson in the best interests of all citizens or do they make it possible for too many criminals to be set free at the expense of law-abiding citizens? Explain your position.

4. We often hear people say: "Better that nine guilty people go free than one innocent person be convicted." Do you agree? Would you agree if the figures were "ninety-nine" and "one?"

5. Can you think of any circumstances where a defendant might not prefer a jury trial? Explain your answer.

6. Some scholars have said that procedural due process is the "keystone of liberty." Others have called it the "heart of the law." Some scholars have said that the degree of due process protections a nation provides for its citizens is an important indicator of whether the nation has a constitutional government or an autocratic or dictatorial government. Why do you suppose the Founders and these scholars would place such a high value on the protection of the rights of people accused of crimes?

Lesson A-2

DRUGS AND THE COURTS: APPLYING THE EXCLUSIONARY RULE

As the drug abuse problem continues, law enforcement efforts have increased, especially to prevent drug dealing. The following case raises important questions about search and seizure protections and came before the United States Supreme Court on January 11, 1988.

The Case of Billy Greenwood

Billy Greenwood lived in Laguna Beach, California. Early in 1984, police there received information that Greenwood was a drug dealer. The information came from a federal drug enforcement agent who had been told by a criminal suspect that a large shipment of narcotics was on its way to Greenwood's house in a truck. In addition, one of Greenwood's neighbors complained to police of a large number of vehicles passing through the neighborhood late at night and stopping briefly at the Greenwood residence. The police watched Greenwood's house and verified what the neighbor had said. Police saw a truck leave the house and followed it to another residence that they had previously investigated as a drug dealing location. The police did not believe that they could get a search warrant without further evidence, however. The criminal informant was not seen as reliable.

On April 6, 1984, police investigator Jenny Stracner, who had been working on the case for several months, asked the trash collector in Greenwood's neighborhood to pick up the plastic garbage bags that Greenwood placed on the curb in front of his house and to give her the bags without mixing their contents with refuse from other houses. The trash collector complied with her request. When Stracner searched through Greenwood's trash, she found items related to use of narcotics. She used this information to obtain a search warrant to search Greenwood's home.

When police officers searched Greenwood's home, they discovered quantities of cocaine and hashish. Greenwood and another person,

Dyanne Van Houten, were arrested on felony narcotics charges but were released after they posted bail.

Neighbors continued to report that many late night visitors still came to the Greenwood house. On May 4, 1984, another investigator, Robert Rahaeuser, again asked Greenwood's regular trash collector to obtain Greenwood's trash. Again, the investigator found evidence of narcotics use. Rahaeuser secured another search warrant for Greenwood's home based on the information from the second trash search. During the second search of Greenwood's house police found additional narcotics and evidence of narcotics trafficking. The police arrested Greenwood again.

Greenwood's lawyers argued that the search of his trash was unconstitutional and that the evidence obtained from the trash search and the subsequent search of his house should be excluded from the trial court. He said that police would not have had probable cause for a warrant to search his house if they had not first obtained evidence illegally by searching his trash. Greenwood also said that the trash collector was acting as an agent of the police and at the request of the police when he singled out Greenwood's trash from other trash. The State of California argued that Greenwood's trash was collected on the street where it had been left for the trash collector. Under these circumstances Greenwood had left his trash in plain sight and had no reason to expect that his trash would remain private. Therefore, the State of California claimed that its case against Greenwood was valid and so was the evidence.

The California Court of Appeals agreed with Greenwood and so did the California Supreme Court. Finally, the State of California appealed the case to the United States Supreme Court. It asked the Supreme Court to decide whether the rights of Greenwood and Van Houten had been violated in searching the trash in front of the house.

The Greenwood case raises an important question about the exclusionary rule and about the privacy of a citizen's trash: **At what point may police search your trash without a warrant**?

- After it is wrapped and tied in opaque garbage bags?
- After it has been placed at the street for collection?
- After it has been picked up by a trash collector?

A Case in Point: You Decide

After reviewing the Greenwood case, the members of the class will serve as Supreme Court justices and petitioners. The Supreme Court's procedures are simplified to the following steps:

1. Attorney teams (4-6 people) for the Petitioner (the party making an appeal) and for the Respondent (4-6 people) prepare arguments to support their positions and make a presentation (no more than four minutes long) to a court of nine justices. Each side is allowed four minutes for its presentation.

2. As the court (nine justices) hear the arguments, any justice can interrupt to ask questions. After all have spoken, the chief justice moderates a five-minute conference in which justices try to change each others' minds. At the end of the conference, the justices take a final vote.

Time Needed:

- Petitioner's Argument - 4 to 5 minutes, including time for Justices' questions.
- Questions/Answers - 2 to 3 minutes
- Respondent's Argument - 4 to 5 minutes
- Questions/Answers - 2 to 3 minutes
- Justices' Discussion/Ruling - 4 to 5 minutes
- Class Discussion - 20 to 25 minutes

Attorneys' Instructions

As attorneys, you are responsible for presenting the court with sound arguments.

If you represent the Petitioner (the State of California), you will argue that the evidence seized in Greenwood's trash should not be excluded from consideration at trial.

If you represent the Respondent (Greenwood) you will argue that the evidence seized in Greenwood's trash should be excluded at trial.

To prepare your argument, work with your team by considering and writing responses to the following:

- A clear, brief statement of your position.
- At least two facts from the case which support your position.
- An explanation of how each fact supports your position.
- One previous court decision which supports your position.
- One reason why your position is fair to the State or Greenwood.
- One reason why a Court decision in your favor will benefit society.

Make an outline ordering this information so that all of it can be included in a four-minute presentation. Decide which team member will present the information. Finally, assign at least one team member to answer the justices' questions. He or she should prepare by carefully reviewing the case description.

Justices' Instructions

When preparing to hear arguments, Supreme Court Justices review documents with their clerks about a case and identify the questions they want to ask the attorneys. Working with your team, write down the following information:

- What don't you understand about California v. Greenwood?
- What facts do you want clarified?
- Which of their clients' actions would you like the attorneys to justify or explain?

Justices also prepare by reviewing previous court decisions. Which of the cases you read about in "The Exclusionary Rule" could be applied to this case? Remember, when you make your decision about California v. Greenwood you must consider these precedents, but you are not bound by them.

The Judgment

- What were the strongest arguments presented by the attorneys for the State of California? What information or argument would have improved their case?
- What were the strongest arguments presented by the attorneys for Greenwood? What information or argument would have improved their case?

- What were the key questions asked by the justices? What other questions, if any, should they have asked? During their conference, what arguments did they consider? Did they ignore any important arguments?
- Does the justices' decision expand or restrict the exclusionary rule? Why? Do you agree with their decision?

U.S. Supreme Court decisions are made by a process similar to one you just tried, except:

- Attorneys for the Petitioner and Respondent must give the Court detailed written arguments, called briefs, before the case is heard. Because Supreme Court decisions set precedents which affect the entire nation, other interested parties can air their views about a case in Friend-of-the-Court briefs.
- During oral arguments, each side is allowed one hour which includes questioning by the Court. This time limit is strictly enforced.
- When the Court reaches a decision, the Chief Justice assigns one of the judges to write an explanation of that decision called the **majority opinion**. Justices who support the decision but differ with the majority's reasoning may write a concurring opinion. At least one of the judges who disagree with the decision will write a **dissenting opinion**.

Do you think this process is fair? Why or why not?

Your teacher will explain the Supreme Court's decision in California v. Greenwood. Compare both the judgment and the reasoning behind it with your own.

Your Opinion

Write a short essay supporting or refuting the statement:

The Supreme Court made a wise decision in the California v. Greenwood case.

In organizing your essay:
- Indicate whether you support or refute the decision of the Court.
- Quickly summarize the Greenwood case.

- List two facts which support your statement.
- Cite a previous court case that supports your statement.
- Develop an argument for fairness which supports your statement.
- Develop an argument to demonstrate how this benefits society.

Do not sign your name, your teacher will give you an ID number to use instead. All papers will be read and critiqued by three students using the student critique sheet.

Student Critique Guidelines

Paper # _____

1. Does the paper (Circle one) SUPPORT/REFUTE the decision of the Court?
2. Is the Greenwood case summarized? YES/NO
   Comments:
3. Are relevant facts presented? YES/NO
   Comments:
4. Is a previous court decision cited? YES/NO
   Comments:
5. Is an argument for fairness given? YES/NO
   Comments:
6. Is an argument illustrating the benefit to society given? YES/NO
   Comments:
7. On the paper mark any spelling, punctuation, or grammatical errors.
8. What is the best part of the paper? What needs improvement?

Lesson A-3

CONSTITUTIONAL RIGHTS IN A TIME OF CRISIS, 1941-1945

LESSON PLAN AND NOTES FOR TEACHERS

Preview of Main Points

This lesson describes the abridgement of the constitutional rights of Japanese-Americans during World War II. It shows the effects of a national crisis on the constitutional rights of an unpopular minority group. Basic questions about civil liberties and rights are raised. The lesson highlights constitutional issues raised by actions of the President, Congress, and Court

Connection to Textbooks

Most American government textbooks say little or nothing about the internment in detention camps of Japanese-Americans during World War II. American history texts mention this event, but do not probe it to examine the profound constitutional issues. Thus, the lesson can be used to provide a detailed study of a significant event in American constitutional history. The lesson can be used with chapters on civil liberties in American government textbooks. Of course, it can be used in connection with chapters about World War II in American history textbooks.

Objectives

Students are expected to:

1. Know about the Executive Order and federal law that established the authority of military commanders to abridge the constitutional rights of Japanese-Americans.

2. Identify reasons used to justify the Executive Order and federal law that led to the evacuation and detention of Japanese-Americans.

3. Know the constitutional issues raised by the evacuation and detention of Japanese-Americans.

4. Know the issues and decisions involved in three Supreme Court cases: (a) *Hirabayashi v. United States*, (b) *Korematsu v. United States* and (c) *Ex parte Endo*.

5. Know the main ideas of the dissenting opinions in the *Korematsu* case.

6. Explain how the government actions toward Japanese-Americans in World War II shaped the meaning of the Constitution.

7. Interpret and appraise the judicial opinions in the cases of *Hirabayashi, Korematsu* and *Endo*.

Suggestions for Teaching the Lesson

Opening the Lesson

- Preview the main parts of the lesson for students.
- Explain how this lesson is connected to the material they are studying in the textbook.

Developing the Lesson

- Have students read this case study. Then ask them to respond to the review questions at the end of the lesson.

- Conduct a discussion of the review questions. The purpose is to make sure that students understand the main ideas and facts of this lesson.

- Have students respond to the questions involving interpretation and appraisal of judicial opinions in the cases of *Hirabayashi, Korematsu* and *Endo*.

- Pay special attention to the dissenting opinions of Justices Murphy and Jackson. Ask students to agree or disagree with the main ideas of these dissenting opinions.

Concluding the Lesson

- Ask students to identify the continuing constitutional significance of the events in this case study about Japanese-Americans in World War II. Ask them to explain what Justice Jackson meant when he referred to the Court's decision in the *Korematsu* case as a "loaded weapon."

- Ask students to speculate about situations in the future that might prompt a governmental response similar to the actions directed toward Japanese-Americans in World War II. What might happen in the future to occasion similar treatment of an unpopular minority group? How might the rights of all citizens be guarded against such a possibility? Ask students to tell what they would do as a member of a minority group facing suspension of constitutional rights. Ask them how they would respond to such a possibility as a member of the majority.

- It has been said that "tyranny can be practiced by a majority against a minority." Ask students this question: Is the treatment of Japanese-Americans during World War II an example of tyranny of the majority?

- Conclude the lesson by pointing out that a true democracy is more than rule by the majority. It also involves protection of the rights and freedoms of minorities.

- Read this quote by the British historian, Lord Acton: "The most certain test by which we judge whether a country is really free is the amount of security enjoyed by minorities." Ask students to discuss Acton's idea with reference to the issues raised by this lesson.

Suggested Readings

Bosworth, Allan R. *America's Concentration Camps.* New York: W. W. Norton & Company, Inc., 1967. This book tells the story of the Japanese-Americans during World War II. Easy to read, it includes discussion of the main constitutional issues and court cases discussed in this lesson.

Irons, Peter. *Justice at War.* New York: Oxford University Press, 1983. The story of the Japanese internment cases. It includes current interviews with people involved in those cases.

Murphy, Paul L. *Constitution in Crisis Times: 1918-1969.* New York: Harper & Row, Publishers, 1972. This is an excellent discussion of constitutional development. Chapter 7 deals with constitutional issues during World War II.

"Commission on Wartime Relocation and Internment of Civilians." *Personal Justice Denied.* Washington, D.C.: U.S. Government Printing Office, 1983. This is a report about the internment of Americans of Japanese ancestry during World War II. It is based on testimony from 750 witnesses and a study of documents.

CONSTITUTIONAL RIGHTS IN A TIME OF CRISIS, 1941-1945

On December 7, 1941, Japanese aircraft attacked Pearl Harbor in Hawaii. The surprised defenders suffered a crushing defeat. The Japanese disabled or destroyed five American battleships and three cruisers, killing 2,355 members of the American armed services. The attack left another 1,178 military personnel wounded.

President Roosevelt denounced the "sneak attack" and Congress declared war on Japan. A few days later Germany and Italy declared war on the United States. Thus, Americans entered World War II.

Within three months, the Japanese overran most of southeast Asia and the American territories of Guam and the Philippine Islands. Americans feared a Japanese invasion of Hawaii, or even of California.

General J. L. DeWitt, responsible for defending the Pacific Coast against enemy attack, feared that the 112,000 persons of Japanese ancestry who lived in the West Coast states might be a threat to national security. General DeWitt recommended that these people be sent away from the region.

Suspension of Constitutional Rights

More than 75,000 American citizens of Japanese ancestry lived on the West Coast of the United States. With a few exceptions, all of these citizens had been born and raised in the United States. The overwhelming majority of them had never seen Japan. Virtually all of them spoke English. These Japanese-Americans considered themselves loyal American citizens.

Over thirty-five thousand Japanese immigrants also lived on the West Coast. These men and women had come to the United States before 1924. Although legally citizens of Japan, most considered themselves loyal to their adopted country.

In the weeks after the bombing at Pearl Harbor, some people pointed out that these older Japanese were not United States citizens, but Japanese citizens, even though they had lived in the U.S. for many years. However, few Americans understood that at the time it was illegal for Japanese nationals to become naturalized citizens. In 1922, in the case of *Ozawa v. United States,* the Supreme Court held that certain Asians (such as Japanese, Chinese, and Koreans) could not become naturalized citizens. Thus, although many of the Japanese immigrants living in the United States had wanted to become citizens, the Court had denied them that right. The government only made exceptions for Japanese immigrants who had fought in World War I. Further examples of discrimination against

the Japanese came in 1924, when the Congress prohibited all Japanese immigration to the United States.

Thus, the government did not allow Japanese immigrants to become citizens and prohibited their relatives from joining them in the United States. Nevertheless, these Japanese were loyal to their adopted country. Born in the United States, the children of these immigrants had, of course, become citizens at birth. They also considered themselves patriotic and loyal. Yet, many American politicians and leaders thought otherwise. Secretary of War Henry L. Stimson urged President Roosevelt to take action to remove all American citizens of Japanese ancestry, as well as all Japanese immigrants, from the West Coast.

On February 19, 1942, The President issued Executive Order #9066 giving authority to military commanders to establish special zones in territory threatened by enemy attack. The order invested the military commanders with power to decide who could come, go, or remain in the special military areas. The President issued this executive order on his own authority, under the Constitution, as commander-in-chief of the nation's armed forces.

On March 2, General DeWitt established Military Areas #1 and #2 in the western part of the United States.

On March 21, Congress passed a law in support of the President's Executive Order and of the subsequent actions of General DeWitt.

On March 24, General DeWitt proclaimed a curfew between the hours of 8:00 p.m. and 6:00 a.m. for all persons of Japanese ancestry living within Military Area #1, which comprised the entire Pacific coastal region.

On May 9, General DeWitt ordered the exclusion from Military Area #1 of all persons of Japanese background. The vast majority of these people were U.S. citizens born on American soil. These people had thoroughly American attitudes, beliefs, and behavior. Most of them would have felt out of place in Japan.

The military sent the Japanese-Americans to the relocation centers far from the coastal region. In effect, this action placed more than 75,000 American citizens who had broken no laws in jail without trials. The government did not charge any of these people with crimes.

They could take with them only what they could carry. A government order dated December 8, 1941, froze their bank accounts leaving them without funds. To raise cash, they had to sell any possessions they could. Other Americans and local governments took advantage of their plight, offering to buy possessions and property at low prices that rarely reflected the value of the goods. These Japanese-Americans could never regain most possessions and property lost in this way.

Constitutional Issues

Military commanders, acting under authority granted by the President and Congress, had denied more than 75,000 American citizens their constitutional rights of "due process." The Fifth Amendment says, "No person shall be...deprived of life, liberty, or property, without due process of law. . . ." Article I, Section 9, of the Constitution grants the privilege of the *writ of habeas corpus,* a written court order issued to inquire whether or not a person is lawfully imprisoned or detained. The writ demands that the persons holding the prisoner either justify his or her detention or release the person.

Had the government taken away the constitutional rights of Japanese-Americans? The Supreme Court finally had to rule on the legality of holding thousands of American citizens in detention camps solely because of their ancestry. Would the Court overturn military actions sanctioned by the President and Congress?

Three notable cases involving the constitutional rights of Japanese-Americans came before the Supreme Court. They were:

1. **Hirabayashi v. United States** (1943)
2. **Korematsu v. United States** (1944)
3. **Ex parte Endo** (1944)

The Hirabayashi Case

Gordon Hirabayashi was an American citizen of Japanese ancestry. Born in the United States, he had never seen Japan. He had done nothing to suggest disloyalty to the United States.

Background to the Case. Hirabayashi was arrested and convicted for violating General DeWitt's curfew order and for failing to register at a control station in preparation for transportation to a relocation camp. At the time Hirabayashi was studying at the University of Washington. He was a model citizen and well-liked student, active in the local Y.M.C.A. and church organizations. Hirabayashi refused to report to a control center or obey the curfew order because he believed both orders were discriminatory edicts contrary to the very spirit of the United States. He later told a court, "I must maintain the democratic standards for which this nation lives. . . . I am objecting to the principle of this order which denies the rights of human beings, including citizens."

The Decision. The Court unanimously upheld the curfew law for "Japanese-Americans" living in Military Area #1. The Court said the President and Congress had used the war powers provided in the Constitution appropriately. The Court also held that the curfew order did not violate the Fifth Amendment.

Speaking for the Court, Chief Justice Stone said discrimination based only upon race was "odious to a free people whose institutions are founded upon the doctrine of equality." However, in this case, Stone said, the need to protect national security in time of war necessitated consideration of race.

The Court only ruled on the legality of the curfew order. It avoided the larger issue of the legality of holding American citizens in detention centers and later in large, barbed-wire enclosures, which the government called relocation camps.

Hirabayashi eventually spent more than three years in county jails and federal prisons for his refusal to go along with a law that made him a criminal simply because of his ancestry.

The Korematsu Case

Fred Korematsu was born and raised in Oakland, California. He could read and write only English. He had never visited Japan and knew little or nothing about the Japanese way of life.

Background to the Case. In June, 1941, before America's official entry into World War II, Fred Korematsu tried to enlist in the Navy. Although the Navy was actively recruiting men in anticipation of entering the war, the service did not allow Korematsu, an American citizen of Japanese ancestry, to enlist. He then went to work in a shipyard as a welder. When the war began, he lost his job because of his Japanese heritage. Korematsu found part-time work as a welder. Hoping to move to Nevada with his fiancee, who was not a Japanese-American, Korematsu ignored the evacuation orders when they came. As an American citizen he felt the orders should not apply to him in any event. The FBI arrested Korematsu, who was convicted of violating orders of the commanders of Military Area #1.

The Decision. By a 6-3 vote, the Court upheld the exclusion of Japanese-Americans from the Pacific coastal region. The needs of national security in a time of crisis justified the "exclusion orders." The war power of the President and Congress, provided by the Constitution, provided the legal basis for the majority decision.

Justice Black admitted that the "exclusion orders" forced citizens of Japanese ancestry to endure severe hardships. "But hardships are a part of war," said Black, "and war is an aggregation of hardships."

Justice Black maintained that the orders had not "excluded" Korematsu primarily for reasons of race, but for reasons of military security. The majority ruling really did not say whether or not the relocation of Japanese-

Americans was constitutional. Rather, the Court side-stepped that touchy issue, emphasizing instead the national crisis caused by the war.

Dissenting Opinions. Three justices—Murphy, Jackson, and Roberts—disagreed with the majority. Justice Roberts thought it a plain "case of convicting a citizen as punishment for not submitting to imprisonment in a concentration camp solely because of his ancestry," without evidence concerning his loyalty to the United States.

Justice Murphy said that the "exclusion orders" violated the right of citizens to "due process of law." Furthermore, Murphy claimed that the decision of the Court's majority amounted to the "legalization of racism. Racial discrimination in any form and in any degree has no justifiable part whatever in our democratic way of life."

Murphy admitted that the argument citing military necessity carried weight, but he insisted that the military necessity claim must "subject itself to the judicial process" to determine "whether the deprivation is reasonably related to a public danger that is so 'immediate, imminent, and impending'. . . ."

Finally, Murphy concluded that "individuals must not be left impoverished in their constitutional rights on a plea of military necessity that has neither substance nor support."

The Endo Case

In 1942, the government dismissed Mitsuye Endo from her civil service job in California and the military ordered her to a relocation center. She had never attended a Japanese language school and could neither read nor write Japanese. She was a United States citizen with a brother serving in the U.S. Army. Her family did not even subscribe to a Japanese language newspaper.

Background on the Case. Miss Endo's attorney filed a *writ of habeas corpus* on her behalf, contending that the War Relocation Authority had no right to detain a loyal American citizen who was innocent of all the various allegations that the Army had used to justify evacuation.

The Decision. The Supreme Court ruled unanimously that Mitsuye Endo "should be given her liberty." The government should release the Japanese-American woman from custody whose loyalty to the United States had been clearly established.

Justice Douglas said, "Loyalty is a matter of the heart and mind, not of race, creed or color. . . ."

Justice Murphy added, "I am of the view that detention in Relocation Centers of persons of Japanese ancestry regardless of loyalty is not only unauthorized by Congress or the Executive, but is another example of the unconstitutional resort to racism inherent in the entire evacuation program. . . . Racial discrimination of this nature bears

no reasonable relation to military necessity and is utterly foreign to the ideals and traditions of the American people."

Shortly after the Court's decision in the *Endo* case, Major General Pratt, commander of Military Area #1 at that time, ordered a suspension of the "exclusion orders" that had resulted in the detention of people such as Korematsu and Endo. Most of the detained "Japanese-Americans" were free to return home.

Constitutional Significance

The Court had not used the Constitution to protect Japanese-Americans from abusive treatment during World War II. There was military interference with civil liberties in the name of a wartime emergency. The Supreme Court allowed the executive and legislative branches of government to engage in behavior that it surely would have found unconstitutional in peacetime.

The Court avoided answering a significant constitutional question in reaching verdicts in the cases of Hirabayashi, Korematsu and Endo. Can military authorities, even if supported by acts of the President and Congress, detain citizens outside of a combat zone without charging them with any crime, merely on grounds of defending the nation during wartime?

By avoiding this question, the Court allowed the Executive and Legislative actions that sanctioned the Relocation Centers during World War II to set a dangerous precedent. The Court established a precedent supporting the evacuation and detention of unpopular minorities during time of war. Will others use this precedent to deny constitutional rights to certain groups of citizens during a national crisis in the future?

Afterward

A government commission formed to investigate wartime espionage reported that no evidence existed of disloyal behavior among the Japanese-Americans on the West Coast. The government did not find a single Japanese-American guilty of spying for Japan during World War II, even though it jailed many as suspected spies. In addition, one of the best fighting units of the U.S. Army in Europe, the Nisei Brigade, was made up of Japanese-Americans. This brigade became the most decorated unit in the history of the U.S. Army. Its soldiers proved their loyalty by fighting for their country even though their families had been jailed without "due process of law."

After release from the detention camps, most Japanese-Americans returned to the Pacific Coast. They began again, resettling in cities and starting new farms. Many initiated legal actions to regain their lost property. In 1948, Congress agreed to pay for some of that property, giving the Japanese-Americans less than ten cents for each dollar they had lost. This action was to prove the only admission Congress made that it had done anything wrong to the Japanese-Americans during the war. This minor recompense was a small way of saying, "We're sorry."

The U.S. Government justified the internment two ways. The government claimed that American citizens of Japanese ancestry, more loyal to Japan than to their own country, would spy for Japan. Second, the U.S. Government claimed that because Japan had attacked the U.S., those Americans of Japanese ancestry might have helped Japan. Yet, many have always questioned the validity of these fears.

No evidence justified fears that American citizens of Japanese descent or Japanese immigrants living in the U.S. supported Japan in any substantial fashion. The few supporters of Japan, mostly old men who posed no danger to the U.S., quickly suffered arrest long before the planning of any mass deportation of Japanese-Americans. No Japanese-Americans or Japanese immigrants committed acts of sabotage during the war.

John J. McCloy, a key advisor to Secretary of War Stimson, was the civilian in the War Department most responsible for the removal. Many years after the war he admitted that the purpose of the internment was "in the way of retribution for the attack that was made on Pearl Harbor." In other words, their own government forced American citizens to leave their homes and property and to spend four years behind barbed wire guarded by armed soldiers, because a foreign country (which most of these citizens had never visited) had attacked the United States.

In 1980, Congress re-opened investigations into the treatment of Japanese-Americans during World War II and created the Commission on Wartime Relocation and Internment of Civilians. After nearly three years of careful examination of the evidence, which included testimony from 750 witnesses, the Commission issued a report on February 25, 1983. The report concluded: "A grave injustice was done to American citizens and resident aliens of Japanese ancestry who, without individual review or any probative evidence against them, were excluded, removed, and detained by the United States during World War II."

EXERCISES FOR LESSON IV-12

Reviewing Main Ideas and Facts

1. Why were Americans of Japanese ancestry sent to Relocation Centers?

2. What legal authority for evacuating and detaining Japanese-Americans did the President and Congress provide?

3. What constitutional issues did the evacuation and detention of Japanese-Americans during World War II raise?

4. What constitutional issue did the Supreme Court address in each of these cases?

   a. *Hirabayashi v. United States*

   b. *Korematsu v. United States*

   c. *Ex parte Endo*

5. What did the Court decide in each of these cases?

   a. *Hirabayashi v. United States*

   b. *Korematsu v. United States*

   c. *Ex parte Endo*

6. What constitutional issue did the Court avoid?

7. What continuing constitutional significance does the treatment of Japanese-Americans during World War II have?

Interpreting and Appraising Judicial Opinions

1. List the main ideas of the dissenting opinions in the *Korematsu* case by Justices Roberts and Murphy.

2. Following is an excerpt from Justice Jackson's dissent in the *Korematsu* case. What is the main idea of this excerpt?

   A military order, however unconstitutional, is not apt to last longer than the military emergency. . . . But once a judicial opinion rationalizes such an order to show that it conforms to the Constitution . . . the Court for all time has validated the principle of racial discrimination in criminal procedures and of transplanting American citizens. The principle then lies about like a loaded weapon ready for the hand of any authority that can bring forward a plausible claim of an urgent need.

3. Do you agree with the decisions of the Court in the cases of Hirabayashi, Korematsu and Endo? Explain.

4. Do you agree with the dissenting opinions of Justices Murphy, Roberts, and Jackson?

Lesson B-1

BILL OF RIGHTS CASES

Introduction

"No unreasonable search and seizure, free speech, no cruel and unusual punishment."
These phrases from the Bill of Rights are often seen by students as just more
information to memorize. To truly understand the importance of the protections in the
Bill of Rights, students must be asked to apply and discuss the amendments. This activity
is designed to help them do just that - apply the amendments to hypothetical situations
and discuss their importance.

Objectives

- To examine the rights contained in the Bill of Rights.
- To understand that many of the rights are not absolute.
- To identify which part of a particular amendment is related to each specific
  situation.

Materials

Handout: Ten Hypothetical Situations

Procedures

1. Either in small groups or individually, have the students read each situation and
   decide if it contains a violation of a right granted by the Bill of Rights.

2. After they have completed the situations, ask them to discuss which situations
   contained violations and which situations were properly conducted under the
   Constitution. A number of questions related to the connection between the
   amendments could also be posed. Asking students to categorize the amendments by
   their results is a useful way for them to remember the amendments.

3. Resource Person: An attorney can help discuss the students' answers and the rationale
   for the protections granted by each amendment. Make sure that students have
   completed this assignment before the lawyer comes in.

BILL OF RIGHTS HYPOTHETICALS

Read the following hypothetical situations and decide whether each one contains a violation of the Bill of Rights. For each, write the number of the amendment and the appropriate phrases from the amendment that relate to the situation.

1. A 20 year old college student starts his own newspaper which often prints articles making fun of the local mayor. The mayor is angry and gets his aides to take the papers off the stands before they can be distributed.

2. A woman is being tried for murder. The prosecuting attorney forces her to take the stand and testify.

3. A student wears a button to school urging people to vote for a certain candidate for President of the United States. Some other students don't like the candidate and ask the principal to force the student to take off the button. The principal refuses to tell the student to remove the button.

4. A dentist is being sued for $500,000. He wants a jury to hear the case but the judge refuses his request.

5. A young woman is being tried for treason. She is accused of selling plans for building a nuclear warhead to Iran. The judge believes it would be dangerous to let the public hear her ideas. He refuses to allow anyone to view the trial.

6. A group of teenagers gather quietly on a street corner. Neighbors complain and ask the police to arrest them for getting together as a group. The police refuse.

7. A town needs more land to build a new elementary school. A woman's property is needed, but she wants to keep it. The town forces her to sell and gives her twice the property's actual value. She sues to get her land back.

8. The government tries a man for murder and loses the case. A jury says he is innocent. The district attorney who prosecuted the case is mad and promises to keep trying him until they get a jury to convict him. The defendant thinks this is unfair.

9. The Postmaster General of the United States has a cross and a nativity scene installed at all Post Offices throughout the country during Christmas time. Government funds are being used to purchase the cross and nativity scene. The mayor of a predominantly Jewish town demands that the cross and nativity scene be removed from her town.

10. A man living on a quiet residential street erects a giant billboard on his front lawn. The billboard has neon lights advertising a new breakfast cereal that the man invented. The city has a zoning law against this type of sign in a residential neighborhood and demands that it be removed.

Answer Key

1. **IS** a violation of the student's First Amendment rights to free press.

2. **IS** a violation of the woman's Fifth Amendment right protecting her from self-incrimination.

3. **IS NOT** a violation. The principal behaved in a constitutional manner by refusing to violate the student's First Amendment right of free speech (wearing a political button is considered political speech protected by the First Amendment). If the principal believed the button could cause a riot or seriously disrupt the school, the principal could prevent the student from wearing it.

4. **IS** a violation. The Seventh Amendment guarantees the right to a jury trial if requested in civil cases where the value in controversy exceeds $20.00.

5. **IS** a violation. The Sixth Amendment guarantees the right to a public trial.

6. **IS NOT** a violation. The police were upholding the teenagers' First Amendment right to assemble when they refused to arrest the teenagers for standing on the street corner. However, if the group was blocking access to a store or house, police have the right to remove them.

7. **IS NOT** a violation. The Fifth Amendment allows the government to take private property for public use, as long as the owner receives a fair price (called **condemnation** of property).

8. **IS** a violation. The Fifth Amendment prohibits a person from being tried twice for the same crime.

9. **IS** a violation of the First Amendment which forbids the government from establishing a religion.

10. **IS NOT** a violation of the First Amendment. This type of zoning law is constitutional. Local governments have the right to enact reasonable zoning ordinances.

Lesson B-2

How does the Constitution protect freedom of expression?

LESSON OVERVIEW

In this lesson students learn about the relationship of freedom of expression to political freedom. Students first read and discuss the freedom of expression portion of the First Amendment. Students learn that this section of the amendment is designed to protect various forms of freedom of expression. They then read and discuss why freedom of expression was viewed as so important by the Founders and explore some of the principal arguments in support of this freedom. Finally, students learn that there are limits on this important freedom when it conflicts with other important rights and interests. The relevance of this right to their own experiences is demonstrated by a reading and discussion of two Supreme Court cases dealing with students' rights to freedom of expression.

LESSON OBJECTIVES

At the conclusion of this lesson:

1. Students should be able to describe the freedoms included under the First Amendment's guarantee of freedom of expression.

2. Students should be able to describe some of the historical incidents that influenced the Founders' position on freedom of expression.

3. Students should be able to explain the benefits of freedom of expression.

4. Students should be able to give reasons for placing limits on freedom of expression.

5. Students should be able to formulate and defend an opinion on whether freedom of expression should be limited in a particular case.

MATERIALS NEEDED

1. Student text

2. Handout

TEACHING PROCEDURES

A. Introductory Activity:
Introducing the First Amendment

Have students read the "Purpose of Lesson" and "What is freedom of expression?" Then review with students the excerpts from the First Amendment included in their text, being sure they understand what each clause relating to freedom of expression means.

Discuss the following questions.

- What basic rights are listed in this portion of the First Amendment?
- Why do you think these particular rights were included?
- Why do you think they were included in this first amendment to the Constitution and not in a later one?

B. Reading and Discussion:
Understanding the importance of freedom of expression

Have the class read the sections, "Why was freedom of expression so important to the Founders?" and "What are some of the benefits of freedom of expression?" In discussing the text, be sure students understand the relationship of freedom of expression to political freedom and the arguments commonly given for the importance of this right.

C. Reading and Discussion:
Deciding when freedom of discussion should be limited

Read with the class the section, "When should freedom of expression be limited?" Ask students to think of situations in which they think freedom of expression might endanger other important values and interests such as national security or public safety. Then discuss with the students other rights that we value that might conflict with freedom of expression, such as the right to privacy and the right to a fair trial.

D. Reading and Group Activity:
Dealing with issues of freedom of expression

Read the section on "Freedom of expression in the schools" with the students. This section summarizes the facts and rulings in the well-known *Tinker* case [*Tinker v. Des Moines School District*, 393 U.S. 503 (1969)]. Then have students complete the "Problem Solving" activity that follows which discusses the 1988 Supreme Court case *Hazelwood School District v. Kuhlmeier*, (88 Daily Journal D.A.R. 564). Divide the class into groups of three to five students each. Ask each group to read both of the cases presented in the text and (1) identify the competing rights and interests they involve, and (2) explain which rights and interests the group thinks should be given priority in each situation.

Then explain to the class that the Court ruled in favor of the principal in the *Hazelwood* case. In the *Hazelwood* case, in a five to three decision, the Court overturned a lower court decision and upheld the school district's right to censor the school newspaper. The newspaper was written and edited by a journalism class, as part of the school's curriculum. Therefore, the Court said, it was not to be considered as a forum for public expression and school officials may impose reasonable restrictions, such as protecting the privacy of pregnant students. Dissenting justices said that the articles deleted by the principal would not have disrupted classroom work nor invaded the rights of others, and were therefore covered by First Amendment protections of freedom of expression.

E. Concluding Activity

Conclude the lesson by leading a discussion of the questions contained in "Reviewing and using the lesson." You also may wish to have the students select one of the freedoms of expression protected by the First Amendment and write a paragraph in their constitutional journals explaining why this freedom is still important today.

OPTIONAL ACTIVITIES

For Reinforcement, Extended Learning, and Enrichment

1. Have the students read the expanded case study, *Tinker v. Des Moines Independent School District* (1969), on Handout 23-1 (immediately following) and discuss its relevance to them and the Constitution. Focus the discussion on some of the reasons why freedom of expression is important and the difference that it might make for their lives.

2. Have students look in magazines and newspapers for articles about contemporary issues of freedom of expression. Have them analyze the articles and create a bulletin board that illustrates a First Amendment theme in today's news.

3. Invite representatives from a newspaper, television station, or radio station to class to talk about the limits government has placed on their freedom of expression. What public interests are these limits designed to protect? Do they feel the limits are justified? Why or why not?

4. If your school has a student-run newspaper, you might ask members of the staff, the faculty adviser, and the school principal to conduct a panel discussion for your class, focusing not only on the recent Supreme Court decision but also on any disagreements or censorship incidents that have occurred in your school. What educational goals have conflicted or might conflict with freedom of expression?

5. Interested students might research cases after the Tinker case dealing with symbolic speech — wearing of headgear or insignia, the use of the American flag on clothing, etc., or the right to free assembly (creating and operating student clubs on campus).

6. Tell students that they are about to take part in an activity that will demonstrate what life might be like in a country without First Amendment rights. Choose one of the following activities to use with the class or divide the class into groups and assign each group one of the activities.

Activity A — "Control the press"

a. Appoint a "Censorship Board" of three class members. They are controlled by only one rule: **Any information allowed to leave the classroom must make the teacher and her/his decisions look good.** Failure to follow this rule will result in a call home and a trip to the principal's office. (Suggest that the new rules are in response to a new schoolwide policy aimed at helping students do better in school.)

b. Appoint four "members of the Free World Press" and have them wait in another classroom for a few minutes.

c. Announce to the class the following three new rules:

   • Anyone talking without permission will get 30 minutes detention.

   • Anyone arguing with the teacher will get 30 minutes detention.

   • Anyone leaving his or her seat for any reason during the class period will get 30 minutes detention.

   Explain that these new rules are designed to keep better order in the classroom. Have pairs of students, acting as reporters, write headlines and brief articles summarizing for the "outside world" (rest of the school or school newspaper) the new rules governing their classroom.

d.   Announce that the Censorship Board will impose punishments for negative articles. If the Censorship Board is unwilling to establish meaningful punishments, they will have to accept the consequences mentioned above. The Censorship Board should then choose the article that shows the teacher and the new rules in the best light as the official version of events. It should also impose penalties on those groups that reported unfavorably on the teacher or the new rules.

e.   Members of the "Free World Press" should then reenter the room and be given the officially accepted version of events. They should write a brief account of the three new rules as they have been allowed to see them.

f.   Discuss the situation by asking the following questions:

   • How would you compare the censored version of events with the actual events?

   • What did you think of the new rules?

   • What would you want to include in an article you were writing about the event?

   • Did the fear of punishment keep you from saying what you wanted to in your article?

   • How do you think fear of punishment affects the press in countries that do not have a free press?

   • Do you think that a Censorship Board is even needed, or would fear keep people from printing what they want?

Activity B — "Divide and conquer"

a.   Put up a poster with the following three "new rules."

   • Anyone talking without permission will get 30 minutes detention.

   • Anyone arguing with the teacher will get 30 minutes detention.

   • Anyone leaving his or her seat for any reason during the class period will get 30 minutes detention.

b.   Allow students to create informal gatherings to discuss the fairness of the new rules.

c.   Tell them that if they can develop a classwide alternative to the rules given, they might be able to convince the teacher to change the rules.

d.   Immediately change your mind about allowing the "assemblies" to take place, citing a need for better order, which was the reason for the rules in the first place.

e.   Solicit individual, written suggestions for change. Suggest that there will be serious steps taken to deal with anyone who suggests something too radical or with critical overtones.

f.   Discuss the fears and frustrations of working alone to confront repressive authority as compared to working with a group.

g.   Discuss the activity using the following questions:

   • How did you feel when you were told you couldn't work together?

   • Did the fear of punishment keep you from arguing about the restriction on group activity?

   • What were the benefits and costs of working alone?

   • What would be the benefits and costs of working with a group?

Activity C — "Suppressing discussion and thought"

a.   Announce the three new class rules noted above. Do not allow discussion.

b.   Assign a short group assignment of your choosing. Reading the student text for this lesson would be appropriate.

c.   Tell the students that they may discuss the assignment but they are not to discuss the new rules. ("It's just something that was necessary for a more orderly and efficient classroom!") Also warn them that there are students throughout the room who have been asked to report instances of unauthorized discussion to you, in secret, at a later time. There will be an unnamed consequence, depending on the severity of the offense, for those who are reported.

d.   After providing a few minutes to complete the group work, move on to a discussion.

e.   Discuss the activity using the following questions:

- Was it hard to refrain from discussing the new rules?

- Did you discuss them anyway? If not, why not? If you did, were you worried about being reported?

- Are there countries where adults face the same problems in discussing and criticizing their government that you just faced with the new rules? Can you name some?

- How can people express their opinions in those countries and avoid being punished by the government? Were there really any "spies" in our class? Does this tell us that sometimes the fear of being caught acts to keep people from speaking freely?

HANDOUT

Tinker v. Des Moines Independent School District (1969)

In December, 1965, a small group of students and their parents decided to express their opposition to the United States' involvement in the Vietnam War by wearing black armbands for about two weeks during the holiday season. Some of the group had participated in similar protest activities before, including Mr. Tinker, a Methodist minister; Mrs. Eckhardt, an official in the Women's International League for Peace and Freedom; and the children of both families. They said the protest would include wearing the armbands to school.

The principals of the Des Moines public schools heard of the plan, and on December 15 adopted a policy specifically prohibiting students from wearing black armbands while at school, and announced the policy in the schools. The Tinker and Eckhardt children knew of the schools' policy. They understood they would be suspended if they disobeyed the rule. On December 16 and 17, seven of the 18,000 students enrolled in the Des Moines public school system wore the black armbands. They attended classes as usual. There were no overt disruptions of classroom activities, no demonstrations, and no threats of violence. Outside the classroom, however, a few angry remarks were directed toward the students with armbands. And a mathematics teacher reported that his lesson period had been practically "wrecked by disputes" with Mary Beth Tinker.

Later in the afternoon, the students wearing the armbands were called into the principal's office and asked to remove them. When they refused, they were suspended until they returned to school without the armbands. John F. Tinker, age 15, and Mary Beth Tinker, age 13, were among the five students suspended. After the planned protest period was over, the students returned to school.

After the suspension, school authorities had prepared a statement listing the reasons for banning black armbands. The statement referred to the fact that a former student, whose friends were still in school, had been killed in Vietnam and that "if any kind of demonstration existed, it might evolve into something which would be hard to control." The school authorities said that the regulation was directed "against the principle of demonstration" itself, that "schools are no places for demonstrations," and "if students didn't like the way our elected officials were handling things, it should be handled with the ballot box and not in the halls of our public schools." They also said their decision to ban black armbands — symbols of opposition to American involvement in Vietnam — was influenced by the fact that the Vietnam War had recently become "the subject of major controversy" — as indicated by mass marches in Washington and draft card burning incidents.

Mr. Tinker filed a complaint on behalf of his children that their right of free expression had been violated. He asked for a small amount of money and requested that the children not be disciplined for their actions.

The case finally reached the Supreme Court, and the Court ruled in the students' favor. Mr. Justice Fortas, writing the majority opinion of the Court, said:

> First Amendment rights...are available to teachers and students. It can hardly be argued that either students or teachers shed their constitutional rights to freedom of speech or expression at the schoolhouse gate....Under our Constitution, free speech is not a right that is given only to be so circumscribed that it exists in principle but not in fact....The Constitution says that Congress (and the States) may not abridge the right to free speech. This provision means what it says.

Reviewing and using the case

1. What does this selection have to do with the Constitution?

2. How does this case show the relevance of the Constitution to your life?

3. Under what circumstances do you think it would be reasonable and fair to limit students' rights to express their political opinions in school?

How does the Constitution protect freedom of expression?

Purpose of Lesson

In this lesson, you will learn why the Founders considered freedom of expression so important. You will also learn why it is important to you as an individual and to the preservation and improvement of our constitutional democracy. When you have completed this lesson, you should be able to explain the importance of freedom of expression. You should also be able to describe situations in which it might be reasonable and fair to place limitations on this freedom.

Terms to know

abridging
petition
"redress of grievances"
freedom of expression

What is freedom of expression?

"...secure the blessings of liberty to ourselves and our posterity [future generations]...." *Preamble of the Constitution*

One of the purposes of government is to protect our liberty. What does "liberty" mean? When you answer this question you are likely to think of some of the freedoms guaranteed by the First Amendment to the Constitution. It is probably the best-known amendment to the Constitution. Here is what one section of it says:

Congress shall make no law... **abridging** [limiting] the freedom of speech, or of the press; or the right of the people peaceably to assemble, and to **petition** [ask] the government for a **redress of grievances** [to correct wrongs].

Freedom of speech, freedom of the press, freedom of assembly, and freedom of petition are all part of the right to **freedom of expression** protected by the First Amendment. It is important to understand that this Amendment limits the powers of Congress. It prevents Congress from placing unreasonable and unfair limits on freedom of expression. That is why the Amendment begins with the phrase, "Congress shall make no law...."

Why was freedom of expression so important to the Founders?

The way the First Amendment was written makes it clear that the Founders believed freedom of expression was very important. They knew this right had to be protected from government interference. Governments had often limited freedom of expression to try to stop people from criticizing their actions. Some of the historical examples the Founders knew about were:

- **Massachusetts Colony - 1660.** Mary Dyer taught that all men and women were equal before God and that slavery, war, and capital punishment were evil.

She was hanged by the Puritans because her ideas were different from many of theirs.

- **Virginia Colony - 1682.** John Buckner was accused of printing the laws without permission of the governor. The governor decided to ban all printing presses in the colony. He said, "Printing has encouraged [the people] to learn and even criticize the best governments. God keep us from free schools and printing."

- **New York Colony - 1735.** John Peter Zenger, a newspaperman, wrote strong criticisms about government dishonesty and incompetence. Zenger was arrested for his statements. After a long trial, he was released because the jury decided that what he had said about the government was true.

Why do you think freedom of the press is an important right?

What are some of the benefits of freedom of expression?

The Founders knew about these and many other events in history where people had been unfairly deprived of their right to freedom of expression. They also believed in natural rights and representative democracy. They believed that the right to hold and express one's beliefs was essential to being a responsible citizen. The following are some of the arguments for the importance of this right.

1. **Individual development and human dignity.** It is important to your growth as a person to have the right to present your ideas and to consider other points of view. Your dignity as a person should be respected by allowing you the freedom to say what you think and to hear what others think.

2. **Advancement of knowledge.** It is easier for new discoveries to be made when ideas can be discussed freely. Even if you disagree with someone, that person may say something that helps you test your knowledge and increase your understanding.

3. **The maintenance of representative democracy.** Individual citizens participate in running our country through their power to vote for government officials and make choices about government policies. In order to make wise choices, you need to have good information. Free expression does not guarantee complete or accurate information, but it increases the chances of getting such information.

4. **Peaceful social change.** Free speech allows you to try to influence public opinion by persuasion without feeling you have to resort to violence to make changes. Also, if you have the opportunity to express your opinions freely, you may be more willing to accept government decisions, even ones you do not agree with.

When should freedom of expression be limited?

Many people believe that freedom of expression is absolutely necessary for the protection of all of our individual freedoms. Does this mean there are no limits to freedom of expression? For example, should you have the right to yell "Fire!" in a crowded theater, even when there is no fire, just to terrify people? Why should this not be allowed as free speech?

Other situations are more complicated. What if you want to convince other people that we should change our way of government? Should the government be able to keep you from doing so just because it doesn't like your ideas? What if you are part of an unpopular group that wants to have a public demonstration? Should the government be able to stop you by saying that your demonstration **may** cause a riot?

When might it be necessary to limit freedom of expression?

Over the years, the courts in our country have developed guidelines to use in limiting freedom of expression. These guidelines are used to decide when the right to free expression interferes with other important rights and interests. For example, suppose your right to freedom of expression in a particular situation is dangerous to public safety, national security, or some other important interest. If the danger is great enough, the courts sometimes allow freedom of expression to be limited.

When have you exercised your right to freedom of speech?

Also, one person's right to freedom of speech may conflict with someone else's right to free speech. If two people attempt to talk at the same time, neither can be heard. For this reason, we accept limitations that are intended to protect everyone's right to speak.

Freedom of expression in the schools

What should be a student's right to freedom of expression in the schools? When should students' freedom of expression be limited? The following are two important Supreme Court cases that deal with these questions.

Tinker v. Des Moines School District (1969)

This case involved a few high school students who wore black armbands to school. They were protesting American involvement in the Vietnam War. The school principal told the students to remove the armbands. They refused and were then suspended from school until they agreed to come back without the armbands. Their parents took the case to court. They argued that the school administration was depriving the students of their right to freedom of expression.

The school administration argued that they were justified in suspending the students. They said the suspension had been necessary to prevent any school disturbance that might have been caused by the wearing of the armbands.

The Supreme Court ruled that the school administration's action was an unnecessary limitation on freedom of expression. The Court's guideline was that a school cannot limit a student's right to freedom of expression unless the student's exercise of that right disrupts the educational process. In this case, the Court said, there was "no evidence whatever of...interference...with the school's work or of collision with the rights of other students to be secure and to be let alone."

Justice Abe Fortas wrote the opinion for the Court. He said, "Any word spoken, in class, in the lunchroom or on the campus, that deviates from the views of another person, may start an argument or cause a disturbance. But our Constitution says we must take this risk...and our history says that it is this sort of hazardous freedom — this kind of openness — that is the basis of our national strength and of the independence...of Americans...."

This opinion of the Supreme Court clearly confirms the Founders' belief in the importance of freedom of expression. The Court said that students do not give up their "constitutional rights to freedom of speech or expression at the schoolhouse gate." Freedom of expression should be protected unless it clearly violates other important rights and interests such as the "school's work or the right of students to be secure and to be let alone."

How might the *Tinker* case be applied to this illustration?

113

Problem solving

Balancing rights and interests

The following case involves a situation in which students' rights to freedom of expression must be balanced against other important rights and interests. Your class should be divided into groups of about five students each to complete this exercise. Each group should read the case and answer the questions which follow it. Then each group should share its answers with the class for further discussion.

Hazelwood School District v. Kuhlmeier (1988)

A high school newspaper was written in the school's journalism class. One issue of the paper contained an article about teenage pregnancy. The principal thought that the story was not appropriate for younger students in the school. The paper also contained another story in which a student wrote about divorce and made negative remarks about her father. The principal said that the newspaper had not given the father a chance to respond to his daughter's remarks. He ordered both stories to be removed from the paper before it was printed and distributed.

1. What are the conflicting rights and interests in this case?

2. In what ways is this case similar to the *Tinker* case? In what ways is it different?

3. If you used the guideline from the *Tinker* case to decide this case, what decision would you make? Explain your reasoning.

4. What other guidelines might be used in deciding this case? Explain them.

5. How would you decide this case?

Reviewing and using the lesson

1. Restate in your own words the sections of the First Amendment that deal with freedom of expression.

2. Reread the four benefits of free expression described in the lesson. Choose the one that you think is most important. Briefly explain your choice, using a real or imaginary example to support your explanation.

3. Under what conditions do you think public school principals should have the right to censor (restrict) school-sponsored newspapers? Explain your answer.

4. A group dedicated to the belief that white people are superior to other races is planning a public meeting. Members of another organization which represents a minority group, have said that if this meeting is held, they will break it up. There is the possibility of a violent clash between the two groups. Should the government prohibit the group from meeting in public? Explain your answer.

Lesson B-3

How does the Constitution protect freedom of religion?

LESSON OVERVIEW

Many of the colonies gave preferential treatment to certain churches. By the time of the Constitution's ratification, however, many in the new nation believed that the federal government should not be allowed to give such status to any one church. Furthermore, many thought that people have a "natural right" to believe whatever they choose. Thus, a part of the First Amendment says that "Congress shall make no law respecting the establishment of religion, or prohibiting the free exercise thereof, ..."

Students first learn why the Founders thought freedom of religion was so important. Then they learn of the conflicts over the interpretation and application of the "establishment" and "free exercise" clauses of the First Amendment. Students learn that the Supreme Court has ruled that while people have the right to hold any belief or no belief, their religious practices can be limited when those practices interfere with other public interests. And, finally, they read a selection about limits on freedom of religion and apply the "Lemon test" — a set of criteria the Supreme Court has developed for use in determining whether laws involving religion are constitutional — to several situations.

LESSON OBJECTIVES

At the conclusion of this lesson:

1. Students should be able to explain why the Founders thought freedom of religion was important.

2. Students should be able to explain the differences between the establishment and the free exercise clauses of the First Amendment.

3. Students should be able to describe reasons for limits on religious practices.

4. Students should be able to apply the Lemon test to cases involving religion and the public schools.

MATERIALS NEEDED

Student text

TEACHING PROCEDURES

A. Reading and Discussion:
Understanding the Founders' beliefs about freedom of religion

Have students read the "Purpose of Lesson" and "Why did the Founders think freedom of religion was important?" Help them understand the factors that contributed to the growth of religious tolerance among the Founders. This should include an understanding of the influence of the ideas they derived from the natural rights philosophy on their idea of the proper role of government in regard to religious beliefs and practices. It should also include an understanding of the Founders' beliefs about the role of religion in the development of the character traits required of republican government.

B. Reading and Discussion:
Understanding the bases of conflicts regarding freedom of religion
and the proper role of government

Have students read and discuss the next two sections, "Conflicts over freedom of religion" and "Conflicts between the establishment and the free exercise clauses." Help students understand the differences between the establishment and free exercise clauses and the conflicts over their interpretation and application. Have the students identify the public interests with which several of the religious practices mentioned in the text would conflict.

C. Reading and Problem Solving:
Dealing with problems of freedom of religion

Have the students read "Should the government be allowed to support religious education?" Discuss the three questions posed.

For each criterion in the Lemon test, ask one student to paraphrase it and another to create an imaginary law that would violate it.

Then, divide the class into groups of three to five. Have each group read the situations in the "Problem Solving" exercise and apply the Lemon test to decide whether the laws and actions cited should be declared unconstitutional. If it can be reproduced for the class, the students can use the reference handout at the end of this lesson for research to support their decisions. Have the groups report their decisions and explain the reasoning they applied to reach their decision in each situation.

D. Concluding Activity

Conclude the lesson by leading a discussion of the questions provided in "Reviewing and using the lesson." You may wish to have students write their positions on one of the constitutional issues dealing with the freedom of religion in their constitutional journals.

OPTIONAL ACTIVITIES

For Reinforcement, Extended Learning, and Enrichment

1. Have students discuss the position that if, as George Washington and other Founders thought, free government depends on virtue and morality, and if they cannot be maintained without religion, our federal and state governments should promote and encourage religion in general, though no one religion in particular.

2. Have students discuss and take positions on the following quotations.

    > Believing with you that religion is a matter which lies solely between man and his God, that he owes account to none other for his faith or his worship... I contemplate with sovereign reverence that act of the whole American people which declared that their legislature should "make no law respecting an establishment of religion, or prohibiting the free exercise thereof," thus building a wall of separation between Church and State... (Thomas Jefferson, Letter to the Danbury Baptist Association, 1802).

    > We are a religious people whose institutions presuppose a Supreme Being....When the state encourages religious instruction...it follows the best of our traditions. For it then respects the religious nature of our people and accommodates the public service to their spiritual needs. (Justice William O. Douglas, *Zorach v. Clauson*, 1952).

3. Have a student report on the religious ideas of Roger Williams, Ann Hutchinson, or Thomas Hooker.

4. Ask several students to find out and report to the class what positions local religious organizations take on the question of prayer in the public schools and the need for a constitutional amendment on this issue.

Reference Section for Problem Solving Situations

1. In *Stone v. Graham* 101 S.Ct. 192(1980), the Supreme Court ruled in a 5-4 decision that a Kentucky law allowing the display of the Ten Commandments in classrooms was unconstitutional.

2. In *Mueller v. Allen* 103 S.Ct. 3062(1983), the Supreme Court in a 5-4 decision allowed Minnesota tax deductions to parents of both public and private/parochial students for educational expenses.

3. In *Aguilar v. Felton* 105 S.Ct. 3248(1985), the Supreme Court voided in a 5-4 decision two programs in New York and Michigan that sent public school teachers to parochial schools to provide remedial instruction.

4. In *Widmer v. Vincent* 102 S.Ct. 269(1981), the Supreme Court by a 8-1 vote held that college officials may not deny student religious groups access to campus facilities. However, the Court has failed to decide a case involving high school students [*Brandon v. Board of Education* 635 F.2d 971(1980) and *Bender v. Williamsport Area School District* 106 S.Ct. 1326(1986)].

Additional Background on the Cases

No. 1: Ten Commandments Case
Citation: *Stone v. Graham,* 101 S.Ct. 192 (1980) 66 L.Ed.2d. 199

Issue: Does the posting of a copy of the Ten Commandments in public school classrooms violate the establishment clause of the Constitution?

Facts: The state of Kentucky passed a law requiring all classrooms to post a copy of the Ten Commandments. The state argued that "secular application of the Ten Commandments is clearly seen in its adoption as the fundamental legal code of Western Civilization and the Common Law of the United States." The copies would be financed through voluntary contributions.

The state law was sustained by a state trial court and was affirmed by a tie vote of the state supreme court.

Decision: In a 5-4 opinion, the state law was overturned with Justices Brennan, White, Marshall, Powell, and Stevens constituting the majority. The Court said, "The Ten Commandmants are undeniably a sacred text in the Jewish and Christian faiths, and no legislative recitation of a supposedly secular purpose can blind us to that fact."

No. 2: Tax Deductions
Citation: *Mueller v. Allen,* 103 S.Ct. 3062 (1983) 77 L.Ed.2d. 721

Issue: Is the establishment clause of the First Amendment violated if a state provides state income tax deductions for educational expenses to parochial schools?

Facts: The Minnesota state legislature passed a law, granting a tax deduction to parents for school expenses in the areas of tuition, transportation, and educational materials at public and private/parochial schools. A cap of $500 for K-6 expenses and $700 for 7-12 expenses was written into the law. 91,000 of

820,000 students in Minnesota were enrolled in private schools, and 95% of that 91,000 were attending parochial schools.

Decision: In a 5-4 decision, Justice Rehnquist for the majority, argued that there was no violation of the *Lemon* test. He noted that Minnesota law provided a wide variety of tax deductions and that this particular deduction was not giving special treatment to parochial school parents but was open to all parents of school- age children. He also argued that the effect of the tax deductions was a well-educated citizenry, which was constitutionally permitted.

No. 3: Public School Teachers in Parochial Schools
Citation: *Aguilar v. Felton,* 105 S.Ct. 3248 (1985) 87 L.Ed.2d. 290

Issue: Can public schools provide instruction in a parochial school setting?

Facts: New York City schools had regularly used Title I funds to send their teachers into parochial schools to provide remedial math, reading, and English instruction during the school day. Grand Rapids schools provided a similar program that offered a wider range of subjects and included paying rent to the parochial schools for the use of their classrooms during the instructional period.

The concept of "shared time" was used in the arguments before the Court. These students were said to be enrolled part-time in the public school and part-time in the parochial school. In both cases, these parochial school classrooms were designated as being public school classrooms and all religious symbols had been draped or removed.

Decision: In a 5-4 decision, Justice Brennan found that the program would cause "excessive entanglement" of the church and state, since teachers would have to be supervised to make sure that no religious instruction was being provided.

No. 4: Equal Access to School Facilities
Citations: *Widmer v. Vincent,* 102 S.Ct. 269 (1981)
Brandon v. Board of Education, 635 F.2d 971 (1980)
Bender v. Williamsport Area School District, 106 S.Ct.1326 (1986)
Lubbock Independent School Board v. Lubbock ACLU, 669 F.2d. 1038 (1982)

Issue: Can schools allow student religious groups the use of school facilities on the same basis as any other student groups on campus?

Facts: In the *Widmer* case, a student religious group at the University of Kansas City had been able to use the campus facilities from 1973-77, although the university had a 1972 regulation that banned the use of campus facilities for the purpose of religious worship or religious teaching. Starting in 1978, the school officials decided to enforce this rule, and rejected the group's future use of campus facilities. The college students filed a suit, claiming violation of their constitutional rights under the First Amendment.

In the *Brandon* case, several students asked the principal for permission to conduct voluntary prayers prior to the start of school each day. The principal, the superintendent, and the school board rejected the request. The students filed a suit, claiming that their rights to free exercise of religion, free speech, and free assembly were being violated.

In the *Bender* case, a student religious group asked to meet during the school's activity period to discuss religion as well as to conduct voluntary prayers. School officials rejected their request and the students filed a suit, claiming that their constitutional rights to freely exercise their religion, to free speech, and to freely assemble had been violated.

In the *Lubbock* case, the school board had allowed school prayers and Bible readings over school public address systems. In addition, Bibles had been distributed to elementary students. The school board was ordered by a U.S. Court of Appeals to stop these practices. As a result, the school board adopted a policy that allowed student groups (including religious ones) to use school facilities for meetings as long as attendance at such meetings was voluntary.

Decisions: In the *Widmer* case, the Supreme Court ruled 8-1 that the college students' rights were being violated because religious and nonreligious speech are protected. (1981)

In the *Brandon* case, the District Court dismissed the case and the Court of Appeals affirmed that dismissal. The appellate court noted that public schools do not have the tradition of being public forums that colleges and universities have, and that students still could freely exercise their religion, although not in a school setting. The U.S. Supreme Court refused to hear the case. (1980)

In the *Bender* case, the students won in District Court but lost in the Court of Appeals. The U.S. Supreme Court ruled that Bender had no standing since he was no longer on the school board nor a parent of one of the affected students. The case was sent back to the U.S. District Court. (1986)

In the *Lubbock* case, the Court of Appeals found that the new policy was a violation of the establishment clause and stated that no use of public school facilities for meetings of student religious groups before or after school hours was constitutionally permissible. The U.S. Supreme Court refused to hear the case. (1983)

How does the Constitution protect freedom of religion?

Purpose of Lesson

This lesson will explain why the Founders thought religious freedom was so important. It will also discuss the difference between religious beliefs and religious practices, and explain why some limits have been placed on religious practices. Finally, the lesson will introduce you to questions about the relationship between religion and education which the Supreme Court has had to consider. It will also discuss the guidelines the Court has followed in these cases.

When you have completed the lesson, you should be able to explain the importance of freedom of religion and describe situations in which it may be limited. You should also be able to explain the present position of the Supreme Court on the relationship between freedom of religion and the schools.

Terms to know

establishment clause
free exercise clause
Lemon test
parochial school

Why did the Founders think freedom of religion was important?

Read the First Amendment. You will see that the very first clauses say, "Congress shall make no law respecting an establishment of religion, or prohibiting the free exercise thereof;..." These clauses show the importance of freedom of religion to the Framers.

Most of the early colonists were Protestant Christians. Few of the early English colonies in North America allowed religious freedom. In several colonies, one religious group dominated the colony, insisting that everyone conform to its ideas. People who disagreed were often persecuted, and sometimes they were forced to leave. Roger Williams, for example, left the Massachusetts Bay colony with a group of his followers and founded Rhode Island.

Was freedom of religion always guaranteed in America?

By the end of the colonial period, however, there were more people who practiced different religious beliefs. Many had become more tolerant (accepting) of religious differences. Groups such as Quakers, Baptists, Catholics, and others made demands for religious freedom.

Many of the Founders held fundamental beliefs that supported tolerance. Perhaps the most important of these beliefs was that people have certain natural rights simply because they are human beings. Philosophers like John Locke argued that society should allow people to live the way their moral principles, guided by the Bible, tell them is right. The best government, therefore, was the one that interfered as little as possible with personal beliefs, including religious beliefs.

In addition, men like Thomas Jefferson and James Madison were greatly concerned about the dangers of religious intolerance (prejudice). They were well aware that throughout history, religious intolerance had often led to conflict and to the violation of individual rights. They thought religious intolerance was a danger to the community and harmful to religion.

Most of the Founders were religious. They believed that religion was essential to develop the kind of character citizens in a free society need to remain free. At the same time, they believed strongly that everyone has a right to his or her own religious beliefs. For example, George Washington believed that without the influence of religion, people would not behave in moral ways. However, he was against the use of taxes in Virginia to support religious instruction for students.

The protections of religious freedom the Framers placed in the First Amendment demonstrate their belief that the government should not interfere with religion.

Conflicts over freedom of religion

Under the Constitution, conflicts over freedom of religion have focused on the following issues:

- **The establishment of religion.** These conflicts have been about whether the government should be allowed to provide any support at all for religion. Questions about government support of religion are dealt with under the clause of the First Amendment that says that "Congress shall make no law...regarding the establishment of religion...." This clause sets forth the idea that in the United States, the government is to be separated from religion. Sometimes this is called the principle of the "separation of church and state." Exactly what this means is not clear and is a continuing source of conflict. For example, does this mean that government may not be involved in any way with religion?

- **The free exercise of religion.** In addition to forbidding the government from establishing religion, the First Amendment says the government shall make no law prohibiting the free exercise of religion. This means that your right to believe as you wish and, in most cases, practice those beliefs, is protected. This idea is also included in Article VI of the Constitution, which says that no religious test shall ever be required as a qualification for any federal government office.

Conflicts between the establishment and the free exercise clauses

Sometimes the free exercise and establishment clauses come into conflict. For example, if the government pays for prison chaplains, it is supporting religion. On the other hand, to prohibit the government from doing this would interfere with the right of prisoners to practice their religion.

Conflicts like these over the relationship between government and religion have caused a number of important cases to be brought before the Supreme Court for settlement. Some of the most controversial cases have dealt with religion and the schools. In each case, the Supreme Court has had the task of deciding how the freedom of religion clauses of the First Amendment should be interpreted.

Should public schools be allowed to set aside time for prayer by students?

Should the government be allowed to support religious education?

At the time the Constitution was written, public schools as we know them did not exist. Children who attended school usually received a great deal of religious training. In fact, their parents wanted the schools to give them religious instruction.

During the 20th century, however, there has been growing disagreement about whether religious teaching should be supported in public schools. In the past 60 years especially, the Supreme Court has heard many cases dealing with this subject. Some of the questions the Court has tried to answer are:

1. Should tax money be used to support parochial schools?

2. Should public schools be allowed to provide certain periods of time during the day when students can attend special classes to receive religious instruction from their own minister, priest, or rabbi?

3. Should public schools be allowed to require students to take part in prayers or the reading of the Bible during regular school hours?

In a 1971 case, Chief Justice Warren E. Burger developed guidelines to be used in deciding if a law involving religion in the schools violated the First Amendment to the Constitution. These guidelines are known as the **Lemon test** because they were written in a case called *Lemon v. Kurtzman* (1971). The three guidelines the law must satisfy to be declared constitutional are:

1. The primary purpose of a law must not be religious. It must have some other purpose, such as furthering education.

As you have learned, the First Amendment originally applied only to the federal government. Many states had laws that in some way limited religious freedom. However, in the 1940s the Supreme Court ruled that the First Amendment applies also to state governments. The case involved freedom of belief.

As late as 1961, Maryland had a law requiring anyone who wanted a job in the state government to swear to a belief in God. The law was challenged. The Supreme Court ruled that the law was unconstitutional because it violated the freedom of religious belief guaranteed by the First Amendment. This decision means that each person has an absolute right to hold any or no religious belief. **Freedom of belief** is an unalienable right that cannot be interfered with by the government in any way.

The Supreme Court has ruled, however, that in some situations the government can make laws limiting your right to **practice your beliefs**. For example, religious practices may be limited if they are contrary to public morals, endanger health, or in other ways harm the common welfare. Supreme Court decisions have said that religious practices involving polygamy (being married to more than one person at the same time) or handling rattlesnakes may be forbidden without violating constitutional rights. Children may be required to be vaccinated against diseases before being admitted to public school, even if this requirement violates their religious beliefs.

Why should the government have the right to require
students to be vaccinated if this is against their religious beliefs?

2. The primary effect of the law must not be to advance (support) or inhibit (restrict) religion.

3. The law must not create an excessive government entanglement with religion.

Problem solving

Religion and the schools

Use the Lemon test to decide if you think the laws and actions described below should be declared unconstitutional. Be prepared to explain your decision to the class.

1. Your state passes a law allowing your public school principal to post a copy of the Ten Commandments in every classroom.

2. Your state passes a law that gives parents who send their children to parochial schools a tax deduction for tuition, transportation, and educational materials.

3. Your state allows your public school's algebra teacher to spend part of the class day at a church school, giving instruction to students having difficulty with math.

4. A group of students at your public school requests permission to use an empty classroom after regular school hours for a voluntary prayer meeting. The principal refuses to make the classroom available to them.

Reviewing and using the lesson

1. Some religious groups have suggested adding an amendment to the Constitution permitting voluntary prayer in public schools. Would you support such an amendment? Why or why not?

2. Should public schools be permitted to close for Christmas? Why or why not?

3. How would the United States be different today if we had an official national religion? What changes would be good ones? What changes would be bad ones? Explain your answers.

Lesson C-1

How does the Constitution protect your right to be treated fairly by the government?

LESSON OVERVIEW

One of the great fears of the Founders and Framers was the tendency of powerful governments to act unfairly and unreasonably. The due process clause in the Fifth Amendment was intended by the Framers to prevent such abuse of power on the part of the federal government.

The due process clause in the Fourteenth Amendment protects against state or local government abuse of power. This clause has been interpreted by the courts to extend most of the rights in the Bill of Rights, that originally applied only to the federal government, to protect people against unfair actions by state and local governments.

Students first read about what due process means. Then they are involved in a problem-solving activity that raises questions about who should have the right to a lawyer in a criminal case. The lesson ends with a discussion of the importance of the right to due process in criminal proceedings, and of other situations in which the right to due process applies.

LESSON OBJECTIVES

At the conclusion of the lesson:

1. Students should be able to state in general terms what due process means.

2. Students should be able to explain the importance of the due process clauses in the Bill of Rights and the Fourteenth Amendment.

3. Students should be able to identify situations in which due process rights are important, particularly the right to a lawyer in criminal proceedings.

MATERIALS NEEDED

1. Student text

2. Handout

TEACHING PROCEDURES

A. Introductory Activity:
Defining due process of law

Ask students to read the "Purpose of Lesson" and "What is due process of law?" Go over with them the location of the two due process clauses and the meaning of the phrase.

B. Problem Solving:
Determining who has the right to a lawyer

Form groups of 3-5 students and assign them the task of reading the problem-solving activity and answering the questions that follow. You might have students write their answers on chartpaper and share their opinions with the rest of the class.

Note: In the case of *Gideon v. Wainwright*, 372 U.S. 335 (1963), the Supreme Court overruled its decision in a case decided twenty years earlier, and held that a state must provide counsel for an indigent accused of a serious crime. This case is an example of how ideas as to what constitutes due process, or fundamental fairness, can change over time.

C. Reading and Discussion:
Understanding the importance of due process in criminal trials

Ask pairs of students to read the sections, "Why is due process important in criminal trials?" and "Other examples of due process rights." They should discuss and answer the questions that follow the first section. Also ask them to write down examples of rights to due process that would be important to school children.

D. Concluding Activity

Have the students answer the questions under "Reviewing and using the lesson." Remind the students of the due date on the collages. Allow time for work on the collages.

OPTIONAL ACTIVITIES

For Reinforcement, Extended Learning, and Enrichment

1. Point out that the public gets much of its information about due process from television programs. Have students watch some currently popular television series about police work, taking notes on procedures followed. Ask the students what they would have done in the situations portrayed. What actions by the police officers were fair or unfair? Then invite a police officer to visit the class and analyze the accuracy of the information conveyed on television.

2. Arrange to have the class visit and observe procedures at a local court hearing. If possible, have the judge discuss procedures with students.

3. A handout has been included for teachers who wish to extend students' knowledge of specific rights included in the Bill of Rights which are applicable to state actions under the due process clause of the Fourteenth Amendment. Distribute Handout 19-1 and allow time for students to complete the worksheet.

Handout

What rights do people have when they are suspected or accused of crimes?

Instructions: Read the protections in the Bill of Rights that are summarized below. Then answer the questions that follow.

Fourth Amendment:

- People, their homes, and their possessions cannot be searched or taken by the government without a good reason.
- In most cases, the police must get a warrant (permission from a judge) before they can conduct a search.

Fifth Amendment:

- People who are accused of crimes do not have to give evidence against themselves.
- People cannot be tried again for a crime for which they have been found innocent.
- People's lives, liberty, or property cannot be taken from them without due process of law.

Sixth Amendment:

- A person accused of a crime has the right to a speedy, public trial by a jury (other citizens).
- People must be told what crimes they are accused of.
- People have a right to question the persons who are accusing them.
- An accused person has the right to have a lawyer.

Eighth Amendment:

- People arrested for crimes are entitled to be free on reasonable bail (money deposited with the court) while awaiting trial.
- If a person must pay a fine, it must be a fair amount.
- People found guilty of crimes shall not be punished in cruel and unusual ways.

Suppose the police think you have committed a crime and come to arrest you. Which of the rights you have just read about do you think would be most important to you? Why?

How does the Constitution protect your right to be treated fairly by the government?

Purpose of Lesson

In the last lesson we looked at how the equal protection clause protects people from unfair discrimination. In this lesson we will look at other words in the Constitution that are about fairness. These words are in the due process clauses of the Constitution. We will see how these clauses help protect our lives, liberty, and property from unfair and unreasonable acts by our government.

What is due process of law?

The **right to due process** is the right to be treated fairly by your government. You will find the words **due process** in two places in our Constitution. They are in both the Fifth Amendment and the Fourteenth Amendment.

* **Fifth Amendment.** It says that no person shall be deprived of life, liberty, or property without **due process of law.** This amendment protects your right to be treated fairly by the **federal** government.

* **Fourteenth Amendment.** This amendment says that **state** governments cannot deprive you of your life, liberty, or property without **due process of law.** It protects your right to be treated fairly by your **state** and **local** governments.

Most people don't know that before the Fourteenth Amendment was passed, the Bill of Rights only protected you from unfair treatment by the federal government. The Fourteenth Amendment has been used to protect you from unfair treatment by state and local governments.

Due process means that members of your government must use fair methods or **procedures** when doing their jobs. They must use fair procedures when they gather information. They must use fair procedures when they make decisions. They must use fair procedures when they enforce the law.

For example, the Bill of Rights says that if you are accused of a crime, you have the right to have a lawyer help defend you. Suppose the government did not allow you to have a lawyer. The government would have violated your right to due process that is guaranteed by the Constitution.

Do you have a right to a lawyer even if you can't afford one?

What does the right to have a lawyer in a criminal case mean? Does it mean the government must pay for a lawyer to help you if you cannot afford to pay for one yourself? The Supreme Court has changed its ideas about this right over a period of years. In 1963, in a famous case, the Supreme Court thought again about what the constitutional right to a lawyer means.

Problem solving

When should you have the right to a lawyer?

Your class should be divided into small groups of three to five students. Each group should read the following case and answer the questions that follow it. Be prepared to explain your answers to the class.

Gideon v. Wainwright (1963)

Clarence Gideon was accused of breaking into a poolroom in Florida. Police said he had stolen a pint of wine and some coins from a cigarette machine. Gideon was a poor, uneducated man who was fifty years old. He did not know much about the law. However, he believed he could not get a fair trial without a lawyer to help him.

When Gideon appeared in court, he asked the judge to appoint a lawyer for him. He was too poor to hire one himself. The judge told him that he did not have the right to have a lawyer appointed for him unless he was charged with murder.

Gideon was tried before a jury, and he tried to defend himself. He made an opening speech to the jury and **cross-examined** the witnesses against him. He then called witnesses to **testify** for him and made a final speech to the jury. The jury decided he was guilty. Gideon was sent to the state prison to serve for five years.

---

cross-examine

to question witnesses testifying for the other side

testify

give information or evidence

130

From prison he wrote a petition to the Supreme Court. It was handwritten in pencil. He argued that all citizens have a right to a lawyer in cases where they might be sent to prison.

1. Should Gideon have been given a lawyer to help him? Why or why not?

2. Should the right to have a lawyer mean the government has to provide one to anyone who cannot afford to hire one? Why or why not?

3. Should lawyers be appointed to help people accused of breaking any laws, even traffic laws? Why or why not?

4. When should a person have the right to a lawyer? Upon arrest? Before being questioned? Before the trial? After the trial, if the person thinks the trial was unfair and wants another trial?

5. Should defendants have the right to have the services of other experts to help them prepare for their trials? Fingerprint experts? People to find witnesses? Psychiatrists?

*Why is it important to protect
your rights to due process?*

To get some idea of the importance of fair procedures in enforcing the law, read the following situations. Then answer the questions that follow them. Suppose you lived in a country in which the following things could happen.

- If the police suspected you of a crime, they could force you by any means to give them information that might show you were guilty.

- If you were taken to court, the judge could use any means to get information from you to decide whether you were guilty.

- The leaders of the country could make decisions about your life, liberty, or property in secret, without allowing you or anyone else to participate.

1. Would you believe that you would be treated fairly if you were accused of a crime? Why or why not?

2. Even if you haven't broken the law or been arrested, would you want other people suspected of crimes treated in these ways? Why or why not?

3. Would you want decisions that affected your life, liberty, or property made in secret? Why or why not?

Other examples of due process rights

Due process means the right to be treated fairly by all agencies of your government. Your right to due process is not limited to making sure you are treated fairly by law enforcement agencies and the courts. The government must treat you fairly whenever it creates laws about your right to travel, raise a family, or use your property. It must also be fair if you apply for a government job or receive government benefits. The right to due process means the right to be treated fairly in all your dealings with your government.

Reviewing and using the lesson

1. Why is the guarantee of due process so important? Give examples to support your position.

2. Look at the Bill of Rights. Find parts of it that are designed to make sure you are treated fairly by your government. Be prepared to explain what you have found to your class.

3. Explain these terms: due process, procedures, cross-examine, testify.

The Bill of Rights

The Constitution deals with the establishment of a system of government with duties and obligations delineated. When signatures were added to the final document, the framers of the Constitution knew the instrument was not yet perfect. One area causing difficulty was the lack of a statement of individual rights. Several state constitutions already had these rights listed.

In order for the convention to move smoothly to closure, an agreement was reached to consider a bill of rights after the Constitution was ratified. Accordingly, the first ten amendments were added on December 15, 1791. In a mere 462 words, they defined the rights of people in the United States.

This lesson is designed to introduce the Bill of Rights to young people. They will learn that their rights are protected by our laws, but they also must act responsibly. Several situations involving personal rights will be studied.

MATERIALS

Copies of "Freedom of Speech, Jr."
Construction paper
Copies of Summary of the Constitution

OBJECTIVES

Students will be able to:
Identify the Bill of Rights as that portion of the Constitution which lists individual freedoms by illustrating three of these.

VOCABULARY

amendments   Bill of Rights

PROCEDURE

1. Distribute copies of "Freedom of Speech, Jr."

2. Explain: "On your sheet there are six situations. You will have several questions to answer about each example. Think carefully before making your decisions. Write your answers on the paper."

3. After students have completed the activity independently, have them assemble in groups of four to discuss their opinions. Instruct them to arrive at a group consensus for each item. Then have groups report to the whole class.

4. Conclude the discussion with these questions.

   Ask: "Can you come up with a general rule stating when people should be allowed freedom of speech?
   "When should it not be allowed?
   "Should adults have more freedom of speech than children?
   "What if the people in the examples had been adults? Would it make any difference? Why or why not?
   "What would happen if people were **not** allowed any freedom of speech?"

5. Say: "A case recently came before the Supreme Court concerning freedom of speech. You might find this interesting since it concerns a speech given by a high school boy in support of his friend's candidacy for vice-presidency of the student body. As I read the newspaper article, listen for the Supreme Court's answers to the questions we discussed on the activity sheet."

6. Ask: "Does this behavior interfere with another individual's rights?
   "Is the action acceptable?

   "If no, should this behavior be regulated by a rule?
   "If a rule is needed, should it be made by individuals or by the government?"

7. Let's think about another situation.

   Read: "The children of Berkshire Elementary School were studying the pioneers. They were asked to write an essay for the school newspaper that included a conversation between two pioneer children. The paper was to be as true to life as possible, but no other directions were given.

   "When Jonathan handed in his paper, the teacher was appalled. Jonathan's essay described a heated argument over a game two pioneer children were playing. The conversation included some swear words — language considered inappropriate for a school situation. The teacher not only verbally scolded him, but also insisted that he redo the assignment for publication. Jonathan had worked hard on the essay. He felt that the conversation was realistic and the language used was appropriate for that particular situation. Thus, he refused to do as the teacher asked."

8. Discuss these questions with the class.

   Ask: "Was Jonathan justified in including swear words in his essay? Should he be allowed to do this?

   "Was his teacher correct in asking Jonathan to rewrite his essay?

   "If the teacher permits Jonathan to include swear words in this essay, should he and other children be permitted to do the same in other essays?

   "Should the swear words be printed in the school paper?

   "Who should decide this issue — Jonathan? The teacher? The principal? Jonathan's parents? A judge? Explain."

9. Say: "In the discussions about Freedom of Speech and Freedom of the Press, we were talking about the right of people to do or not to do something.

   "The writers of the Constitution were concerned with the rights of individual people living in the United States. Several states already had a list of those rights in their state constitutions. Some suggested that such a list be part of the United States Constitution, but others did not feel it was necessary.

   "A compromise was once again reached. Remember that a compromise is putting together an idea by using parts of two different ideas. Each side gives up part of its idea to reach an agreement. Those wanting a bill of rights agreed to sign the Constitution if it would be added later. Those who felt it was unnecessary agreed to the addition of a bill of rights, if that would make the participants sign the Constitution. The first ten **amendments,** or additions, to the Constitution were added on December 15, 1791. They list rights of citizens of the United States. We call these ten amendments **"The Bill of Rights."**

10. Say: "So far, we've discussed two different rights listed in the Bill of Rights — freedom of speech and freedom of the press. Congress may not make laws limiting these freedoms. However, this does not give individuals the right to say or print false things. Nor does it allow people to endanger others by speech or writing.

"One example of abusing freedom of speech is yelling 'FIRE!' in a crowded theater. Such irresponsibility could cause people to panic and result in death."

11. Say: "Let's list some of the other rights found in the Bill of Rights. One is freedom of religion, which means we can each worship as we want, at the church we choose. It also means that we have the right not to worship.

"People are protected from unreasonable searches and seizures. Police are not allowed to enter and search a person's home without a warrant signed by the court. This order states what is expected to be found. This same rule applies to the person's possessions.

"We are guaranteed the right to a fair trial if we have to go to court.

"Cruel and unusual punishment may not be used. For instance, hanging a person by the thumbs would not be a correct punishment for speeding.

"With each of the rights listed, there are responsibilities. It is up to each person living in the United States to consider others. We must not interfere with their rights, if we want to maintain our own freedom."

12. Pass out construction paper. Instruct students to label this, "Our Freedom: Our Bill of Rights." Fold paper in thirds. Illustrate three individual rights guaranteed by our Constitution. Use the summary of the Constitution for reference.

EXTENSION ACTIVITIES

☆ Ask each student to prepare a "Bill of Rights for Students." Post these on the bulletin board.

☆ Review a newspaper article dealing with a right.

Students can be suspended for vulgar, offensive language

The Associated Press

WASHINGTON — The Supreme Court today significantly broadened the disciplinary powers of public school administrators, ruling that students may be suspended for using "vulgar and offensive" language.

By a 7-2 vote, the court upheld the three-day suspension in 1983 of a Spanaway, Wash., high school senior for giving an assembly speech filled with crude sexual allusions.

"Surely it is a highly appropriate function of public school education to prohibit the use of vulgar and offensive terms in public discourse," Chief Justice Warren E. Burger wrote for the court.

Matthew Fraser's one-minute speech in support of a friend's candidacy for student body vice president of Bethel High School contained no dirty words, but it caused a brief uproar among his fellow students.

His friend won the election by a wide margin.

Officials at the school in suburban Tacoma suspended Fraser for violating the school's disruptive conduct rule in "materially and substantially" interfering in the educational process.

Now a student at the University of California at Berkeley, Fraser sued school district officials with help from the American Civil Liberties Union.

A federal judge ruled that Bethel High officials had violated Fraser's free-speech rights by disciplining him, and the 9th U.S. Circuit Court of Appeals upheld that ruling by a 2-1 vote.

School officials were ordered to pay Fraser $278 in damages and $12,750 in legal costs.

Today, the Supreme Court said the lower courts were wrong.

The Reagan administration had urged the court to rule against Fraser. Justice Department lawyers argued that student speech may be restrained "if officials have a reasonable basis for the regulation grounded in the maintenance of an atmosphere of civility or the transmission of basic societal values."

They said such regulations should not be used to suppress "student expression of a particular political viewpoint."

Burger wrote: "The determination of what manner of speech in the classroom or in (a) school assembly is inappropriate properly rests with the school board."

He was joined by Justices Byron R. White, Lewis F. Powell, William H. Rehnquist and Sandra Day O'Connor.

Justices William J. Brennan and Harry A. Blackmun voted against Fraser but did not join Burger's opinion.

Justices Thurgood Marshall and John Paul Stevens dissented.

NAME _____

FREEDOM OF SPEECH, JR.

Directions: Read the situations below. Answer each question.

Example: Tommy swears at the principal.

Does this behavior interfere with another individual's rights?

Yes, the principal's rights are violated.

Is the action acceptable?

No, this language is unacceptable.

If no, should this behavior be regulated by a rule?

Yes, a rule could be written.

If a rule is needed, should it be made by individuals or by the government?

Individuals should write the rule.

---

1. Jimmy, a real joker, stands up during math time in Mrs. Snorgweather's class and yells, "I smell smoke!" (He really didn't.)

Does this behavior interfere with another individual's rights?

_____

Is the action acceptable?

_____

If no, should this behavior be regulated by a rule?

_____

If a rule is needed, should it be made by individuals or by the government?

_____

2. Mary thinks there is not enough peanut butter in the sandwiches at the lunchroom, so she makes a protest sign and puts it up in the cafeteria. It reads: "We want more peanut butter!"

Does this behavior interfere with another individual's rights?

_____

Is the action acceptable?

_____

If no, should this behavior be regulated by a rule?

_____

If a rule is needed, should it be made by individuals or by the government?

_____

IN-LAW RELAT-ED.

A Marriage of Law & Education in Indiana

THE INDIANAPOLIS STAR
THE INDIANAPOLIS NEWS

3. Susie walks up to her grandmother, takes a sniff, and announces, "Grandma, you smell funny."

Does this behavior interfere with another individual's rights?

_____

Is the action acceptable?

_____

If no, should this behavior be regulated by a rule?

_____

If a rule is needed, should it be made by individuals or by the government?

_____

5. Alan and his friends are playing jumprope and singing loudly outside of the library window.

Does this behavior interfere with another individual's rights?

_____

Is the action acceptable?

_____

If no, should this behavior be regulated by a rule?

_____

If a rule is needed, should it be made by individuals or by the government?

_____

4. Mr. Swartz' class wants to play softball instead of kickball at recess time. They ask Mr. Swartz if they can have a class meeting to decide.

Does this behavior interfere with another individual's rights?

_____

Is the action acceptable?

_____

If no, should this behavior be regulated by a rule?

_____

6. Annie's teacher tells her to be quiet. Annie takes a big piece of tape and puts it over her mouth in mock protest.

Does this behavior interfere with another individual's rights?

_____

Is the action acceptable?

_____

If no, should this behavior be regulated by a rule?

_____

If a rule is needed, should it be made by individuals or by the government?

_____

IN-LAW RELAT-ED.

A Marriage of Law & Education in Indiana

THE INDIANAPOLIS STAR
THE INDIANAPOLIS NEWS

Lesson C-3

How does the Constitution protect
your freedom of expression?

LESSON OVERVIEW

When the Founders chose to amend the Constitution through the addition of the Bill of Rights, they placed in the First Amendment the right to freedom of expression. Some scholars argue that this indicates the importance the Founders placed upon this freedom. In this lesson, students will first read sections dealing with the forms of expression protected by the Constitution, the benefits resulting from freedom of expression, and the need to protect this right. The lesson ends with a problem-solving activity that explores the limits to free expression.

LESSON OBJECTIVES

At the conclusion of the lesson:

1. Students should be able to state the various forms of expression covered by the First Amendment.

2. Students should be able to describe the benefits of freedom of expression to the individual and to a democratic society.

3. Students should be able to discuss and explain what they might consider reasonable limits on freedom of expression.

MATERIALS NEEDED

Student text

TEACHING PROCEDURES

A. Introductory Activity:
Exploring the meaning of expression

Write the word "expression" on the chalkboard, and explore with your students its meaning. Brainstorm with them the various ways students express themselves through actions, speech, songs, word games, art, movement, writing, attires, etc.

B. Reading and Discussion:
Identifying freedom of expression

Ask students to read the "Purpose of Lesson" and "What is freedom of expression?" Review with them the four forms of freedom of expression. You might wish to explore with them derivative forms of speech—for example, buttons, attire with slogans, protest signs, and picketing.

C. Reading and Discussion:
Understanding the benefits of freedom of expression

Assign students to read the sections "What are the benefits of freedom of expression?" and "Why is it necessary to protect freedom of expression?" Review with them the four benefits of freedom of expression and historical incidents of intolerance toward free expression. (A famous example is Galileo, who was forced to recant his view that the earth was not the center of the universe but instead moved around the sun.)

You might wish to explore with them some of the possible costs of free expression that is unpopular — public disapproval, job loss, disruptive demonstrations, etc. — and balance these costs, some to the individual and some to the public, against the benefits enumerated.

D. Reading and Discussion:
Discovering the limits to freedom of expression

Have the students read the section, "Should freedom of expression ever be limited?" Review with them the two examples given, then explore with them other possible situations where limits might be placed on expression. Possible situations might be:

- One student dislikes another in his class. He calls the other student offensive names whenever he has the chance. Should offensive names be protected by freedom of expression?

- A rock band practices at 2 a.m. out in the backyard or in the local neighborhood park. Is it reasonable to limit this "freedom of expression"? Is there a better time or location to practice?

- The student newspaper prints lies and rumors about a student. Do the student reporters have a responsibility to tell the truth? Should they print both sides to a story? Should they be stopped from printing lies?

- A group of students are angry at a store in the mall, which refuses to hire nonwhites as clerks. After being unsuccessful in persuading the store management to change its policy, they protest by sitting down in the middle of the shopping mall and at all entrances to the store. They also carry signs that explain their complaints. Their action effectively prevents business from being conducted. Is this a reasonable way to express their protest? What other steps could they have taken?

- A group of students protests the bad food in the cafeteria by starting a food fight. Is this a reasonable way to express an opinion about the quality of the food? What else could the students have done?

E. Problem Solving:
When should freedom of expression be limited?

Organize the class into groups of 2-3 students and ask them to read through the problem-solving activity. Have them write out a group answer to the four questions on either binder paper or chart paper. Each group will then choose one member to present the group's answers to the class.

F. Concluding Activity

Conclude the lesson by leading a discussion of the questions contained in "Reviewing and using the lesson." If the students have been assigned the unit project, have the groups begin collecting clippings for their collages. Encourage them to group the clippings according to the right being illustrated.

OPTIONAL ACTIVITIES

For Reinforcement, Extended Learning, and Enrichment

1. Students might debate the issue of the motion picture ratings system that limits the movies that young persons can view, or the issue of a proposed rating system for rock music recordings.

2. Invite a local law enforcement official or lawyer to speak on local guidelines regarding public demonstrations.

3. Invite representatives from local newspapers, television, or radio stations to speak to the class on limits that the government places on freedom of expression in their fields. Students could also examine the limits placed on expression in student-run newspapers and other publications.

How does the Constitution protect your freedom of expression?

Purpose of Lesson

In this lesson, you will learn why freedom of expression was important to the Founders. You also will learn why it is so important today, both to you and to our nation. When you have completed this lesson, you should be able to explain the benefits of freedom of expression. You should also be able to explain when it might be reasonable to limit this freedom.

What is freedom of expression?

Suppose someone asked you to make a list of some of the freedoms you think are very important. Most Americans would say they think it is important to have freedom of:

> **speech** - the right to say whatever they wish to say

> **press** - the right to read and write whatever they wish

> **assembly** - the right to meet with others to talk about whatever they wish

> **petition** - the right to ask the government to correct things that they think are wrong

These rights—freedom of **speech, press, assembly,** and **petition**—are part of the right to **freedom of expression.** Our right to freedom of expression is protected by the First Amendment of the Bill of Rights.

How does the Bill of Rights protect freedom of speech?

144

Our Constitution limits the powers of our government in order to protect these freedoms. Under our Constitution, the government cannot interfere with these rights except under very special circumstances.

What are the benefits of freedom of expression?

Freedom of expression is important to us as individuals and as citizens. The following are some of the reasons it is so important.

Freedom of expression supports our democracy. Our democratic system of government depends on the people's ability to make good decisions. To make good decisions, you need to be able to get enough information to make up your mind. You need to hear and discuss different ideas and opinions. When you are able to vote, discussing different points of view will help you decide which are the best people or laws to vote for.

Why is it important to be able to exchange ideas freely?

- **Freedom of expression helps us grow as individuals.** When you express your thoughts and listen to the ideas of others, you learn and become more mature. Hearing and discussing different points of view helps you make thoughtful choices about what you think is right. You mature as a person when you make choices for yourself rather than just accepting what others tell you.

- **Freedom of expression advances knowledge.** It is easier for you to make new discoveries and gain new knowledge when you can suggest ideas and exchange information freely. Even if some ideas do not work, they provide a way of testing the truth of other ideas.

- **Freedom of expression makes peaceful change in society possible.** If you are free to try to persuade others to change things, you are less likely to use violence. We have improved many things in our country by using our right to freedom of expression. And, if we can criticize things we can't change, we may be willing to accept them until we can get them changed.

Why is it necessary to protect freedom of expression?

The Founders of our nation knew it was necessary to protect freedom of expression. Throughout history governments had often tried to stop people from spreading new ideas or criticizing government actions.

For example, the Founders knew that in the American colonies, people had suffered—and sometimes died—for saying what they thought. In the Massachusetts Colony in 1660, a woman named Mary Dyer had been hanged by the Puritans for teaching that slavery, war, and **capital punishment** were evil.

capital punishment
death as a legal punishment for a crime

146

What do you think the Founders learned from the experiences of people like Mary Dyer?

That is why the Founders insisted that freedom of expression be protected in the Constitution.

Should freedom of expression ever be limited?

As you have learned, our democracy depends on freedom of expression. However, sometimes it is fair to limit freedom of expression to protect other rights. For example, you may not cry "Fire!" in a crowded theater when there is no fire, just to frighten people. Someone might be hurt rushing to get out.

You are also not allowed to tell military secrets to foreign countries. This could be dangerous for the entire nation.

Can you think of any other situations in which it might be fair to limit freedom of expression?

When do you think the government should have the right to limit your freedom of expression?

Problem solving

When should freedom of expression be limited?

Read the situation below. Then, in small groups, discuss answers to the questions that follow it. Be prepared to present your answers to the class.

One morning in 1961 about 200 black high school and college students met in front of a church in Columbia, South Carolina. They planned to walk to the State House and march around it carrying signs protesting unfair treatment. Some of the signs said, "Down with **segregation!**"

segregation

separation of people in public places because of their race

When the group reached the State House they walked back and forth carrying their signs. They did not stop traffic or block the sidewalks. After a few hours, about 200 to 300 people gathered to watch the students. Some were unfriendly to the students. The police, fearing trouble, told the students they would be arrested if they did not leave within fifteen minutes. The students did not leave. They listened to a speech by one of their leaders. Then they sang the "Star Spangled Banner" and other patriotic songs.

The police arrested 187 of the students and took them to jail. The students were tried and convicted of disturbing the peace. They were fined and given sentences of 5 to 30 days in jail.

The students said that their rights to freedom of speech and assembly had been taken unfairly from them. They appealed their convictions to the Supreme Court.

1. Should groups of people be allowed to do what these students did? Why or why not?

2. How are speaking and carrying signs the same?

3. Should the police be allowed to stop people from speaking or carrying signs if the people watching them become angry? Why or why not?

4. Suppose a small group of people in an audience get angry at a speaker and try to stop the person from speaking. Whose rights should the police protect? Give the reasons for your answer.

Reviewing and using the lesson

1. What types of expression are protected by the First Amendment? Give examples of each type you mention.

2. Which of the four benefits of free expression described in this lesson do you think is most important? Why? Give an example.

3. In what kinds of situations do you think it is fair and reasonable to limit freedom of expression? Give examples.

4. What advantages are there to letting everyone speak or write his or her ideas? What disadvantages?

5. Explain these terms: freedom of expression, capital punishment, segregation.

Part V
Papers in ERIC on Constitutional Rights

V

Papers in ERIC on Constitutional Rights

The papers on constitutional rights in the following list and several items in the annotated bibliography of curriculum materials (Part VI) can be obtained through ERIC. These items in the ERIC database can be recognized by the ED numbers that are printed at the end of the annotations in the bibliography of curriculum materials and at the end of the citations in the following list. What is ERIC? How can constitutional rights materials in the ERIC database be obtained?

ERIC (Educational Resources Information Center) is a nationwide educational information system operated by the Office of Educational Research and Improvement of the U.S. Department of Education. ERIC documents are abstracted monthly in ERIC's *RIE* (*Resources in Education*) index. *RIE* indexes are available in more than 850 libraries throughout the country. These libraries may also have a complete collection of ERIC documents on microfiche for viewing and photocopying.

ERIC documents may be purchased from the ERIC Document Reproduction Service (EDRS), 7420 Fullerton Road, Suite 110, Springfield, VA 22153-2852, in either microfiche (MF) or paper copy (PC). The telephone number is (703) 404-1400. The FAX number is (703) 404-1408. When ordering, be sure to include the ED number, specify either MF or PC, and enclose a check or money order. EDRS also provides a toll free number (1-800-443-3742) for customer service and phone orders.

The ERIC documents included in this publication are merely a few of the many constitutional curriculum materials and background papers that can be found in the ERIC database. These items exemplify the large pool of constitutional rights resources that can be obtained through ERIC. Additional resources on the Bill of Rights can be found by searching the monthly *RIE* index using the partial list of "constitutional rights" descriptors listed below. These descriptors may also be used to do a computer search of the ERIC database.

List of ERIC Descriptors on Constitutional Rights

Academic Freedom	Discriminatory Legislation
Bill of Rights	Drug Legislation
Childrens Rights	Due Process
Citizenship	Educational Legislation
Citizenship Education	Equal Education
Citizenship Responsibility	Equal Protection
Citizen Participation	Freedom of Speech
Citizen Role	Intellectual Freedom
Civics	International Crimes
Civil Disobedience	International Law
Civil Liberties	Justice
Civil Rights	Laws
Civil Rights Legislation	Law Related Education
Constitutional History	Legal Education
Constitutional Law	Parent Rights
Controversial Issues	Privacy
(Course Content)	Sanctions
Courts	School Law
Court Judges	Search and Seizure
Court Litigation	Sex Discrimination
Criminal Law	Student Rights
Democracy	Teacher Rights
Demonstrations (Civil)	Voting Rights

The papers in the following annotated list were selected because of their relevance to social studies teachers in elementary and secondary schools. Some of these papers were presented at meetings of major professional associations, such as the American Historical Association, American Political Science Association, and the National Council for the Social Studies. Other papers on this list were developed through projects of universities, state-level departments of education, and the U.S. Department of Education.

Barham, Frank E., et al. *The Equal Access Law: One Nation Under God?* Flagstaff, AZ: Paper presented at the Annual Meeting of the National Conference of Professors of Educational Administration, 1986. ED 275 043.

Although schools cannot actively promote religiously oriented activity, neither can they prohibit such activity. The ninety-eighth Congress passed the Equal Access Act in an attempt to ground students' rights to practice religion in the schools in well-established constitutional principles requiring equal treatment, protecting student-initiated meetings, and preserving local control of schools. This paper reviews a number of legal issues associated with implementation of the new law. Among these issues are the extent to which schools are justified in limiting student activities, and under what circumstances; the extent to which participation in such activities by staff members may be construed as state support or approval; the form to be taken by official responses to violations of the new law; and the ability of students to make mature decisions concerning participation in religiously related activities.

Bartlett, Larry D. "Student Press and Distribution Issues: Rights and Responsibilities." *Legal-Memorandum* (April 1984): 9. ED 243 215.

This review analyzes case law in the area of student press and distribution, and offers some guidelines for developing and implementing school policy and rules. Litigation is reviewed in order to clarify students' rights, limitations and administrative authority in matters of censorship and prior restraint, and actions in connection with writing and distributing publications for which students may be disciplined. It is recommended that school rules clearly state that students will not be punished for views they express in printed materials and that school officials attempt to persuade students to employ tact and restraint in the exercise of their First Amendment rights. Rules requiring approval of student publications before distribution are not advised, for although the theoretical concept of prior restraint in the school setting has sometimes been upheld in court, specific instances usually have not. The policy of holding students accountable after printed materials have been distributed and for their actions, rather than for their words, is supported by case law. Students should be reminded that they have a legal responsibility to refrain from actions resulting in disruption of the educational environment or infringing on the rights of other students, and

they should be held accountable when they breach it.

Beezer, Bruce. *U.S. Supreme Court Decisions in Bethel and Hazelwood: Is the Pig in the Parlor Gone?* Chicago, IL: Paper presented at the Annual Meeting of the American Educational Studies Association, 1989. ED 313 792.

The "pig in the parlor" refers to a growing area of censorship. In this paper, "parlor" stands for public schools, and "pig" for speech that need not be protected if it occurs at an inappropriate time or place (i.e., if such speech is not considered to bear the "imprimatur" of the schools). A review of the U.S. Supreme Court decisions affords insight into the meaning of free speech as a democratic value in the context of the public school setting. This review of Court cases focuses on: (1) a brief overview of the law governing free speech; (2) specific legal concepts pertinent to free speech in the context of the public schools; (3) a discussion of two recent Supreme Court decisions on free speech in schools and subsequent lower court decisions; and (4) some general conclusions concerning issues related to the conference's theme of "Ethics and Democratic Values in the Education Profession." The two cases discussed are the *Bethel School District No. 403 v. Fraser* (1986) and *Hazelwood School District v. Kuhlmeier* (1988).

Brennan, William, Jr. *Teaching the Bill of Rights*, Anti-Defamation League of B'nai B'rith, 1963. ED 001 997.

This article discusses the idea that the anxiety to win the race of space and technology may cause the United States to neglect the struggle of values which is crucial in winning the war for freedom. The author suggests that the most useful materials for the teaching of civil rights are case studies, either reports of actual cases or hypothetical studies, designed to present unsettled legal questions.

Bullock, Angela, and Charles F. Faber. *The Right of Privacy of Public School Employees*, 1989. ED 303 861.

A nationwide controversy over the right of privacy has arisen as a result of companies probing into their workers' habits and health through such means as mandatory drug tests, electronic databases, and lie detector tests. The legal claims arising from these civil suits against employers for invasion of privacy have established precedents that are now being applied to schools and their personnel. These cases are reviewed in this paper. It begins with a historical background on the legal right of privacy, starting with Hebrew and Roman law, and moving through European legal concepts to the United Nations covenant on human rights and the American experience from 1890 to the present. The next section discusses constitutional bases for the right of privacy, deriving from Supreme Court cases that interpret the First, Fourth, Fifth, Ninth, and Fourteenth Amendments. The following section then specifically addresses privacy concerns for educators. The tradition of the teacher as exemplar for behavior standards is first reviewed, followed by a discussion of the current view that if a teacher is to be disciplined for private conduct, there must be a connection between the act and his or her role as an effective teacher. Cases are reviewed that construe various aspects of this standard. The final section addresses four areas of future privacy concerns for educators: (1) drug testing; (2) search of employees' desks and files; (3) the use of audiotape recorders in schools; and (4) the schools and children with AIDS. The Ninth Amendment, allowing for implicit rights not explicitly recognized in the Bill of Rights, suggests that other rights may yet surface.

Carter, T. Barton, et al. *The First Amendment and the Fourth Estate; The Law of Mass Media*, 4th ed. 1988. ED 293 175.

This book examines U.S. Supreme Court opinions on the First Amendment involving the topics: 1) the American legal system and freedom of expression; 2) privacy; 3) copyright and trademarks; 4) national security; and 5) obscenity. The book includes a glossary of legal terms and a table of cited cases.

Civil Rights Division. *Enforcing the Law, January 20, 1981—January 31, 1987.* Washington, DC: Civil Rights Div., Department of Justice, 1987. ED 281 925.

This document describes the enforcement activities and accomplishments of the Civil Rights Division of the United States Department of Justice between January 20, 1981 and January 31, 1987. Emphasis is placed on describing the enforcement responsibilities and programs, not on listing comprehensively cases and activities. The report is divided into the following nine sections: (1) a general introduction; (2) Criminal Civil Rights Violations, especially those involving racial violence; (3) Educational Opportunities, with emphasis on desegregation enforcement; (4) Equal Employment Opportunities, covering discrimination cases and back pay awards; (5) Fair Housing/Consumer Credit/Public Accommodations; (6) Rights of Institutionalized Persons; (7) Voting Rights, including proposed changes in law; (8) Civil Rights Appeals; and (9) Coordination of Civil Rights Enforcement Activity. The report is illustrated with maps and charts.

Dale, Michael, et al. *Your Rights: A Handbook for Native American Youth in Arizona.* Phoenix, AZ: Phoenix Indian Center, 1982. ED 238 660.

This handbook for Arizona Native Americans under eighteen years old explains rights and responsibilities of young people, Native Americans, tribal members, and residents of Arizona. Rights as a family member are discussed, as well as changes in family structure, adoptions, step-parents, and leaving home. A section on education covers the rights of a student, Bureau of Indian Affairs boarding schools, special education, school discipline, suspension, expulsion, and constitutional rights. "Youth and the Criminal Justice System" outlines legal rights of juveniles, arrest procedures, and hearings and appeals. Health care rights and the Indian Health Service are discussed. Employment rights of young people are explained, including minimum wages, hours and kinds of work, exceptions of child labor laws, job discrimination, rights to wages, workmen's compensation, unemployment compensation, and social security. Other rights and privileges including marriage, driver's licenses, bicycles, glue sniffing, alcoholic beverages, gambling, traffic violations, firearms, hunting, fishing, tobacco, voting, draft registration, lawsuits, obscene materials, name changes, curfews, and contracts are discussed. Twelve Arizona agencies that can help young people are listed and described. Federal regulations on students' rights and due process are appended.

Dickson, Tom. *How Advisers View the Status of High School Press Freedom Following the Hazelwood Decision.* Washington, DC: Paper presented at the Annual Meeting of the Association for Education in Journalism and Mass Communication, 1989. ED 308 524.

To examine how the decision in *Hazelwood School District v. Kuhlmeier* (1988) affected high school advisers' views of their role in controlling content in their school newspapers and what they see as objectionable content, a study surveyed 100 Missouri high school advisers randomly selected from a list of 573 Missouri public high schools (with a 56% response rate). Each respondent was sent a cover letter and a thirty-four-item questionnaire. Results indicated that schools have a variety of means for controlling newspaper content, but that there was no significant difference between advisers at small and large schools on the questions concerning how advisers oversee their newspapers' content. In addition, findings indicated that the *Hazelwood* decision would not affect the content of school publications. A table provides responses of advisers to sixteen of the survey questions.

Drechsel, Robert E. *Some Second Thoughts about Hustler v. Falwell.* Washington, DC: Paper presented at the Annual Meeting of the Association for Education in Journalism and Mass Communication, 1989. ED 310 392.

In 1984, a jury awarded $200,000 to the Rev. Jerry Falwell for emotional distress intentionally inflicted by a parody depicting Falwell as a drunkard who had incestuous relations with his mother in an outhouse. In 1988, in *Hustler v. Falwell*, the U.S. Supreme Court struck down the verdict on First Amendment grounds. Although the *Hustler* decision has been widely hailed as a major victory for freedom of expression, this view needs qualification, and subsequent cases in the lower courts support such qualification. A critical examination of the Supreme Court's decision suggests that the decision confuses the concepts of falsity, believability, and opinion. Analysis reveals the Court's opinion to be far from clear. The Court addresses neither the question of how much protection the First Amendment grants to opinion, nor the question of what constitutes opinion, nor the more general problem of plaintiff's use of alternate theories of liability to avoid First Amendment obstacles to claims for libel. One result is that *Hustler v. Falwell* may not effectively discourage attempts to use intentional infliction of emotional distress as an end-run around difficult constitutional defenses to libel and invasion of privacy.

Durham, Robert, et al. *Problems in the Workplace: Aids, Drug Testing, Sexual Harassment, and Smoking Restrictions.* LERC Monograph Series No. 7. Second Edition. Eugene, OR: Oregon University, Labor Education and Research Center, 1989.

This document presents discussions of four problems that may be found in the workplace. "AIDS in the Workplace: Employee Safety and Rights" by Robert Durham and Burton White explores issues of employee/employer relationship and the issue of Acquired Immune Deficiency Syndrome (AIDS) in the workplace. "Legal Challenges to Drug Testing in Public Employment" by Gene Mechanic examines the relationship of the Fourth Amendment and drug testing. Other constitutional challenges to drug testing and challenges under state constitutions are also discussed. The article concludes that it is crucial for employers and employees to work together to achieve a reasonable approach for dealing with drug use problems in the workplace. "Technical Issues and Proce-

dural Safeguards in Workplace Drug Testing" by Steven Hecker discusses analytical methods for drug testing, capabilities and limitations of drug screening techniques, and labor and management considerations in designing drug screening programs. "Sexual Harassment in the Workplace: Eliminating the Offensive Working Environment" by Paula Barran discusses the development of legal standards and the employer's responsibilities to take prompt, appropriate, remedial action. "Overview of Legal Issues Relating to Smoking in the Workplace" by Jeffrey Merrick discusses legislation on smoking, worker's compensation, and constitutional rights of workers.

Edwards, Floyd H. *Tennessee's Student Drug Testing Law.* Tuscaloosa, AL: Paper presented at the Annual Meeting of the National Council of Professors of Educational Administration, 1989. ED 310 550.

In 1988, the Tennessee Legislature passed permissive legislation (TCA 49-940) that allows school officials to test suspected students for using drugs. The law provides that testing is optional, with each local education agency deciding whether or not to adopt the policy. Twelve school systems chose to adopt the legislation as board policy. This paper explores precedents of the law and describes its basic provisions. Detailed standards include: (1) search standards; (2) individualized suspicion requirement; (3) collection of specimen procedures; (4) reasonableness scope requirement; and (5) reasonable suspicion requirement. The law further provides that only students under "particularized suspicion" may be tested. The law raises constitutional questions in regard to the legality of such a policy under the reasonable suspicion interpretation of the Fourth Amendment as well as the due process provisions of the Fourteenth Amendment.

Ehrhardt, Cathryn. *Religion in Public Schools: Free Exercise, Information, and Neutrality.* Alexandria, VA: Educational Policies Service, National School Boards Association, 1990. ED 313 813.

Politics and sex are regular entrees on the school curriculum menu, but since the Supreme Court's 1960s revival of the "wall of separation" between church and state, religion has been censored from the curriculum as well as from the school routine. The free exercise of religion, guaranteed by the First Amendment, is accommodated in U.S. school systems; however, the prohibition against establishment of religion in schools (prohibited by the First Amendment), while theoretically simple, is difficult in practice. The exclusion of the role of religion in society's past and present in school textbooks, courses, libraries, and class discussions has resulted in "ethically illiterate" students. Policy development in religious studies should follow the same processes chosen for other new initiatives. A public information program as well as teacher training should be included in religion curriculum planning.

Faber, Charles F., et al. *School Law for Kentucky Teachers and Administrators*. Third Edition. Lexington, KY: University of Kentucky, College of Education, 1989. ED 310 506.

Intended for use in school law courses of a primarily informative nature with some attention given to attitudinal concerns, this book is designed for teachers and educational administrators. The content is divided into thirteen units that contain information regarding education and the American legal system, certification and employment, religion and the schools, First Amendment rights of teachers, First Amendment rights of students, search and seizure, legal issues related to supervision of pupil conduct, tort liability, racial segregation, equal opportunity under the law, the law relating to instruction, the law relating to attendance, and the law relating to education of children with handicaps. The appendices detail selected provisions of the United State Constitution and provide a glossary of terms.

Goldstein, William. *Controversial Issues in Schools: Dealing with the Inevitable*. Fastback No. 288. Bloomington, IN: Phi Delta Kappa Educational Foundation, 1989. ED 306 693.

Several of the current controversial issues are discussed. Chapters are devoted to: (1) religion in the schools; (2) freedom of expression; (3) textbook censorship; and (4) compensatory social programs (including drug testing, drug problems, and bilingual education). In each of these areas, the issues surrounding the controversies are examined and ways educators can respond to them are suggested.

Gore, Deborah, ed. "Constitutional Issues and Iowa." *Goldfinch* 8 (February 1987): 25. ED 282 807.

Important constitutional issues are presented in a manner appropriate for use in the classroom. Case studies and events from the history of Iowa are used to illuminate the Constitution and Bill of Rights. Freedom of expression and students' rights are discussed in *The Black Armband Case*; free exercise of religion as won by the Iowa's Amish is described in "Religious Rights"; and the women's suffrage movement as it occurred in Iowa is outlined in "Amending the Constitution: Woman Suffrage." A play on equality of education which can

be read or performed by students is included. There are also selections discussing the development and evolution of both the United States Constitution and the Constitution of Iowa.

Hepburn, Mary A., ed. *Constitution 200: A Bicentennial Collection of Essays*. Athens: Georgia University, Carl Vinson Institute of Government, 1988. ED 295 891.

Constitutional essays which formed the basis of public assemblies throughout three states are compiled in this book. The first three essays consider the principles of federalism, judicial review, and the separation of powers. Michael L. Benedict proposes that the question of ultimate sovereignty has been answered differently by various groups according to their political needs. Martha I. Morgan examines the source and extent of the power of the U.S. Supreme Court to review the constitutionality of state and federal acts. Richard H. Cox discusses the principle of the separation of powers. The remaining essays review issues related to the rights of the individual. The fourth essay by L. Carter discusses separation of church and state. Procedural guarantees and the extension of the protections to the states through Supreme Court interpretation of the Fourteenth Amendment are outlined in essay five by S. Talarico and E. Fairchild. The sixth essay by T. Freyer traces the development of black voting rights. Essay seven by C. Bullock III traces the expansion of the equal protection clause of the Fourteenth Amendment. The closing essay by J. Soma and S. Oran discusses privacy rights as they relate to personal information in an advanced information technology era.

Hoffman, Frank. *Intellectual Freedom and Censorship: An Annotated Bibliography*. Metuchen, NJ: Scarecrow Press, Inc., 1989. ED 307 652.

Intended to act as a general introduction for high school and college students, this book presents an annotated bibliography of books, periodical articles, legal materials, and other documents dealing with the subject of intellectual freedom and censorship. The book is divided into five parts: (1) "The Theoretical Foundations of Censorship and Intellectual Freedom"; (2) "Key Court Cases Relating to Censorship and Intellectual Freedom"; (3) "Professions Concerned with Intellectual Freedom" (Journalism, Librarianship, and Politics and Government Service); (4) "Pro-Censorship/Anti-Censorship: Representative Individuals and Groups"; and (5) "Cases of Censorship in the Mass Media." The book concludes with a personal name index and a subject index.

Hunter, Richard J., Jr. *A Discussion of School Law and Other Related Topics*. New York: Paper presented at the Annual Meeting of the National Catholic Educational Association, 1988. ED 298 637.

A discussion of school law, defined as how the educational system is impacted upon by the law, is addressed as it relates two major issues to the Catholic or parochial schools. In an overview of the legal system, the types of courts, the nature of legal precedents, and the levels within the judiciary are reviewed. The first major issue centers around the question of due process as it relates to students' rights. Based on current educational law, a student may not expect to have general protection of the Fourth Amendment while attending parochial school. It is recommended, therefore, that school administrators establish a system of discipline based on principles of equity and fairness, and that this system be published as a handbook for all parents and students. Private schools also have the right to hold secular goals, to emphasize moral development and discipline, to discourage criticism, and to impose conformity of dress, speech, and action. The second major issue discussed regards the liability question. In this area, the factor that determines liability is negligence. To prove that one is negligent, four factors must be present: there must be a clear duty to be performed, an individual must be shown to have breached this duty, the person in charge must be shown to have had substantial effect in producing the injury, and the incident must result in damage. An outline of suggestions regarding field trips and playground supervision is given.

Hyman, Ronald T. *Educational Beliefs of Supreme Court Justices in the 1980s*. San Francisco, CA: Paper presented at the Annual Meeting of the National Organization on Legal Problems of Education, 1989. ED 313 784.

The educational beliefs of Supreme Court Justices in the 1980s are examined (i.e., the explicitly stated beliefs, rather than any inferred beliefs based on legal decisions). In particular, the focus is on beliefs expressed only in the major Court opinions rendered in the 1980s. Issues discussed include the definition of education, its relation to the First and Fourth Amendments, and its role in democracy. Discipline and education are considered as well as the power of educational decision making, curriculum, school leadership, and students' rights. The emphasis in the justices' educational viewpoints has turned in general to an emphasis on control, discipline, order, authority, and the inculcation of traditional values.

It's the Law: Students' Rights and Responsibilities! Oklahoma City: Oklahoma Bar Association, Oklahoma State Department of Education, 1982. ED 240 008.

Secondary-level learning activities dealing with youth and the law are included in this resource guide. Although the guide was written specifically for use in Oklahoma schools, it can, with modifications, serve as a model for other states. There are seven sections dealing with: 1) youth and employment law; 2) business rights and responsibilities; 3) property; 4) school; 5) relations between people; 6) arrest; and 7) the court system. Each section is comprised of two parts, one containing questions and answers, the second containing learning activities. Students are expected to read and then use the materials provided in a question and answer section in many of the learning activities. For example, in the section on youth and crime, students learn the definitions of various types of crimes. A learning activity then asks them to read about criminal acts and identify the crime. Examples of other activities include involving students in discussing specific court cases, taking matching tests, and analyzing crime statistics. A selected bibliography is provided.

Johnson, T. Page. *Procedural Due Process and Fairness in Student Discipline: A Legal Memorandum*. National Association of Secondary School Principals, 1990. ED 315 888.

When the Supreme Court decided that the Constitution requires public school principals to follow procedural due process in suspension and expulsion cases, the Justices recognized a link between procedural due process and the fairness of effective discipline. This report reviews the constitutional due process required when public school officials are investigating allegations of student misconduct and determining disciplinary sanctions, and advocates its use, even when not legally required, as a step toward ensuring fairness in every disciplinary decision. The following topics are discussed: (1) codes and student conduct; (2) constitutional due process and fundamental fairness; (3) constitutional due process for long-term suspensions and expulsions; (4) suspension or expulsion of handicapped students; and (5) conclusion and recommendations.

Klauke, Amy, and Margaret Hadderman. *Drug Testing*. ERIC Digest Series Number EA35 (Revised). ERIC Clearinghouse on Educational Management, University of Oregon, 1990. ED 316 957.

This document suggests that despite privacy concerns, school administrators are feeling pressure to adopt urgent measures to keep drugs and alcohol from further endangering our youth's well-being and undermining staff performance. This urgency is reinforced by a national anti-drug campaign and Congressional passage of the Drug-Free Workplace Act (1988) and the Drug-Free Schools and Communities Act (1986, with 1989 amendments) tying institutional compliance to federal funding eligibility requirements. Drug testing raises issues pertaining to the First and Fourteenth Amendments. Although an earlier appellate court case upheld the need for a "factual basis" of suspicion before subjecting a teacher to urinalysis, two 1989 U.S. Supreme Court cases involving public employees ruled that public safety considerations outweighed privacy and individualized suspicion requirements. The document also suggests that attempts to pretest student athletes raise the issue of whether extracurricular activities are rights or privileges. Also, urinalysis and breathalyzer tests can inaccurately reflect an individual's use or abuse of a controlled substance, particularly marijuana. According to one case analysis, school officials have no authority to stipulate off campus conduct having no bearing on properly maintaining the educational process. Mandatory urinalysis should be based only on individualized suspicion and satisfy both prongs of the *T.L.O. v. New Jersey*, 1985 test for search and seizure constitutionality (i.e., reasonable suspicion and appropriate circumstances).

Magsino, Romulo F. *Student Rights in Newfoundland and the United States: A Comparative Study*. St. John's, Newfoundland: Memorial University, Faculty of Education, 1980. ED 240 017.

Official policies concerning students' rights in Newfoundland and in the United States are examined, and standards of justification for students' rights are discussed. A questionnaire was sent to each school district superintendent in Newfoundland and to 100 selected superintendents in the state of Wisconsin. The response rate from Newfoundland was 66%; from the United States, 56%. The superintendents were asked to indicate policies concerning students' rights to free speech, free press, association membership, personal appearance and behavior, reasonable punishment, privacy, due process, and academic matters. Results showed that, in spite of the many U.S. Supreme Court rulings on student rights, only in the area of due process do over 50% of the Wisconsin school boards have an officially adopted policy. In Newfoundland, even fewer school boards have official policies. The study concludes that many current standards of justification for students' rights

(e.g., the student as a constitutional person, the student as a human person, the Rawlsian standard), are inadequate. A preferred justification is the utilitarian standard, which is based on a committed concern for the greatest welfare of the greatest number. Appendices contain the research proposal, the questionnaire, and statements on students' rights.

McCarthy, Martha M., and Nelda H. Cambron-McCabe. *Public School Law: Teachers' and Students' Rights*. Second Edition. Newton, MA: Publication Sales, Allyn and Bacon, Longwood Division, 1987. ED 283 243.

This text is designed to assist school personnel in understanding current application of the law, provide an awareness of rights and responsibilities, motivate educators to translate basic concepts into actual practice, and generate an interest in further study of the law. Legal issues involving the rights of students and teachers in daily school operations are examined in fourteen chapters: (1) "The Legal Foundation of Public Education" (examining the state and federal role in educational law; (2) "Church-State Relations"; (3) "School Attendance and Instructional Issues"; (4) "Students' Rights in Noninstructional Matters"; (5) "Student Classification Practices"; (6) "Student Discipline"; (7) "Terms and Conditions of Employment"; (8) "Teachers' Substantive Constitutional Rights"; (9) "Discrimination and Employment"; (10) "Termination of Employment"; (11) "Collective Bargaining"; (12) "Tort Liability"; (13) "School Desegregation"; and (14) "Conclusion: Summary of Legal Generalizations." Each chapter includes a conclusion and explanatory notes to aid in further research. A glossary of basic terms and a table of cases are provided.

Miller, Phyllis. *The Burning of the Banner: The Press and the Government in Conflict*. Washington, DC: Paper presented at the Annual Meeting of the Association for Education in Journalism and Mass Communication, 1989. ED 311 437.

Brenham, Texas, in 1866, was a newspaperman's town. In addition to *The Weekly Southern Banner*, Brenham citizens read the *Lone Star*, the *Christian Advocate*, and the *Brenham Enquirer*. The events of 1866 bring into sharp focus the struggle between the First Amendment and the federal government. This struggle, fueled by verbal battles and physical violence, centered on the sacred right to freedom of the press. The combatants, journalist Daniel Leonidas McCary and a newly formed governmental agency, the Freedmen's Bureau, engaged in a classic, period confrontation between the federal government and the local press in a South Central Texas town struggling to survive the manifold problems of Reconstruction.

Overduin, Henry. *Titus Brandsma 1881-1942: An Enduring Symbol for Freedom of the Press*. Washington, DC: Paper presented at the Annual Meeting of the Association for Education in Journalism and Mass Communication, 1989. ED 311 439.

Titus Brandsma, a Dutch Carmelite priest, philosopher, educator, and active journalist, was killed by the Nazis in Dachau on July 26, 1942. Beatified by the Catholic Church in 1985, he was hailed as a potential second patron saint for journalists and unofficially adopted as such by some organized groups. The incident that precipitated his arrest and death was his organized opposition to a Nazi order. His story is especially relevant for the North American context of today, where the social responsibility theory of the press postulates a secular press serving a pluralistic society. Within that context, the "right of access" to the editorial and advertising columns is a controversial issue. The story of Brandsma's life and his final refusal to accept reasoning that explicitly forbade appeal to principles demonstrate the seriousness of principled journalism and publishing. The principle that the Nazis rejected and Brandsma was ready to die for was the principle of a free press—not just a Catholic press, but any press based on principles that go beyond commercial considerations. Thus he emerges as an enduring symbol of freedom of the press, one whose life and death transcend his own time and situation.

Paraschos, Manny. *Constitutional Provisions on the Press: A World View*. Washington, DC: Paper presented at the Annual Meeting of the Association for Education in Journalism and Mass Communication, 1989. ED 310 387.

The study examines the legal treatment of the press in constitutions or other basic legal institutional documents from around the world. Sixty-three constitutions or basic documents from the Western World, the Communist Bloc, the Middle East, Africa, Southeast Asia, and Latin America were analyzed. Analysis revealed that most constitutions open with a freedom-guaranteeing clause and proceed (with great diversity in length, language, and priorities) to define the exceptions to that freedom. Findings suggest that it is not the length or the eloquence of the provision but the spirit behind its enforcement that measures a nation's dedication to the freedom of expression.

Phillips, Kay D. *Freedom of Expression for High School Journalists: A Class Study of Selected North Carolina Public Schools*. Washington, DC: Paper presented at the Annual Meeting of the Association for Education in Journalism and Mass Communication, 1989. ED 310 385.

The study examines the freedom of the high school press in North Carolina to determine whether publication guidelines should be in place, and if so, what those guidelines should contain. High school newspaper advisers, high school principals, and high school newspaper editors from large and small, urban and rural, eastern and western high schools were interviewed on several occasions. The nine advisors interviewed for this study attended the North Carolina Scholastic Press Association Workshop at the University of North Carolina at Chapel Hill in June, 1987 and to that extent are not representative of North Carolina high school newspaper advisors, most of whom are untrained and have never attended a journalism workshop. But, although better informed than average, results indicate that few of the study advisers are well informed on matters of journalistic importance (North Carolina has no certification requirements for secondary journalism teachers), all practice prior review, and all censor student writing by cutting controversial material and instituting an atmosphere of intimidation that causes students to refrain from printing certain materials in the school newspaper. Findings suggest that most of the problems that confront the high school newspaper adviser and staff can be avoided if every high school adopts a clear, legally explicit set of guidelines and if advisers are required to be well trained.

Price, Janet R., et al. *The Rights of Students. The Basic ACLU Guide to Students' Rights*. Third Edition. An American Civil Liberties Handbook. Washington, DC: American Civil Liberties Union, 1988. ED 302 887.

This book, addressed directly to students, defines the scope of school officials' power to regulate students' lives and these officials' responsibilities to provide services and protection to students. The chapters outline the law in specific areas, but they all reflect a common theme: school officials can make and enforce only reasonable rules of behavior that are directly related to the students' education. Information is accordingly provided, through a question-and-answer format, on the following topics: (1) the right to a free public education; (2) First Amendment rights; (3) personal appearance; (4) discipline and due process; (5) law enforcement and searches; (6) corporal punishment; (7) tracking and competency testing; (8) students with handicapping conditions; (9) sex discrimination; (10) marriage, pregnancy, and parenthood; (11) school records; (12) grades and diplomas; and (13) private schools. Appended are instructions on how to use this book and proceedings from two prominent Supreme Court cases, *Tinker v. Des Moines Independent Community School District* (1969) and *Goss v. Lopez* (1975). A bibliography is included.

Rossow, Lawrence F. *Search and Seizure in the Public Schools*. Topeka, KS: National Organization on Legal Problems of Education, 1987. ED 281 305.

This monograph attempts to provide clear understanding of the standards presented by the Supreme Court in *New Jersey v. T.L.O.* (1985) relative to search and seizure in public schools, and suggests practical ways of applying search and seizure law to situations in the school setting. After an introduction, section two examines students' rights and the Fourth Amendment, describing the Amendment's source and applicability in public schools. The reasonableness standard is examined in the third section, applying the standard to *New Jersey v. T.L.O.* (1985) and detailing a two-pronged test, the TIPS formula. Taking into account certain variables, the TIPS formula aids in search and seizure decisions by defining reasonable search as comprising two elements: (1) reasonable suspicion, examining the thing to be found and the information source; and (2) reasonable scope, involving the place or person being searched and the measures used in the actual search (TIPS stands for the thing to be found, the information source, the place or person being searched, and the search methods). Considerations of penalties, involvement of the police, and common errors are examined in section four. Section five focuses on application of the reasonableness standard after the *New Jersey v. T.L.O.* (1985) case and discusses other cases involving search and seizure and/or drug testing. Sections six and seven contain a summary, and conclusion and remarks, respectively.

Ryder, Bernard F. "This School Drug Search Made a Point: We Care Enough to Get Tough With Kids. The Endpaper." *Executive Educator* 4 (September 1982): 40. ED 236 757.

The following is the full text of this document: A parent who notices a gun in his child's room would not hesitate to ask questions and demand answers about its presence. As a school administrator, I believe it is my responsibility to ask questions and take action when I find an equally destructive weapon—drugs—in my schools. The zealous protection of student rights by some

courts unfortunately has dampened many school administrators' spirits in this regard. But this is not the time to look the other way. We must renew our commitment to protect children and to eliminate drugs from schools. In my community of Dover, New Hampshire, the local police and the schools have an excellent working relationship. So I recently involved the police chief and several police officers in a school drug search that might well help accomplish those goals. Immediately after school was dismissed one afternoon—while some students still were in the buildings—the police and I together searched the school buildings thoroughly, using police dogs trained to detect the presence of heroin, cocaine, hashish, and marijuana. When the dogs signaled that a specific locker or desk contained illegal substances, we noted the name of the student assigned to that locker or desk. Then, we telephoned these students and their parents and asked them to view the results of our search. Students were asked to open their lockers in front of their parents and to turn over the contraband to the police. The purpose of this search was not to have kids arrested. The students, in the presence of parents, received warnings. No police records were kept because this exercise was purely an administrative search. I'm pleased to report that a sizable cache of hard drugs was not found—only traces. Out of 1,500 lockers, only twenty-two contained drugs. But it was enough to prove that drugs were being used in school. After the search, we asked parents to work with their children through counseling and drug-awareness programs to see if anything could be done about the students' drug use. Finally, we informed students and parents that the next time we conducted a drug search at school, it would be treated as a police investigation. As you undoubtedly are aware, several courts have split in their rulings concerning the use of dogs in searching students and school lockers for drugs. So before I began my experiment, I checked with local attorneys and police to make sure I was not violating a law or students' rights. Administrators, of course, should not attempt the kind of search I conducted without knowing their legal rights and responsibilities—fully understanding the possible consequences (including public outcry) of such a search. In my case, the support I received from the community was gratifying. I realize that attempting to curb the flow of drugs in schools is a tricky business, but I believe we owe it to students—and ourselves—to make schools as free of drugs as possible. In Dover, my experiment shocked and scared some kids. That's what I wanted to do. Students and their parents learned two lessons: First, parents now know that our schools are willing to work with them to make sure children spend the school day in a drug-free atmosphere. Second, drug "salesmen" in the schools now recognize that administrators once again have assumed the role of protecting students. And everyone—parents, the police, teachers, and children—knows we care enough to get tough on drugs. After the drug search, a local newspaper had this comment: "In the corridors of our local high school, an unspoken notice has been given. Drugs and schools do not mix. . . . While it is true that life contains many gray areas, drugs in a public school is not one of those grays."

Sneed, Don, and Harry W. Stonecipher. *Prisoner Fasting as Symbolic Speech: The Ultimate Speech-Action Test*. Washington, DC: Paper presented at the Annual Meeting of the Association for Education in Journalism and Mass Communication, 1989. ED 309 485.

The ultimate test of the speech-action dichotomy, as it relates to symbolic speech to be considered by the courts, may be the fasting of prison inmates who use hunger strikes to protest the conditions of their confinement or to make political statements. While hunger strikes have been utilized by prisoners for years as a means of protest, it was not until 1982 that the courts attempted to define the rights of such protesters or to sort out the countervailing state interests leading to force-feeding, the state's usual response to such dissent. The central question is: How have the courts in recent decisions balanced the expression and privacy claims of the fasting prisoner with the state's interest in suicide prevention, maintaining order and security in prisons, and the state's obligation to protect the health and welfare of persons in its custody? Recent court decisions that involve inmate hunger-strikers who claim that their fasting deserves constitutional protection as symbolic speech and that force-feeding amounts to an invasion of privacy indicated that the balance has tipped strongly in favor of prison officials who carry out state interests. It is also evident from recent cases that when free expression consists largely of conduct, the courts feel the state has a broad power to regulate such conduct without infringing upon First Amendment protection.

Spicola, Rose, and Carolyn Stephens. "Intellectual Freedom: The Censorship War Continues." *Texas Reading Report* 11 (May 1989): 7-8. ED 305 700.

Censorship efforts are taking place throughout the country in spite of greater activism among anti-censorship forces. One of the alarming trends is that many of the censors are now attacking the curriculum of the schools, challenging textbooks in reading, literature, history, science, health, and social studies. The International Reading Association has developed a censorship statement which very clearly states that any type of censorship infringes upon the freedom of speech, thought, and inquiry guaranteed in the First Amendment of the United States Constitution. Schools should develop procedures for dealing with book challenges, and should also adopt procedures to support teachers who wish to implement broad literature-based programs in their reading curriculum. Parents will need to be informed and teachers will need to be careful not to use trade books that have not been adopted through the regular adoption routine. A list of sources of information concerning censorship is included.

Students' Rights and Responsibilities Handbook. 1986 Edition. Sacramento: California State Department of Education, 1986. ED 278 135.

This handbook informs the reader of the provisions of the constitutions and statutes of California and the United States as they are interpreted by the courts to affect the rights and responsibilities of public school students. The first of the handbook's seven sections reviews the constitutional rights of students, their right and their duty to attend school, their right to an education, and their basic responsibilities. Section two concerns discipline, transfers to continuation schools, corporal punishment, student appearance codes, and smoking regulations. The third section focuses on proficiency standards, independent study, physical education options, special programs, married or pregnant students, and the exclusion of students from school. The topics of section four are refusal to salute the flag, student involvement in school affairs, student representation on district governing boards, and students' freedoms of expression, religion, and association. Section five examines the legalities of searches and seizures, and considers the presence of law enforcement officers in schools. The sixth section discusses the levying or requiring of fees, deposits, and other charges, and reviews the prohibitions against sex discrimination. Section seven covers parents' and guardians' rights to be informed of district policies affecting their children and to obtain access to their children's records.

You Have the Right if You Know it: A Rights and Responsibilities Handbook for Virginia Teenagers. Richmond: Virginia State Department for Children, 1987. ED 311 312.

Two hundred sixty questions and answers on the rights and responsibilities of Virginia youth are presented in this document. Questions and answers are presented in these twelve categories: transportation, juvenile justice, drugs, education, employment, financial responsibility, sexual conduct, health, parental responsibilities, family planning, legal change, and miscellaneous. In the category of education these issues are presented: (1) legal obligation to attend school and exceptions to this law; (2) availability of homebound education; (3) legality of corporal punishment in schools; (4) responsibility of students to pay for damage to school property; (5) legality of student appearance rules; (6) right of students to assemble, to petition, and to express opinions; (7) students' rights concerning search and seizure; (8) rights of students to access their records; (9) students' rights regarding expulsion and suspension; and (10) post-high school educational opportunities. The section on drugs defines five classes of drugs, explains the physical and psychological effects of using them, and identifies whether or not they are addictive. The section on sexual conduct provides a brief description of some of the laws and court procedures about sexual conduct. The section on family planning answers questions about marriage, birth control, foster care, and adoption.

Part VI
Select Annotated Bibliography
of Curriculum Materials on Constitutional Rights

VI

Select Annotated Bibliography
of Curriculum Materials on Constitutional Rights

The Bicentennial of the Bill of Rights has been a catalyst for the development of many high-quality commercial and non-commercial curriculum materials designed to facilitate better understanding of constitutional issues based on the Bill of Rights. The materials highlighted in this publication do not represent an exhaustive list of materials available. The ones chosen for inclusion, however, do meet certain criteria.

1. *The materials are intended for teachers and students in grades K-12.* Learning about the Bill of Rights is appropriate at all levels of instruction. During the elementary years the foundation for understanding, applying, and evaluating constitutional issues related to the Bill of Rights can be laid. Middle school/junior high affords the perfect opportunity to teach students to understand, apply, and evaluate provisions of the Bill of Rights. High school provides students with the opportunities to develop their knowledge of Bill of Rights topics and issues. Mock trials, moot court simulations, simulated congressional hearings, case studies, and role playing are all excellent ways of deepening understanding.

2. *The materials are published by non-commercial publishers and non-profit educational agencies.* Many excellent materials are available through large-scale commercial textbook publishing companies that have sizable budgets to advertise their products. The intent of this publication is to highlight equally exceptional products, but ones developed by non-profit educational agencies and agencies that do not advertise and market products on the scale of big commercial publishers.

3. *The materials included in this bibliography emphasize a variety of instructional strategies.* Understanding, applying, and evaluating Bill of Rights issues cannot be accomplished through lectures and recitation alone. Cooperative learning strategies, role playing, and case studies that include active participation by students can enhance the study of the Bill of Rights.

Therefore, the materials selected for inclusion stress student involvement in the process of learning rather than requiring students to act merely as receptacles of information.

4. *The materials included in this bibliography represent three broad instructional formats*: (a) printed materials, including books, lessons, and curriculum packages; (b) video programs; and (c) poster sets. Just as instructional strategies must vary, so too must instructional formats. The various learning styles of students and teaching styles of instructors require that instructional materials used in a classroom exhibit more than one form. Therefore, the annotated lists in this part include a variety of curriculum materials that emphasize a variety of instructional formats.

In addition to the items included in these three broad formats, two outstanding periodicals are highlighted. *The Bill of Rights in Action* (BRIA) and *Update on Law-Related Education* are included in this publication because they regularly feature lessons on Bill of Rights issues designed for students and teachers.

The citations for all materials included in the following annotated bibliography are listed in alphabetical order by title. Several citations included in this bibliography are also available through ERIC (Educational Resources Information Center). They are noted by an ED number at the end of the citation. Information about the ERIC database, and how to obtain items in it, is presented in Part V of this publication.

America Becomes a Nation: A More Perfect Union (1989) by The Motion Picture Studio.

This entertaining and educational two-hour videotape is a dramatic production which relives the Constitutional Convention and the actions of men who represented differing viewpoints but finally, through a number of compromises, agreed on a document that would ultimately guide this nation. The suggested audience is secondary students and beyond. The videotape can be obtained by contacting the Motion Picture Studio, 207 MPS, Brigham Young University, Provo, UT 84602, (801) 378-2525.

American Law Source Book (1989) by Pamela J. Brown, James A. Snyder, and Rick Mibrison.

This publication provides sources on American law which can be easily used by a secondary teacher on a unit or subject basis for any relevant part of a traditional curriculum. The materials selected and the method of presentation have been specifically designed for student use in the classroom. Leading cases in major areas of the law are presented in summary form for analysis and discussion by students. Where possible, cases with contrasting results are placed side-by-side, so the student can learn to distinguish between what is permissible and what is prohibited under the law. The purpose of this juxtaposition is to demonstrate that legal rights coexist with legal responsibilities. Following each section of cases is a set of discussion questions, a brief summary of the decision of the court, a commentary on the historical background and some of the important principles governing that area of the law, and a brief list of other significant or similar cases of interest. Also included is an entire chapter devoted to instructional methods that can be successfully employed in teaching about the fundamental principles of American law and the dynamics of our legal system. In addition, there are other sections on subjects which will enable the teacher to obtain a better understanding of the operation of our legal system (e.g., "The Legal Profession in Today's Society" and a glossary of the most commonly used legal terms). The text provides a bibliography of publications and materials which may be of assistance to teachers who are interested in locating additional sources. The text can be obtained by contacting the Young Lawyers Division of the American Bar Association, 750 North Lake Shore Drive, Chicago, IL 60611-4497, (312) 988-5555.

American Viewpoint (1987) by Milton B. Hoffman.

This video highlights a series of sixty-second commentaries designed to review the importance of the First Amendment. The video features PBS newsman Jim Hartz and can be obtained by contacting the Public Affairs Department of American TV and Communication, 300 1st Stamford Place, Stamford, CT 06902, (203) 328-0620.

America's Conscience: The Constitution in Our Daily Life (1987) by the Anti-Defamation League of B'nai B'rith.

This educational program is designed to inform high school students of citizens' rights protected by the Constitution and Bill of Rights; educate students about the importance and meaning of these rights; and sensitize students to the certain dangers of loosing them. The material is divided into two sections. Activities one through thirteen explore the Bill of Rights, and activities fourteen through twenty show the importance of the Thirteenth and Fourteenth Amendments. The materials are designed to be used in sequence, but lend themselves to use in a more flexible way. The kit is self-contained, but certainly could be supplemented with additional research on the part of students. A glossary is included that contains all words that students are asked to define within the activities. This educational program can be obtained by contacting the Anti-Defamation League of B'nai B'rith, 823 United Nations Plaza, New York, NY 10017, (212) 490-2525.

Becoming Informed Citizens: Lessons on the Constitution for Junior High Students (1988) by Kenneth A. Wagner, John T. Hyland, Donald O. Dewey, and Virginia S. Retlinger.

This publication was developed by teachers in the Los Angeles Unified School District who were sponsored by the National Endowment for the Humanities and the Commission on the Bicentennial of the United States Constitution, and California State University, Los Angeles. The teachers designed curricula plans to teach substantive historical material about the Constitution and Bill of Rights for eighth-grade students. The publication can be obtained by contacting Regina Books, P.O. Box 280, Claremont, CA 91711, (714) 624-8466.

Bicentennial Funbook (1987) by Harriet Bickleman Joseph.

This activity workbook is designed for elementary school students studying the Constitution. This workbook contains fun, but enlightening activities that foster a better understanding of constitutional issues and questions. The workbook can be obtained by contacting the Law, Youth and Citizenship Program, New York State Bar Association, One Elk Street, Albany, NY 12207, (518) 474-1460.

Bill of Rights: K-12 Resource Packet (1990) by the Michigan Commission on the Bicentennial of the U.S. Constitution

This publication includes twenty-two lessons for elementary school students and twenty-five lessons for secondary school students. Various teaching strategies and types of learning activities are presented. Active learning by students is emphasized. Funding for this project was provided by the Commission on the Bicentennial of the United States Constitution. This resource packet can be obtained from the Michigan Commission on the Bicentennial of the U.S. Constitution, P.O. Box 30026, Lansing, MI 48909, (517) 335-4460.

Bill of Rights, vol. V no. 1 Summer, 1990 *Magazine of History: For Junior and Senior High School Teachers*, by the Organization of American Historians (OAH).

This special edition of the OAH's quarterly journal includes three introductory essays. The first, "Trial Rights of the Accused" is written by David J. Bodenhamer. The second, "The Religion Clauses" is written by Melvin I. Urofsky and the third, "Teaching and Learning the Bill of Rights" is written by John J. Patrick. The special issue also includes three teacher-developed lesson plans written about understanding religious freedom, The Establishment Clause, and school prayer. The lessons emphasize the use of a courtroom simulation and primary sources. Also included in this issue are details about National History Day 1991 and educational resources gathered by the Indiana Historical Bureau. This special edition can be obtained by contacting the Organization of American Historians, 112 N. Bryan Avenue, Bloomington, IN, (812) 855-7311.

The Bill of Rights: An Introduction (1990) by Gordon B. Baldwin.

This booklet is intended to assist in celebrating the Bicentennial of the Bill of Rights. It is designed for use by schools and other organizations. The booklet discusses each of the first ten amendments and includes relevant cases as footnotes. The booklet can be obtained by contacting the Wisconsin Bar Foundation, 402 W. Wilson Street, Madison, WI 53703, (608) 257-9569.

The Bill of Rights and Beyond (Calendar) by the Commission on the Bicentennial of the United States Constitution.

This 1991 calendar, devoted to a study of the Bill of Rights and subsequent amendments, is an excellent teaching tool for students of all ages. The calendar is available in limited quantities by contacting the Commission on the Bicentennial of the United States Constitution, 808 17th Street, NW, Washington, DC 20006-3999, (202) 872-1787.

Bill of Rights and Beyond (Poster) by Betty Debnam and the Commission on the Bicentennial of the United States Constitution.

This poster was developed as an incentive to encourage schools to participate in the national "Teach About" on the Bill of Rights and subsequent amendments. The poster depicts all twenty-six amendments to the Constitution and includes learning activities and resource information on the back side. During 1991, the poster will be distributed to all schools in the country along with a supplement presenting a simplified explanation of the Bill of Rights for elementary students. Additional copies may be obtained by contacting the Commission on the Bicentennial of the United States Constitution, 808 17th Street, NW, Washington, DC 20006-3999, (202) 872-1787.

The Bill of Rights and Beyond, 1791 to 1991: 200 Years of the Bill of Rights (1991) by "Scholastic" magazine and the Commission on the Bicentennial of the United States Constitution.

This publication is a sequel to a series of educational materials on the three branches of government. The materials include background information and learning activities appropriate for both elementary and secondary schools. "Scholastic" is distributing editions to approximately 150,000 teachers nationwide in the Spring of 1991. A video documentary on the founding of our national government has been developed as a supplement to the series. Both the elementary and secondary editions can be obtained by contacting Information Services, Commission on the Bicentennial of the United States Constitution, 808 17th Street, N.W., Washington, DC 20006, (202) 653-9800.

The Bill of Rights and Beyond: A Resource Guide (1990) by the Commission on the Bicentennial of the United States Constitution.

This resource guide features programs and plans for 1990-1991, a section on how to get involved with activities related to the Bill of Rights, resources including educational materials, organizations, bibliographies, and audio-visual programs. The guide also includes a brief introduction and history of the Bill of Rights and a list of significant dates. The guide can be obtained by contacting the Commission on the Bicentennial of the United States Constitution, 808 17th Street, NW, Washington, DC 20006-3999, (202) 872-1787.

The Bill of Rights (1990) by the National Archives and Records Administration of the United States.

This teaching unit is designed 1) to help students of U.S. history, government, and economics understand the process by which history is written; and 2) to develop analytical skills. The unit contains fifty reproductions of documents-charts, photographs, letters, drawings, and posters—and a detailed teacher's guide. The materials deal with certain key issues of the period, governmental and political responses to these issues, and public attitudes. The teaching unit can be obtained by contacting SIRS, Inc., P.O. Box 2348, Boca Raton, FL 33427-2348, 1-(800)-327-0513. Alaska and Florida call collect (407) 994-0079.

The Bill of Rights: A Law-Related Curriculum for Grades 4-6 (1986) by Fran Reinehr.

This educational package focuses on the individual and personal freedom as guaranteed by the U.S. Constitution and as interpreted by the courts—namely, the idea of fundamental rights as expressed through the concepts of liberty, justice, and equality. Student materials include readings, worksheets, hypothetical problems, and case studies. The teacher's guide contains goals and objectives for each of the ten lessons, points of law which explain the legal concepts involved in each lesson, which are intended as background information for the teacher, and an explanation of and recommended directions for each activity. The lessons have been designed for use either with or without outside resources. The educational package can be obtained by contacting the Director of Law-Related Education, Nebraska State Bar Association, P.O. Box 81809, Lincoln, NE 68501, (402) 475-7091.

The Bill of Rights: A Law-Related Curriculum for High School Students (1988) by Steve Jenkins, Wayne Kunz, and Alan H. Frank.

This package includes twelve lessons on the Bill of Rights that cover topics such as freedom of speech, freedom of the press, fair trials, freedom of religion, the right to bear arms, due process of law, search and seizure, the Fifth Amendment, the Sixth Amendment, excessive bail, cruel and unusual punishment, and equal protection. Each lesson includes goals and objectives, teaching instructions, student materials, activities, and media resources. This compilation of lessons can be obtained by contacting the Nebraska State Bar Association, Law-Related Education Project, 635 South 14th Street, P.O. Box 81809, Lincoln, NE 68501, (401) 475-7091.

The Bill of Rights: A Law-Related Curriculum for Primary Students (1986) by Wilma Boles.

This educational unit focuses on the individual and personal freedom expressed in the Bill of Rights. Through a story format of an animal community, primary students will make decisions about important fundamental freedoms by considering conflicts in which the animals find them-

selves. Included in each of the nine lessons is a set of objectives, teacher instructions, stop and think questions, think and act, think and write, and alternative and supplemental activities. This unit can be obtained by contacting the Director of Law-Related Education, Nebraska State Bar Association, P.O. Box 81809, Lincoln, NE 68501, (402) 475-7091.

The Bill of Rights: Acting on Principle (1990) by the Virginia Commission on the Bicentennial of the United States Constitution and the Virginia Institute for Law and Citizenship Studies.

This program offers teachers an innovative strategy for teaching the Bill of Rights. The program encourages students to discuss and try to resolve rights-related issues; that is, actively interpreting the Bill of Rights in a local government setting. *Acting on Principle* converts the classroom into a hypothetical community whose school board and municipal government must decide on a variety of public policies that involve making choices about the rights of citizens. Students take the roles of the council and board members and citizens with interests at stake in policies regarding gun control, drug testing, jail overcrowding, a smoking ban, control of the curriculum, AIDS notification, surveillance in the schools, and use of the schools for a bible study class. Acting out these roles within the above context, students work to accommodate both the purposes of government and the protection of individual liberties. The program provides an approach to the teaching of constitutional law that focuses on Bill of Rights and Fourteenth Amendment issues; focuses attention on the local government process, so often given inadequate attention in the curriculum; and shows students the very real influence that individuals can bring to bear in the resolution of local issues, thereby encouraging participation in the democratic process. The program also demonstrates the complexity that attends any discussion of rights issues—that rights can conflict with each other and with the aims of government—and to analyze how political and moral values can affect interpretations of the Bill of Rights; and provides an opportunity for students to experience the process by which issues are confronted and resolved. Student involvement in this process requires public speaking, analysis of the issues, interpretation, and debate. The program can be obtained by contacting the Virginia Institute for Law and Citizenship Studies, Virginia Commonwealth University, School of Education, 1015 West Main Street, Richmond, VA 23284-2020, (804) 367-1322.

The Bill of Rights and You (1990) by Steve Jenkins, Linda Riekes, Roger Goldman, and Patricia C. McKissack.

This junior high/middle school text is about history and how that history affects our everyday lives. The text will help students to develop a new understanding of the crucial relationship between the past and the present; develop problem-solving and critical-thinking skills that will enable them to explore important historical and contemporary issues and themes; develop a greater understanding of the historical origins, fundamental principles, and present-day applications of the Bill of Rights; recognize that the protection of the Bill of Rights depends upon active citizen involvement; and apply their understanding of the Bill of Rights to their rights and responsibilities as citizens. *The Bill of Rights and You, A Teacher's Resource Manual*, includes background information, teaching strategies, and help in using legal citations and fostering community and family involvement. The text and the resource manual can be obtained by contacting the Law and Citizenship Education Unit of the St. Louis Public Schools, 5183 Raymond, St. Louis, MO 63113, (314) 361-5500.

Bill of Rights in Action (BRIA) by the Constitutional Rights Foundation.

This free newsletter is published several times a year by the Constitutional Rights Foundation (CRF). Each issue of *BRIA* provides in-depth coverage of an amendment. Lessons are designed for U.S. History, World History, and U.S. Government emphasizing the particular amendment highlighted in each issue. *BRIA* also gives teachers suggestions for further reading, classroom activities, discussion, and hypothetical legal dilemmas. *BRIA* can be obtained by contacting CRF, 601 South Kingsley Drive, Los Angeles, CA 90005, (213) 487-5590.

Blessings of Liberty, (1987) by the National Park Service.

This sixteen-minute video program is a chronicle of the creation of the Constitution and Bill of Rights and the basic rights and freedoms promised to all Americans. This program, produced by the National Park Service to commemorate the Bicentennial of the Constitution, features many national historic sites where events leading to the signature of these two charters of freedom occurred. The video can be obtained by contacting the National Archives National Audio-visual Center, (800)-638-1300 or Eastern National Parks and Monuments Association, P.O. Box 47, Yorktown, VA 23690, (804) 898-3383 or (800) 821-2903.

By and for the People: Constitutional Rights in American History (1991) by the Organization of American Historians.

This collection of eleven essays by noted historians places the constitutional rights of individuals in historical perspective. The essays also treat current controversies about constitutional rights. Secondary school teachers of history will be able to use these essays to plan lessons and conduct classroom discussions; glossaries, bibliographies, and court case lists are included. Contributing authors are Kermit L. Hall, Melvin I. Urofsky, Norman Rosenberg, Lawrence Delbert Cress, Sam Walker, David J. Bodenhammer, Gordon Morris Bakken, Sandra F. VanBurkleo, Paul Finkleman, and Paula Petrik. This volume can be obtained from Harlan Davidson, Inc., 3110 North Arlington Heights Road, Arlington Heights, IL 60004.

Constitution Sampler: In Order To Form A More Perfect Lesson Plan (1988) by SPICE II classroom teachers for the Center for Research and Development in Law-Related Education (CRADLE).

The mission of CRADLE is to encourage the development and dissemination of innovative instructional materials which focus on the law, the legal process, and the fundamental principles on which the legal system is based. To this end, CRADLE has sponsored Special Programs in Citizenship Education (SPICE). A week-long institute involved teachers from throughout the nation. At the conclusion, participants developed and field tested instructional materials which are then published and disseminated by CRADLE. The publication, therefore, represents the efforts of elementary and secondary educators from all regions of the United States. The publication is organized by content according to constitutional issues to be taught. The Table of Lessons designates the theme or major concepts contained in each lesson and the instructional level intended by the author. Much of the material in this book is easily adaptable to a variety of grade levels; therefore, elementary lessons may be entirely appropriate for middle school instruction, and vice versa. The lessons are organized in an easy-to-follow format beginning with an overview of the content, including a rationale for integrating it into the curriculum. Each lesson designates an instructional level and recommended length of instructional time. Student "handouts" and other materials are identified along with step-by-step instructional procedures. A special section, Tips from the Teacher, offers suggestions based on the author's experience using the material in the classroom. Users of the materials in this publication are encouraged to communicate their recommendations to CRADLE. A brief evaluation detailing successes, problem areas, and suggestions and insights would be most valuable for CRADLE and future SPICE participants. This publication can be obtained by contacting CRADLE, Wake Forest University School of Law, P.O. Box 7206, Reynolda Station, Winston-Salem, NC 27109, (919) 759-5872. ED 301 529.

Constitution Minutes (1987) by Lou Reda.

This thirty-minute video, features twenty-six sixty-second video spots on the Constitution, the Constitutional Convention, and issues of the day. The Discovery Channel and other local stations will be airing the twenty-six sixty-second spots during 1991 and 1992. The video is hosted by noted personalities and can be obtained by contacting Lou Reda Inc., Lou Reda Building, Box 68, 4 N Street, Easton, PA 18042, (215) 258-2957.

The Constitution Is for Kids Too (1987) by the Pennsylvania Department of Education.

This packet for elementary students includes ways to use the book, teaching strategies and fourteen activities designed to actively engage students in learning about rights of individuals in a democratic society. The packet can be obtained by contacting the Pennsylvania Department of Education, 333 Market Street, Harrisburg, PA 17126-0333, (717) 783-6788.

The Constitution. . .Let's Talk About It (1990) by The Commission on the Bicentennial of the United States Constitution.

This community education project is designed to help people rediscover fundamental constitutional principles and understand how the United States Constitution and Bill of Rights affect them. The project includes four illustrated discussion booklets that weave together a discussion of the American political heritage, system of government and evolving contemporary social and political issues. The titles are, *The Constitution Works: Our Nation's Charter Through Two Hundred Years; Human Rights Under the Constitution; The Spirit of the Constitution: Fundamental Principles;* and *Being An American: Citizenship and the Constitution Today.* A four-page outline for discussion leaders accompanies each booklet. To assist the discussion leader, available optional materials include five discussion trigger videos, an introductory video, and a handbook for discussion leaders. The five trigger videos, each approximately four minutes in length with a discussion trigger question at the end, follow a simulated news report format and are designed to encourage discussion of relevant constitutional issues for the four discussion booklets. The four discussion booklets are available in two editions—one for the general audience, and a simpler, abridged edition for use in intermediate literacy and GED classes. This program can be obtained by contacting Virginia DeRoze, Adult Education Programs, Commission on the Bicentennial of the U.S. Constitution and Bill of Rights, 808 17th Street, NW, Suite 800, Washington, DC 20006, (202) 653-7469.

Democracy and Rights (1989) by the Anti-Defamation League of B'nai B'rith.

This thirty-three-minute video and discussion guide tells the story of the "Little Rock Nine," the Black youngsters who in 1957 were the first to integrate Little Rock's Central High School. The case, narrated by Supreme Court Justice Sandra Day O'Connor, serves as an excellent way of examining civil rights under the Constitution. The video and discussion guide can be obtained by contacting the Anti-Defamation League of B'nai B'rith, 823 United Nations Plaza, New York, NY 10017, (212) 490-2525.

A Design for Liberty: The American Constitution (1987) by Liberty Fund Inc.

This twenty-eight-minute video program, using pictures and quotations from the founding period of the United States, discusses the idea of liberty as it was understood by the revolutionary generation and how the concern for the preservation of liberty culminated in the writing of the Constitution in 1787. Among those heard from are Joseph Warren and John Adams of Massachusetts, David Ramsey of South Carolina, Richard Henry Lee of Virginia, and John Dickinson of Delaware. The script was written by professor Forrest McDonald of the University of Alabama with the advice of Professor William B. Allen of Harvey Mudd College. The video can be obtained by contacting Modern Talking Picture Service, 5000 Park Street, N., St. Petersburg, FL 33709, (800) 243-6877.

Empire of Reason (1988) by the Law, Youth and Citizenship Program of the New York State Bar, and the New York State Education Department.

This sixty-minute video depicts the ratification of the Constitution through the eyes of "modern day" news media coverage. The video, through the media coverage of Walter Cronkite, William F. Buckley, Jr., Phil Donahue and others, follows the struggle and debate in New York over the ratification of the Constitution. The video and teacher's guide can be obtained by contacting the Law, Youth and Citizenship Program of the New York

State Bar, One Elk Street, Albany, NY 12207, (518) 474-1460.

Equal Justice Under Law—A Series (1977) by the Judicial Conference of the United States.

This video series highlights four landmark cases from the court of Chief Justice Marshall. This nationally acclaimed series produced by WQED/Pittsburgh for PBS is designed to promote discussion and thought about the Constitution. Particular emphasis is given to the Supreme Court's reinforcement of the separation of powers, as well as the specific constitutional prohibitions and limitations on the exercise of official authority. A teacher's guide written by Dr. E. Susanne Richert is also available. The four programs in this video series are listed and described below.

1) *Marbury v. Madison*. In 1803, the Supreme Court in this case, established its authority to review the constitutionality of acts of Congress. The controversy of two great statesmen, President Thomas Jefferson and Chief Justice John Marshall, over the relative power of the judiciary is discussed.

2) *McCulloch v. Maryland*. In this decision, the Supreme Court, using the Supremacy Clause, dealt a great blow to a claim of state rights by striking down Maryland's attempt to tax a federally chartered bank. This decision enhanced congressional power and reaffirmed the vitality of the federal government.

3) *Gibbons v. Ogden*. In this precedent setting case, which linked states' authority to license steamboats in federal waters with the seemingly unrelated issue of slavery, Chief Justice Marshall interpreted the Constitution to give the federal government the duty to determine the rules of commerce, thereby laying the foundation for an American "Common Market" nearly a century before Europe enjoyed it.

4) *United States v. Aaron Burr*. Chief Justice Marshall presided over the trial of Aaron Burr and in strictly adhering to the Constitution stepped between Burr and death. The case established precedent over government abuse of the treason charge.

Each video tape is thirty-six minutes long, except *United States v. Aaron Burr* which is seventy-six minutes long. The videos can be obtained by contacting WQED/Pittsburgh, 4802 Fifth Avenue, Pittsburgh, PA 15213, (412) 622-1467.

The First Amendment: Free Speech and A Free Press (1985) by Thomas Eveslage.

This curriculum guide is intended to encourage students to learn how everyone benefits when cit-izens and media exercise the constitutional rights of free speech and free press. This curriculum guide for high school teachers reflects the thinking of 129 educators in thirty states who responded to a two-page questionnaire mailed in 1981. Besides background on free speech issues, the guide includes classroom activities, discussion questions, and worksheets. The broad approach to the First Amendment allows teachers flexibility while offering useful content for each section. The guide can be obtained by contacting the School of Communications and Theater, Temple University, Philadelphia, PA 19122. ED 261 929.

First Amendment Congress Newsletter by the First Amendment Congress Board of Trustees.

This newsletter includes teacher resources, current publications, and updates on Supreme Court decisions and opinions. Also included is relevant information for educators who deal with First Amendment issues in their classrooms. This publication can be obtained by contacting Claudia A. Haskel at the University of Colorado at Denver Graduate School of Public Affairs, 1250 14th Street, Suite 840, Denver, CO 80202, (303) 556-4522.

Forgotten Freedoms (1989) by Kenneth Barder, Young Lawyers Division, American Bar Association.

This videotape and discussion guide depicts scenarios in which constitutional rights basic to our personal freedoms are violated. The video is suitable for secondary students and adult audiences, and can be obtained by contacting the Young Lawyers Division, American Bar Association, 750 Lake Shore Drive, Chicago, IL 60611-4497, (312) 988-5555.

Four National Civics Lessons and *Four More National Civics Lessons* (1990) by the South Carolina Bar Foundation with funding from the Commission on the Bicentennial of the United States Constitution.

These eight sixty-minute TV programs for K-12 teachers are designed to increase the background knowledge and understanding of the Constitution and Bill of Rights. The first forty-five minutes of each program highlights a leading scholar who responds to in-depth questions posed by executive director, Jack C. Hanna, and the demonstration of two lessons by master teachers. The final fifteen minutes of the program features student actors portraying characters from key cases on the Constitution and Bill of Rights. The eight TV programs can be obtained by contacting the South Carolina Bar Association, 950 Taylor Street, P.O. Box 608, Columbia, SC 29202-0608, (803) 799-6653.

From the School Newsroom to the Courtroom (1989) by the Constitutional Rights Foundation.

What had begun in a small high school newsletter in Missouri, with a few ideas for feature articles, has now became a matter of national importance. The case of *Hazelwood School District v. Kuhlmeier* has significantly affected First Amendment law and the rights and responsibilities of students and administrators across the United States. The five lessons in this packet ask students to consider the facts of the *Hazelwood* case and reach a decision in a process modeled on that used by the U.S. Supreme Court. The lesson packet contains two classroom simulation activities—a Supreme Court hearing, and a school board policy debate. They each raise issues about student rights of free speech in public schools. The lesson packet can be obtained by contacting the Constitutional Rights Foundation, 601 South Kingsley, Los Angeles, California 90005, (213) 487-5590 or 407 South Dearborn, Suite 1700, Chicago, IL 60605, (312) 663-9057.

This Honorable Court by WETA.

Two one-hour programs, hosted by Paul Drake, explore the history and function of the Supreme Court. The video can be obtained by contacting WETA, P.O. Box 2626, Washington, DC 20013, (202) 988-2626.

How to Teach the Bill of Rights (1991) by John J. Patrick with the assistance of Robert S. Leming.

Chapters 1-6 of this publication examine main ideas and issues about the origins, enactment, and development in U.S. History of the federal Bill of Rights. There is a lengthy discussion about what and how to teach about the Bill of Rights in secondary school social studies courses. In addition, twelve original lesson plans and learning activities are included. Chapter seven is an annotated listing of high-quality curriculum materials. A table of Supreme Court cases is also included. This publication can be obtained by contacting the Anti-Defamation League of B'nai B'rith, 823 United Nations Plaza, New York, NY 10017, (212) 490-2525.

Law in a Changing Society (1988) by Public Service/Law-Related Education, State Bar of Texas.

These materials are excellent supplemental lessons on the Constitution and Bill of Rights. The lessons use case studies and interactive strategies to teach legal concepts in history and government courses. This K-12 series includes twelve different packets which can be ordered individually. The curriculum materials can be obtained by contacting Public Service/Law-Related Education, State Bar of Texas, P.O. Box 12487, Austin, TX 78711, (512) 463-1388.

The Leaders of 1787 Constitutional Convention by the Pennsylvania Humanities Council.

This poster-set and discussion guide feature twelve posters, each displaying an artist-rendered painting of a constititutional leader. The discussion guide, written by Robert G. Crist, contains historical vignettes and classroom suggestions. The poster set and discussion guide can be obtained by contacting the Pennsylvania Humanities Council, 401 N. Broad Street, Suite 818, Philadelphia, PA 19108, (215) 925-1005 or (800) 462-0442.

Lessons on the Constitution (1985) by John J. Patrick and Richard C. Remy.

Project '87, a joint effort of the American Historical Association and the American Political Science Association, is the sponsor of this text, for students, teachers, and curriculum developers. The *Lessons* are an integral part of Project '87's program on behalf of the Constitution's Bicentennial. They are meant to be supplementary instructional materials that can be easily adapted by teachers for use by their students in classes on civics, American history, and American government. A total of sixty lessons are included in this text which is divided into five chapters. Chapter One, entitled "Documents of Freedom" includes selected *Federalist Papers*. Chapter Two, entitled "Origins and Purposes of the Constitution," includes twelve lessons, one of which discusses the decisions made during the debate over the Bill of Rights. Chapter Three, entitled "Principles of Government in the Constitution" includes fourteen lessons, of which five are directly related to civil liberties and rights. Chapter Four entitled "Amending and Interpreting the Constitution" includes fourteen lessons, of which nine lessons relate to Bill of Rights issues. Chapter Five entitled "Landmark Cases of the Supreme Court" includes twenty lessons, all of which relate to constitutional issues regarding the Bill of Rights. This text can be obtained by contacting the Social Science Education Consortium (SSEC), 3300 Mitchell Lane, Boulder, CO 80301-2272, (303) 492-8154. ED 258 891.

Liberty and Order in Constitutional Government: Ideas and Issues in the Federalist Papers (1989) by John J. Patrick.

This publication provides a brief introduction to core ideas of constitutional government in the United States, which are treated in depth in *The Federalist* by Alexander Hamilton, James Madison, and John Jay. The Anti-Federalist perspective is also presented, because without it *The Federalist* can neither be fully understood nor appreciated. Both sides to the great debate of 1787-1788 which shaped our American political tradition, and the ideas and issues addressed long ago are interesting and relevant to citizens today. This booklet presents information and ideas that can be used in a Federalist/Andi-Federalist Forum—an open discussion on questions and issues about constitutional government in the United States. The primary focus of the Forum proposed in this publication is a perennial problem of constitutional government: how to adequately provide both liberty and order for all individuals living under a government's authority. The Federalist/ Anti-Federalist Forum of this publication is similar in spirit and style to the Jefferson Meeting on the Constitution, a program of the Jefferson Foundation of Washington, DC and the Virginia Jefferson Association. Like the Jefferson Meeting, the Forum is designed to promote reflective thinking, deliberation, and discourse on ideas and issues of constitutional government in the United States. Unlike the Jefferson Meeting, which is concerned with proposed amendments to the Constitution of the United States, this Forum addresses alternative positions on a fundamental question in political theory and practice: how to establish a constitutional government that provides both liberty and order, freedom and stability. Furthermore, this Forum emphasizes acquisition and application of knowledge about core ideas in *The Federalist* and essays of the Anti-Federalists. The "Guide for Teachers and Forum Leaders" in the Appendix, provides directions and suggestions for use of the booklet and management of the Federalist/Anti-Federalist Forum. It is expected that teachers and Forum leaders will modify suggestions presented in this guide in order to meet the interests and needs of different groups of students and participants in this program. This volume can be obtained from the Virginia Jefferson Association, P.O. Box 1463, Richmond, VA 23212. ED 313 315.

The Living Constitution Poster Series (1988) by Howard J. Langer, editor, the Anti-Defamation League of B'nai B'rith.

This series includes fifteen posters which highlight constitutional issues. The series is appropriate for classes in American history, American government, civics, problems in American democracy, world history, political science, law, economics, society and current affairs. Junior high, senior high, and college level students will find the posters intriguing. Teachers can develop entire lessons surrounding each of the fifteen posters. The series can be obtained by contacting the Anti-Defamation League of B'nai B'rith, 823 United Nations Plaza, New York, NY 10017, (212) 490-2525.

Miracle at Philadelphia: *Educational Materials* by the National Endowment for the Humanities.

This educational package includes *The Confederation Chronicle*, Delegate Biography cards, a map of Philadelphia in 1787, the Delegates Library, the bicentennial bookshelf, and a teacher's packet. Each item can be ordered separately or together. The teacher's packet provides teaching suggestions and class activities for each individual item. The materials can be obtained by contacting Eastern National, 313 Walnut Street, Philadelphia, PA 19106, (800) 821-2903.

More than Mere Parchment Preserved Under Glass: The United States Constitution: Cases and Materials (1987) by Eric S. Mondschein, E. Rick Miller, Jr., and Beth A. Lindeman.

This book is designed for use in secondary school social studies classes, primarily in the areas of American history and American studies. Political science and/or law electives that focus on the evolution of the Supreme Court could likewise use the materials. The book consists of ten landmark cases that the Supreme Court heard, examined, and struggled with from 1803 to 1974. The historical setting is examined and significant portions of the actual decisions are included. Suggested teaching strategies are shared along with a chronological law and American history table, a glossary of legal terms, the United States Constitution, and a selected bibliography. The book facilitates the use of case study methods. Students are given the opportunity to determine the facts, state the issues, and understand the decisions. In addition, students will acquire the ability to understand the social, political, and economic environment out of which the cases emerged. Students will also have the opportunity to analyze and assess the impact of the decisions upon the American society. This publication can be obtained by contacting the Law, Youth and Citizenship Program, New York State Bar Association, One Elk Street, Albany, NY 12207, (518) 474-1460.

A More Perfect Union: The Constitution at 200 (1987) by Cable News Network.

This twenty-two week series of two minute vignettes examines specific sections of the Constitution, Bill of Rights, and landmark Supreme Court decisions. The series can be obtained by contacting CNN, 100 International Blvd., Atlanta, GA 30348, (404) 827-1700.

The National Repository Catalog of Teacher Developed Lesson Plans on Law and the Constitution (1989) by the Center for Research and Development in Law-Related Education (CRADLE).

CRADLE, in conjunction with Wake Forest University School of Law, has been designated by the Commission on the Bicentennial of the United States Constitution and Bill of Rights as a repository for teacher-developed lesson plans and materials on law and the Constitution. The repository collects and makes available teacher-developed lesson plans. The catalog and supplement are produced three times a year. The catalog is divided into three divisions: Elementary school lesson plans, grades K-4; middle school lesson plans, grades 5-8; and high school lesson plans, grades 9-12. Each lesson plan lists the code number, grade level, author, title, and a brief description of the lesson plan. Teachers are encouraged to submit lessons plans for inclusion in the repository. If a teacher submits a lesson plan, he/she may receive ten free lesson plans from the repository, otherwise, there is a minimal charge for each lesson. The catalog, with lesson plan entry forms and order forms for lessons can be obtained by contacting CRADLE, Wake Forest University School of Law, P.O. Box 7206, Reynolda Station, Winston-Salem, NC 27109, (919) 759-5872.

Our American Rights (1990) by "Learning" Magazine and the Commission on the Bicentennial of the United States Constitution.

This publication for elementary and middle school teachers and students includes learning activities designed to stimulate thinking about rights and responsibilities. The publication also includes poster illustrations that enhance understanding. The publication can be obtained by contacting the Commission on the Bicentennial of the United States Constitution, 808 17th Street, NW, Washington, DC 20006-3999, (202) 872-1787.

Pennsylvania and Constitutional Development 1776-1794. A Lesson Packet for Secondary Schools (1987) by the Pennsylvania Department of Education.

This packet, which includes nine lessons about early Pennsylvania and constitutional development, is designed in an effort to provide teaching material that demonstrates how the Constitution is an integral part of a society. The packet can be obtained by contacting the Pennsylvania Department of Education, 333 Market Street, Harrisburg, PA 17126-0333, (717) 783-6788.

Righting Your Future (1989) by SPICE III Classroom Teachers.

Over fifty lessons written by classroom teachers are included in this CRADLE publication. The lessons are designed for grades 6-12 and are intended to prepare students for the challenges of the twenty-first century. The book can be obtained by contacting the Center for Research and Development in Law-Related Education (CRADLE), Wake Forest University School of Law, P.O. Box 7206, Reynolda Station, Winston-Salem, NC 27109, (919) 759-5872.

Rights in History (1990) by the Commission on the Bicentennial of the United States Constitution.

This resource book was developed for use in the National History Day Competitions held during the 1990-1991 school year. The book includes a background essay, primary source material, suggested research activities for students, and a bibliography. A limited supply of this book is available by contacting the Commission on the Bicentennial of the United States Constitution, 808 17th Street, NW, Washington, DC 20006-3999, (202) 872-1787.

The Road to Brown (1989) by William A. Elwood.

This video depicts the story of segregation and the legal assault on it which helped launch the Civil Rights movement. Charles Houston, a former editor of the Harvard Law Review and Dean of Howard University Law School, realized that an attack on the legal basis of segregated education would undermine the whole Jim Crow social structure. The video includes clips from a film Houston shot in South Carolina in 1934 documenting separate but unequal schooling. John Hope Franklin, Juanita Mitchell, and Jack Bass recall how Houston, eschewing the limelight himself, energized a generation of black jurists to wage the battle against Jim Crow. Houston died in 1950 at the age of 54, just as his long legal campaign was reaching its climax. The video is a constitutional detective story, untangling the cases which led to the landmark *Brown v. Board of Education* decision. The video can be obtained by contacting Resolution Inc./California Newsreel, 149 Ninth Street/420 San Francisco, CA 94103, (415) 621-6196.

A Salute To Our Constitution and the Bill of Rights: 200 Years of American Freedom Volume I: Grades 1-3 and Volume II: Grades 4-6 (1987) by Connie S. Yeaton and Karen Trusty Braeckel.

These two elementary texts emphasize using the newspaper to discover how the Constitution and Bill of Rights work. The first section of both texts consists of a set of model lessons demonstrating the use of various parts of the newspaper to study the Constitution. They include techniques and sample articles to show how a teacher can use current affairs to make this great document of the eighteenth century relevant to twentieth century students. Each lesson is based on a specific part of the newspaper and is outlined in a step-by-step procedure that includes a sample newspaper item to show how it works. All questions are generic, so that teachers can use them with current newspaper articles. Following each question is a specific answer based on the sample item. Several of the lessons suggest the use of the "DECISION T" activity sheet. This is a device to help children test possible solutions to problems and become better problem-solvers. The second section of each text helps teachers introduce the United States Constitution and Bill of Rights to elementary students. The lessons take children on a journey, beginning with their present-day experience, back to the time when the Constitution was written. By first examining today's problems, it is easy for young people to understand the need that existed for a written framework of government. The lessons are outlined in a step-by-step procedure. Materials needed are listed at the beginning of each plan. Activity sheets to be copied for students appear throughout and the appendices contain helpful background information. A mixture of materials and techniques is used throughout the lesson plans. Newspapers, library books, and filmstrips are integrated into the theme. Role-playing, games, puzzles and mock hearings actively involve students. Teachers are highly encouraged to use field trips, guest speakers, and resource persons as enrichment. Both texts can be obtained by contacting the Indianapolis Star and News, P.O. Box 145, Indianapolis, IN 46206-0145, (317) 633-9005. ED 280 759.

Shaping American Democracy (1990) by the Citizenship Law-Related Program for the Schools of Maryland, Inc. of the Maryland State Bar Association, the Maryland State Education Department and the Law, Youth and Citizenship Program of the New York State Bar Association and the New York State Education Department.

The format of this resource guide is designed to assist teachers and students in the study of key Supreme Court cases. Each of the ninety-three cases is presented with facts, issues, and the decision of the Court. Secondly, twenty-five commonly used textbooks were analyzed to determine the extent to which Supreme Court cases are cited. To assist teachers, the first section includes a table that indicates which cases are cited in which text-book. The table is developed topically, according to the major concept around which the cases have been categorized. Specific legal case citations are also included. The second section contains the bibliography of coded textbooks. The third section provides a brief synopsis of the ninety-three Supreme Court cases. Since they are listed by category, teachers or students can review preceding or following cases to consider changes in precedents and also gain a quick reference for further legal research. The four sections include a number of strategies and activities highlighting the case study method. Teachers are encouraged to adopt or adapt these single activities to fit their students' needs. The appendices include a copy of the U.S. Constitution and Bill of Rights and subsequent amendments, and a glossary of legal terms. This resource guide can be obtained by contacting the Law, Youth and Citizenship Project, New York State Bar Association, One Elk Street, Albany, NY 12207, (518) 474-7460.

Supreme Court Holy Battles (1989) by the Anti-Defamation League of B'nai B'rith.

This sixty-minute video examines Thomas Jefferson's piece of legislation that suggests that religion is a purely personal, private matter between the individual and God, and government has no right to intrude. The video discusses the many historical struggles that ensued over this issue and present day examples that bring the issue up-to-date. The video and discussion guide can be obtained by contacting the Anti-Defamation League of B'nai B'rith, 823 United Nations Plaza, New York, NY 10017, (212) 490-2525.

This Is a Free Country (1991) by The Educational Excellence Network of Vanderbilt University; the American Federation of Teachers; Freedom House; and the JHM Corporation and funded by the Commission on the Bicentennial of the United States Constitution.

This set of interactive computer-based instructional materials is designed for secondary students. The set includes ten lessons that incorporate text material and still images to help students learn about their fundamental rights and responsibilities as United States citizens. The set of ten computer-based lessons can be obtained by contacting Educational Excellence Network, 1112 Sixteenth St., NW, Suite 500, Washington, DC 20036, (202) 785-2985.

T.J.'s Rights (1990) by Maryland Instructional Technology.

This eighteen-minute dramatic video for 5th-8th grade social studies classes helps students understand their personal relationship to the Bill of Rights. The video follows T.J. (short for Thomas Jefferson) as he goes to his school library to check out *To Kill a Mockingbird* by Harper Lee. To his surprise, the book has been removed from the shelves for review because some parents have expressed concerns about its content. The video deals with how T.J. learns about censorship and what it is like to participate in the American democratic process. Also included is a teacher's guide. Both the video and the teacher's guide can be obtained by contacting Maryland Instructional Technology, 11767 Owings Mills Blvd., Owings Mills, MD 21117, (301) 581-4207.

To Preserve These Rights: The Bill of Rights Exhibit (1989) by the Pennsylvania Humanities Council.

This display consists of three kiosks displaying four mounted posters. Each panel explains a particular set of rights and illustrates those rights through the text of relevant amendments, captioned photos, drawings, and quotations. The final panel (which focuses on civic responsibility) asks the exhibit visitor: What can we, as Americans, do to preserve these rights? A companion publication *To Preserve These Rights User's Guide* has been developed to augment the exhibit. The guide looks at the historical development of the concept of rights and liberties, and at the importance of the judicial system in upholding the Constitution. It suggests related educational activities and provides bibliographies. The display and *User's Guide* will enhance any classroom's or school's celebration of the Bill of Rights and can be obtained by contacting Susan Halsey, The Pennsylvania Humanities Council, 320 Walnut Street, Suite 305, Philadelphia, PA 19106, (215) 925-1005.

To Secure the Blessings of Liberty: Rights and the Constitution (1989) by Russell L. Hanson and W. Richard Merriman, Jr.

This discussion guide is one in a series on constitutional reform issues developed by the Jefferson Foundation as part of the Jefferson Meeting on the Constitution project. The guide examines different kinds of rights: the rights of individuals accused of committing a crime, political rights, civil liberties, economic rights, and civil rights. The discussion guide can be obtained by contacting the Jefferson Foundation, 1529 18th Street NW, Washington, DC 20036, (202) 966-7840.

The U.S. Constitution (1987) by the Agency for Instructional Technology.

This six-part video series, featuring Bill Moyers, is designed to show students that the Constitution is an enduring and fundamental document that

can change and is changed as a result of the need to resolve conflict and because of changing political, economic, and social situations. Three of the six videos involve Bill of Rights issues. *Limited Government and the Rule of Law* depicts the U.S. Constitution as a provider of power sufficient to rule according to limits established by law. *Freedom of Expression* deals with the constitutional right that raises questions about security and liberty. *Equal Protection of the Laws* explains how after the Civil War the American ideal of equality under the law was embodied in the Fourteenth Amendment to the Constitution. These three videos plus the other three in the series and the *Teacher's Guide*, written by John J. Patrick, can be obtained by contacting the Agency for Instructional Technology (AIT), Box A, Bloomington, IN 47402, (800) 457-4509 or (812) 339-2203. ED 286 820.

U.S. Supreme Court Decisions: A Case Study Review for U.S. History and Government (1989) by Project P.A.T.C.H. of the Northport-East Northport U.F.S.D. and the Law, Youth and Citizenship Program of the New York State Bar Association and State Education Department.

This constitutional casebook was prepared by eleventh-grade students. It provides junior high/ middle and high school students and teachers with a summary review of fifty-one cases that can enhance any U.S. History and Government course. Appendix A includes answers to the pre-post evaluation quiz, a glossary, and a format for written certiorari briefs. Appendix B includes the Constitution of the United States and the Bill of Rights. The text can be obtained by contacting Project P.A.T.C.H., 110 Elwood Road, Northport, NY 11768, (516) 261-9000 Ext. 284.

Update on Law-Related Education by the American Bar Association Special Committee on Youth Education for Citizenship.

This journal, published three times a year, helps elementary, middle school and high school teachers educate students about law and legal issues. Although it is not specifically designed to center on the Bill of Rights, many of the lessons included in each issue are based upon cases that have a direct relationship to Bill of Rights issues. Back issues and subscription information can be obtained by contacting the American Bar Association, 541 North Fairbanks Court, Chicago, IL 60611-2314, (312) 988-5735.

We the People . . . (1987) by the Center for Civic Education.

The *We the People . . .* curriculum is available at three instructional levels: upper elementary, middle school and high school. At each level, a variety of suggested teaching strategies are employed to encourage student participation and involvement. Illustrations in the texts highlight and enhance comprehension of the key concepts. The curriculum examines the basic philosophical ideas that influenced the development of the Declaration of Independence, the Constitution, and the Bill of Rights; the evolution of constitutional government and the historical experiences that influenced the development of the Declaration of Independence, the Constitution, and the Bill of Rights; the principal issues and debates of the Philadelphia Convention, and the struggle between the Federalists and Anti-Federalists over ratification; the organization of the new government and the development of judicial review; the protection of freedom of religion, freedom of expression; due process of the law, equal protection of the laws; the right to vote; and the role of the citizen in our constitutional democracy; and the rights and responsibilities of citizenship. A special Bill of Rights edition entitled *With Liberty and Justice For All* will be published for the 1991-1992 school year. The text does not limit its attention solely to the first ten amendments to the Constitution, but deals with the "extended Bill of Rights." It also directs attention to the protections of individual rights included in the body of the original Constitution and amendments subsequent to the Bill of Rights. It also discusses the broader concept of human rights. Rather than focusing on each of the many specific rights contained in the Constitution, the book focuses upon several overarching topics which encompass the most important of these rights. The curriculum also introduces students to an analytic framework or set of intellectual tools to assist them in thinking critically about constitutional issues. These "tools of the mind" can help students develop reasoned and responsible positions on the important topics presented in the program. Cooperative learning strategies, such as simulations, debates, mock trials, and government hearings, are used. It provides young people with both the knowledge base, and the personal and group interaction skills required for successful social and political participation in our constitutional democracy. The *We the People* . . . curriculum can be used in conjunction with the National Bicentennial Competition. The competition, designed to simulate a congressional hearing, is held before a panel of judges. The entire class works together as a team, so that all students participate rather than a select few. Classes divide into groups, each making a brief presentation and responding to questions on one of the topics covered in the instructional program. At the high school level, competitions are held at the congressional district, state, and national levels. Classes that win the district competition go on to the state contest and winning state teams compete each spring in the national finals held in Washington, D.C. The texts and information about the National Bicentennial Competition can be obtained by contacting the Center for Civic Education, 5146 Douglas Fir Road, Calabasas, CA 91302, (818) 340-9320. ED 292 692.

We the People: *Students, Teachers, Lawyers Working Together. Law-Related Lessons on Teaching the Constitution* (1987) by the Constitutional Rights Foundation.

In cooperation with the Young Lawyer's Section of the Chicago Bar Association and the Chicago Schools, the Constitutional Rights Foundation has developed a set of fifteen interactive lessons for junior high school students. The lessons, designed to fit into existing curriculum, and the activities are devised as exemplary lessons to infuse the study of the Constitution and Bill of Rights into U.S. history and government classes. The lessons are intended for use with a resource person to provide realism and positive role models. Each lesson includes specific suggestions for the types of resource persons and the activities in which they can participate. The materials encourage inquiry and critical thinking, so that teachers can build support for democratic values while at the same time develop skills needed for effective citizens. The *We the People* lessons can be obtained by contacting the Constitutional Rights Foundation, 407 South Dearborn, Suite 1700, Chicago, IL 60605, (312) 663-9057. ED 301 502.

Without Them the Bill of Rights Would be a Bill of Wrongs (1990) by the Pennsylvania Academy for the Profession of Teaching.

This book of twenty activities for elementary and middle school students actively engages students in thinking, discussing, and problem solving with issues that are related to their basic rights and freedoms as individuals in a democratic society. Each lesson revolves around hypothetical situations relevant to elementary and middle school students. The book of twenty lessons can be obtained by contacting the Pennsylvania Department of Education, 333 Market Street, Harrisburg, PA 17126-0333, (717) 783-6788.

Part VII
Periodical Literature on Teaching the Bill of Rights

VII

Periodical Literature on Teaching the Bill of Rights

The following annotations of articles from journals in the ERIC database represent an extensive sample of articles written during the 1980s about the Bill of Rights. All of the annotations appear in the *Current Index to Journals in Education (CIJE)*, which is published on a monthly basis and is available at libraries throughout the country. The annotations are intended to briefly describe the contents of the articles in general terms. Therefore, it is suggested that the reader locate the entire article in a library. Reprints of the articles may be available from University Microfilms International (UMI), 300 North Zeeb Road, Ann Arbor, MI 48106, (800) 732-0616.

Readers are encouraged to complete their own searches of the ERIC database to discover new articles which are constantly being added to the system. Various types of articles are represented in Part VII of this publication, including research studies, conference papers, lesson plan ideas, and articles that focus on historical documents as primary sources. Educators will find these articles a valuable resource for fostering understanding, application, and evaluation of the Bill of Rights.

Aldridge, Kathy, and Jeanne Wray. "Students' Constitutional Rights." *Update on Law-Related Education* 12 (Winter 1988): 30-33. EJ 368 161.

Centering on a role-play simulating the search of students suspected of possessing illegal drugs, this lesson focuses on students' rights and calls upon students to argue landmark cases involving students' rights to enhance critical thinking skills.

Anderson, Charlotte C., and Charles Williams, eds. "Supreme Court Docket: Drug Testing and the Fourth Amendment." *Social Education* 53 (April-May 1989): 229-32, 50. EJ 391 389.

The article focuses upon classroom involvement in issues related to the Fourth Amendment of the Constitution. It presents a description of a drug test case simulation, a case involving drug testing in the public sector which is to be heard by the

Supreme Court, other teaching strategies, and provides a guide for finding Supreme Court cases.

Arnold, Jay. "How to Enforce Discipline Rules Without Trampling Kids' Rights." *Executive Educator* 11 (April 1989): 34-35. EJ 387 032.

A Georgia school district standardized discipline procedures, codified offenses, and published the results in booklet form. A clear hierarchy of offenses specifies problems to be handled at the local school, at formal hearings, or at a special disciplinary committee.

Baxter, Maurice. "The Northwest Ordinance — Our First National Bill of Rights." *OAH Magazine of History* 2 (Fall 1988): 13-14. EJ 366 743.

The article describes the Northwest Ordinance as the nation's first bill of rights and discusses the similarities between the Ordinance and state constitutions. It states that neither the Ordinance nor the state constitutions mentioned freedom of speech. The article contends that the Ordinance was one of the "foundation stones" in the structure of American liberty.

Beezer, Bruce. " 'Teachers and the Law' by Louis Fischer, David Schemmil, and Cynthia Kelly. Book Review." *West's Education Law Reporter* 53 (July 6 1989): 381-83. EJ 392 071.

The authors state their book's main purpose is to assist teachers to become "legally literate." The reviewers describe the book as a wide-ranging, narrative approach to teachers' legal rights. However, those who want an in-depth and technical discussion on substantive and procedural issues are advised to look elsewhere.

Birch, I. K. F. "Divining the Impact on Education of an Australian Bill of Rights with an American Rod." *Unicorn, Bulletin of the Australian College of Education* 12 (November 1986): 221-25. EJ 343 801.

The article explores the common law bill of rights debate in Australia and the probable impacts of extending constitutional and statutory rights to the educational system. It also closely examines compulsory education, the court's role, children's rights, and the law and education interface, with reference to equality and quality issues in the United States.

Bowen, John. "Captive Voices: What Progress, Change Has Occurred in 10 Years?" *Quill and Scroll* 59 (February-March 1985): 14-16. EJ 313 620.

The article suggests that conclusions drawn from a new survey indicate that student editors are less willing to tackle sensitive topics, that administrators will honor First Amendment rights until there is a conflict, and that advisers continue to support students' rights.

Burkholder, John David. "Religious Rights of Teachers in Public Education." *Journal of Law and Education* 18 (Summer 1989): 335-74. EJ 395 042.

Religious rights of teachers are affected in three primary areas of activities: (1) outside the school environment; (2) inside the school environment; and (3) inside the classroom. These issues are examined from the perspective of the constitutional principles involved.

Butts, R. Freeman. "A History and Civics Lesson for All of Us." *Education Leadership* 44 (May 1987): 21-25. EJ 353 881.

Advocating the complete separation of church and state, the author outlines the history of the present debate over the school-religion controversy. The article includes a detailed discussion of interpretations of the First Amendment (especially the Establishment Clause) and Supreme Court decisions related to the issue.

Carr, Patricia. "Why Not Vote?" *Learning* 13 (October 1984): 80, 82, 84. EJ 305 983.

The article suggests that students need to learn about the real-world issues our nation faces. They need to understand how concerned individuals gather information, consider opposing opinions, come to conclusions, and act on their beliefs. Background information, resources, and classroom activities are provided to help students understand the importance of voting.

Cooper, Dolores J. and John L. Strope, Jr. "Long Term Suspensions and Expulsions after *Goss.*" *West's Education Law Reporter* 57 (January 18, 1990): 29-42. EJ 402 348.

The article suggests that in *Goss v. Lopez* (1975), the Supreme Court held that more formal procedures would be required for longer school suspensions or expulsions. The article reviews more than forty cases that address the question of procedural due process required for long-term suspension or expulsion and summarizes findings.

Cowen, Zelman. "Written Constitution or None: Which Works Better?" *Update on Law-Related Education* 11 (Fall 1987): 9-11, 49. EJ 360 038.

The article explores the difference between the U.S. Constitution and British constitutional law. It specifically examines the concept of the U.S. Bill of Rights in relation to the United Kingdom's common law doctrine of parliamentary sovereignty.

Delon, Floyd G. "*Clayton v. Place*: Shall We Dance?" *West's Education Law Reporter* 57 (February 1, 1990): 341-49. EJ 402 420.

The article addresses the issue of a school dance in Purdy, Missouri, that occurred only because a federal district court prohibited enforcement of the school board's policy barring social dancing on school property. The article examines the district court opinion, subsequent events in the community, the appeal, and the Eighth Circuit Court's holding in the case.

DeLoughry, Thomas J. "Colleges Told to Uphold Rights of Students with AIDS Despite Public Outcry." *Chronicle of Higher Education* 35 (May 3, 1989): 33-34. EJ 389 214.

A civil-rights lawyer advises that institutions will be legally obligated to support the rights of students with AIDS. The campus health center is one part of an institution that has a legitimate reason to know whether a student has AIDS, but it should gather such information on its own.

Dickens, Bernard M. "Legal Rights and Duties in the AIDS Epidemic." *Science* 239 (February 5, 1988): 580-86. EJ 366 658.

The article provides an overview of some major areas of legal concern in which the Acquired Immune Deficiency Syndrome (AIDS) epidemic is having an impact. It also reviews rights of confidentiality and nondiscrimination regarding access to health care, employment, housing, education, and insurance.

Dorros, Karen and Patricia Dorsey. "Whose Rights Are We Protecting, Anyway?" *Children Today* 18 (May-June 1989): 6-8. EJ 392 577.

The article discusses the way in which the legal system perpetuates child abuse and protects parents' rights more than children's rights. It also discusses the difficulties social services encounter in dealing with these children and parents.

Eastman, Wayne, et al. "Civil Liberties and Human Rights in Education." *Education Canada* 29 (Summer 1989): 20-23. EJ 395 664.

The article finds that among 429 senior education majors, high school teachers, and administrators in Newfoundland there was: (1) little awareness about human rights, particularly students' rights; (2) no greater awareness among social studies teachers or administrators; and (3) a wide range of opinions on specific human rights issues.

Eiserloh, Carole De Angelis. "Civil Liberties and the Bill of Rights." *Social Studies Review* 27 (Fall 1987): 69-79. EJ 369 569.

The article presents a three-day lesson that requires students to evaluate selected Supreme Court cases and determine how they think the cases were decided and which amendments were applicable. The article includes eighteen cases for student deliberation, followed by the actual Supreme Court decisions.

Epstein, Terrie and Heidi Hursh. "National Organization for Women (NOW) Bill of Rights for 1969." *OAH Magazine of History* 1 (April 1985): 27-28. EJ 319 093.

As early as 1848, women organized into groups to assert their rights as citizens. In 1969, the National Organization for Women developed a bill of rights. The document is presented here, accompanied by learning activities, discussion and debate questions, and research topics for use with high school students.

Eshleman, Kenneth L. "Student Voting Rights and Patterns: A Research Project." *Political Science Teacher* 1 (Summer 1988): 19-21. EJ 376 926.

The article presents five projects on student voting rights recommended for college students in U.S. government and constitutional law courses. Projects include reading the state's residency law, investigating state and local interpretation of student voting rights, researching the constitutional issues involved in voting rights, and surveying students as to their voting choices.

Fisher, Louis. "When Courts Play School Board: Judicial Activism in Education." *West's Education Law Reporter* 51 (April 13, 1989): 693-709. EJ 388 707.

The article examines the general concept of judicial activism, then looks at three specific areas where charges of usurpation of policy-making power have been leveled at the courts: (1) racial desegregation; (2) due process for students; and (3) religion in public education. The article concludes that judicial involvement in school policy occurs when explicit constitutional rights are addressed.

Flygare, Thomas J. "Texas Supreme Court Upholds 'No Pass/No Play' Rule." *Phi Delta Kappan* 67 (September 1985): 71. EJ 326 615.

The Texas Supreme Court ruled that students' rights to participate in extracurricular activities were not on the same level as rights to free speech

and found that the state law barring failing students from extracurricular activities was rationally related to a legitimate state interest in educational quality.

Franklin, John Hope. "Race and the Constitution in the Nineteenth Century." *Update on Law-Related Education* 12 (Fall 1988): 8-13. EJ 380 980.

The article examines the impact of race on Nineteenth century politics and social order. It discusses the denial of voting rights and due process to free Blacks prior to the Civil War and the "unkept promises" of the Thirteenth, Fourteenth, and Fifteenth Amendments to the U.S. Constitution. The article also lists books on the nineteenth century Black experience and identifies significant individuals in Black history.

Hindman, Sara E. "The Law, the Courts, and the Education of Behaviorally Disordered Students." *Behavioral Disorders* 11 (August 1986): 280-89. EJ 341 315.

The article reviews and synthesizes judicial rulings related to corporal punishment, behavior management strategies, suspension and expulsion, and residential placement. Recent court decisions are discussed; issues related to behaviorally disordered students' rights are examined; and recommendations for practice are presented.

Horner, Jeff. "Access to Educational Facilities for School and Public Groups." *West's Education Law Reporter* 54 (August 17, 1989): 1-5. EJ 395 059.

The article suggests that school districts have broad discretion in using school facilities as they see fit, even for activities not specifically connected to the educational program. However, selective discrimination between public groups, employee groups, or religious groups is not permitted by legal authority.

Horowitz, Robert. "Tighten Standards for Termination of Parental Rights." *Children Today* 18 (May-June 1989): 9-11. EJ 392 579.

The article discusses the way in which child abuse cases should be dealt with legally in order to improve the effectiveness of intervention programs. The article also suggests the tightening of legal standards for parental rights to custody of their children in neglect cases.

Hubsch, Allen W. "Education and Self-Government: The Right to Education under State Constitutional Law." *Journal of Law and Education* 18 (Winter 1989): 93-140. EJ 387 077.

The article examines state court jurisprudence in three areas: (1) classical liberalism and republicanism; (2) the current understanding of federal equal protection and due process through United States Supreme Court decisions; and (3) school finance cases litigated in state courts.

Isherwood, Geoffrey B. "Students' Rights, Principals' Responsibilities." *Education Canada* 28 (Fall 1988): 4-8. EJ 380 708.

A recent Canadian Charter gives students new status in schools and places additional responsibilities on principals and teachers. The article helps administrators and teachers create school policy taking new legislation into account and examines new student status and "right to schooling" included in the Charter. The article also recommends possible elements of school policies.

Jacobsen, Margaret. "Giving Women the Vote: Using Primary Source Documents to Teach about the Fight for Women's Suffrage." *OAH Magazine of History* 3 (Summer-Fall 1988): 50-52. EJ 391 316.

The article presents a lesson in which students use primary sources to learn about the organizing strategies used in the fight for women's suffrage. These sources will provide insights into the past and help students develop appreciation for the hardships suffragists endured. Included in the article are objectives, procedures, and suggestions for activities.

Justice, William Wayne. "Teaching the Bill of Rights." *Phi Delta Kappan* 68 (October 1986): 154-57. EJ 341 182.

The article suggests that like other institutions, schools are occupied by people whose duties and liberties are in conflict. Understanding the Bill of Rights can help resolve school problems as well as major social problems outside the court system.

Kniker, Charles R. "Accommodating the Religious Diversity of Public School Students: Putting the Carts before the Horse." *Religion and Public Education* 15 (Summer 1988): 304-20. EJ 361 411.

The article suggests five guidelines teachers and local school district policy committees can use to accommodate the religious diversity of students while meeting five historic goals of public schools. The article also points out emerging issues facing those concerned about religion and First Amendment rights of students and parents.

Lanier, Gene D., et al. "Censorship." *North Carolina Libraries* 45 (Fall 1987): 15-30; 133-35; 137-47. EJ 361 411.

Seven articles discuss censorship, intellectual freedom, and information policy in the context of federal and state legislation. They also examine humanism and the religious right, technological advancement, the author's point of view, current

school policies, and the Library Bill of Rights for elementary and secondary schools.

Larrabee, Marva J., and Cynthia K. Terress, eds. "Ethical and Legal Issues in Elementary and Middle Schools." *Elementary School Guidance and Counseling* 19 (February 1985): 172-216. EJ 316 394.

The article discusses how a changing conception of the counselor role may affect a counselor's functions, responsibilities, and ethical guidelines. The article deals with students' rights, the law and ethical practices with children in school, ethics surrounding group work, referrals, children with special needs, and school records.

Lederman, Douglas. "Supreme Court Rejects Coach's Plea, Exempts NCAA from Constitution's Due-Process Requirement." *Chronicle of Higher Education* 35 (January 4 1989): A35-36. EJ 384 177.

The Supreme Court ruled that the National Collegiate Athletic Association is not a governmental entity, enhancing the NCAA's powers by exempting it from constitutional guarantees that governments must act according to due process of law. A dichotomy between the abilities of various universities to implement NCAA penalties is discussed.

Levin, Sandy. "Teaching Criminal Law." *History and Social Science Teacher* 24 (Winter 1989): 66-69. EJ 383 112.

The article presents learning activities and resources for teaching senior level criminal law courses. Topics covered include arrest, search and seizure, bail, trial procedures, sentencing, and prisons. One objective is to encourage students to address societal issues.

Lincoln, Eugene A. "Mandatory Urine Testing for Drugs in Public Schools and the Fourth Amendment: Some Thoughts for School Officials." *Journal of Law and Education* 18 (Spring 1989): 181-88. EJ 392 024.

In 1985 the United States Supreme Court concluded that the Fourth Amendment's prohibition against unreasonable searches and seizures applies to public school officials. The article offers some hypothetical examples for public school officials to consider regarding mandatory urine testing and the reasonable suspicion standard.

Marshall, Thurgood. "The Evolving Constitution." *Update on Law-Related Education* 11 (Fall 1987): 3; 48. EJ 360 035.

The article argues that bicentennial celebrations of the U.S. Constitution should be focused on struggles throughout the life of the document rather than the "miracle" of its birth. The article illustrates this point by reference to changes in the voting rights and citizenship for Black Americans.

McDonald, Frances M. "Technology, Privacy, and Electronic Freedom of Speech." *Library Trends* 35 (Summer 1986): 83-104. EJ 342 844.

The article explores five issues related to technology's impact on privacy and access to information—regulation and licensing of the press, electronic surveillance, invasion of privacy, copyright, and policy-making and regulation. The importance of First Amendment rights and civil liberties in forming a coherent national information policy is stressed.

McGovern, Judith C. "The Bill of Rights." *Social Studies Review* 27 (Fall 1987): 66-68. EJ 369 568.

The article presents a lesson which will help students understand the importance of the Bill of Rights in their everyday lives. The article outlines the procedures for a five-day teaching unit, assignment of a student project, and discussion of two problems dealing with freedom of expression.

Menacker, Julius. "Activist Conservation in the Driver's Seat: Supreme Court Erosion of Student Expression Rights." *Urban Education* 24 (July 1989): 199-214. EJ 394 549.

The development of students' rights to free expression is explored through a historical review of judicial decisions on the subject from 1943 to 1988. The analysis shows that student civil rights have been eroded by the Supreme Court while other types of civil liberties in education have been protected.

Moss, Lee A. "A Case Against Censorship of School Libraries." *Georgia Social Science Journal* 20 (Winter 1989): 4-6. EJ 395 867.

The article argues that parents and special interest groups should not be allowed to ban books from school libraries. The article suggests that an uncensored school library contributes to freedom of speech, freedom of thought, freedom to understand other cultures, and freedom to examine controversial issues. The article concludes that these freedoms contribute to helping children become informed adult citizens.

Nichols, David. "How Five (Partly True) Myths Can Help Teachers Teach about the Constitution." *OAH Magazine of History* 3 (Winter 1988): 31-37. EJ 374 159.

The article uses five myths about the Constitution of the United States to help students better understand the basis for and the ratification of this important historical document. Among the myths included are: 1) the heart of the Constitution is the Bill of Rights and 2) the Constitution was cre-

ated by reactionary commercial interests to maintain the status quo.

O'Connor, Karen. "The Impact of the Civil Rights Movement on the Women's Movement." *Update on Law-Related Education* 12 (Fall 1988): 34-37. EJ 380 984.

The article states that the civil rights movement served as a catalyst to women in working for their own rights. The article also points out that the American Civil Liberties Union (ACLU) Women's Rights Project, modeled after the National Association for the Advancement of Colored People (NAACP) Legal Defense fund, led the litigation battles for women's rights. Suggested readings on the subject are listed.

Phillips, James. "Is Drug Testing Constitutional?" *Update on Law-Related Education* 13 (Spring 1989): 14-16. EJ 392 955.

The article examines the role of the friend of the court, "amicus curiae", by discussing the filing of a brief in a drug testing case currently under consideration by the U.S. Supreme Court. The article explores the issue of drug testing for employment, suggests possible outcomes, and provides ten discussion questions for use with students.

Richmond, Douglas R. "Instructional Liability for Fraternity Hazing: *Furek v. University of Delaware.*" *West's Education Law Reporter* 50 (January 19, 1989): 1-8. EJ 383 886.

Institutional responsibility for hazing injuries was called into question in a Delaware Superior Court in the case of *Furek v. University of Delaware.* In ruling in the university's favor, the Court signaled that universities may move to eliminate hazing without unreasonable fear of creating institutional liability for hazing incidents.

Rodriguez, Kenneth, and Alita Letwin. "Developing Constitutional Literacy: Examining Concepts and Principles through Student Involvement." *Georgia Social Science Journal* 20 (Winter 1989): 15-22. EJ 395 869.

The article describes the National Bicentennial Competition on the Constitution and Bill of Rights, a Center for Civic Education project. It includes two lessons from the "We the People. . . ." text which focus on the U.S. Constitution as an instrument to protect individual freedom at the middle school level, and features the founding philosophies of the Constitution at the high school level.

Russo, Elaine M. "Prior Restraint and the High School 'Free Press': The Implications of *Hazelwood School District v. Kuhlmeier.*" *Journal of Law and Education* 18 (Winter 1989): 1-21. EJ 387 075.

In *Hazelwood School District v. Kuhlmeier* (1988) the Supreme Court held that school authorities did not violate students' First Amendment rights by censoring a high school newspaper. The article traces the history of the decision and contends that the Court has effectively curbed the role of the school newspaper as a student voice.

Sacken, Donald M. "Due Process in Student Discipline." *West's Education Law Reporter* 50 (February 2, 1989): 305-16. EJ 383 903.

The article discusses how the Sixth Circuit Court approved an expulsion process even though the student was "convicted" on hearsay testimony alone and denied the opportunity to confront and cross-examine witnesses. The explanation and rationale for the Court's decision is viewed against prior case law.

Scherer, Joseph, and Jim Stimson. "Supreme Court Decision Rekindles Debate over Handicapped Students' Rights." *School Administrator* 42 (August 1985): 19-20. EJ 323 651.

The article discusses how the Supreme Court denied fees for administrative hearings as well as court proceedings for parents of a disabled child who prevailed in court against a school district. Bills introduced in Congress by Senator Lowell Weicker (S.415) and Representative Pat Williams (H.R.1523) address the issue.

Seefeldt, Carol. "Perspectives on the Pledge of Allegiance." *Childhood Education* 65 (Spring 1989): 131-32. EJ 385 992.

The article presents various perspectives on public school children's recitation of the Pledge of Allegiance, and ways to turn this ritual into a meaningful act for those who wish to participate.

Shah, Dorothie C. "Individual Rights: Freedom of the Press." *Update on Law-Related Education* 13 (Spring 1989): 51-53. EJ 392 961.

The article outlines a lesson plan for discussing the civil rights of public school students and uses the U.S. Supreme Court decision in *Hazelwood School District v. Kuhlmeier* (1988) as a basis for discussing freedom of expression protected by the First Amendment. The article also provides materials for student use and detailed directions for implementation of the lesson.

Sorenson, Donna. "Introducing the First Amendment." *Update on Law-Related Education* 11 (Winter 1987): 25. EJ 351 632.

The article offers a lesson plan for teaching upper elementary and middle school students about the First Amendment.

Sparks, Richard K. "Before You Bring Back School Dress Codes, Recognize that the Courts Frown upon Attempts to 'Restrict' Students' Rights." *American School Board Journal* 170 (July 1983): 24-25. EJ 285 262.

The article suggests that courts will support school boards' dress codes if based on needs rather than opinions. Courts have affirmed that minors have constitutional rights. Hair length, clothing style, and beards may be protected by students' right to freedom of expression. Codes must be carefully written and consistent with schools' legitimate goals.

Splitt, David A. "Affirmative Action, School Law." *Executive Educator* 11 (October 1989): 11. EJ 396 517.

To pass the Supreme Court's "strict scrutiny" test and be held constitutional, an affirmative action minority-set-aside program must satisfy a two-part test. Remedies must address past records of local discrimination and be aimed only at specific groups victimized by such discrimination. Impacts on schools are assessed.

Sprang, Kenneth A. "Balancing Power and Liberty in the School." *Update on Law-Related Education* 11 (Winter 1987): 35-38. EJ 351 637.

The article presents a brief conceptual background on the First Amendment freedoms and due process. The article offers three case studies to help students explore the issue of balancing First Amendment freedoms with the governmental responsibility for the common good.

Starr, Isidore. "Great Constitutional Ideas: Justice, Equality, and Property." *Update on Law-Related Education* 2 (Spring 1987): 2-7. EJ 354 894.

The article examines the ideas of justice, equality, and property as they are represented in the Declaration of Independence, the U.S. Constitution, and the Bill of Rights. It discusses how these ideas affect the way public schools operate and the lessons educators teach or don't teach about our society. The article also includes ideas for classroom activities.

Starr, Isidore. "The Five Ideas of Our Constitution." *Update on Law-Related Education* 11 (Winter 1987): 3-5, 48-49. EJ 351 623.

The article identifies five great ideas of the Constitution as power, liberty, justice, equality, and property. The article focuses on how ideas of power and liberty are presented in the Constitution. It also discusses how people may exercise power through voting and public protest, and liberty through freedom of speech and press.

Stelly, Philip. "Okaying the Use of Metal Detectors Proves Easier than Actually Using Them." *American School Board Journal* 171 (March 1984): 47. EJ 294 969.

The article discusses legal problems of a policy permitting the use of metal detectors to search students suspected of carrying concealed weapons. A wholesale search policy was challenged as a violation of students' rights; therefore, the board adopted a selective search policy based on reasonable suspicion.

Stevens, Richard G. "Due Process of Law and Due Regard for the Constitution." *Teaching Political Science* 13 (Fall 1985): 25-35. EJ 330 538.

The article discusses the relation between the due process clause of the Fourteenth Amendment and the provisions of the Bill of Rights.

Tarr, G. Alan. "Civil Liberties under State Constitutions." *Political Science Teacher* 1 (Fall 1988): 8-9. EJ 383 025.

The article discusses "new judicial federalism" as the rediscovery of state bills of rights for protecting civil liberties and analyzes the differences in protection under state and federal bills of rights.

Tatel, David S., and Elliot M. Mincberg. "The 1987-1988 Term of the United States Supreme Court and Its Impact on Public Schools." *West's Education Law Reporter* 55 (Nov. 9, 1989): 827-45. EJ 383 943.

This report of the Supreme Court's 1987-88 term is organized by subject matter with summaries of the key cases the court decided, lower court decisions the Court refused to review, and decisions to be reviewed in the 1988-89 term. A list of all cases discussed, including case citations, is included.

Thomas, Stephen B. and Renne E. Weisbaum. "Legal Update—The Censorship of Library Books: *Board v. Pico*." *Texas Tech Journal of Education* 10 (Fall 1983): 189-93. EJ 288 997.

The Supreme Court's opinion is reviewed in a case that involved the Island Trees Union Free School District (New York) Board of Education's decision to remove ten books from school libraries. The Court did not reach a majority decision. Various justices' views on students' rights, censorship, and school board authority are discussed.

Vile, John R. "Religious Expression in High School Valedictory Addresses: *Guidry v. Calcasieu Parish School Board*." *West's Education Law Reporter* 53 (August 3, 1989): 1051-65. EJ 395 040.

The article summarizes court cases bearing on religion in the school setting and the use of the three-part "Lemon test" in Establishment Clause cases and examines a Louisiana District Court decision that affirmed the action of a school principal prohibiting a religiously oriented valedictory address.

Vos, Valerie. "Let Freedom Ring." *Social Studies* 78 (March-April 1987): 97-99. EJ 354 916.

This play, designed for grades four to six, is a reenactment of the Constitutional Convention of 1787. It shows how the proposals for equal representation, a governmental balance of powers, and the Bill of Rights led to the ratification of the Constitution.

Walter, Gail A. "Substantive Rights for the Developmentally Disabled: Conditions for Receipt of Federal Funds." *Journal of Education Finance* 8 (Fall 1982): 216-22. EJ 279 559.

The article discusses the U.S. Supreme Court decision in *Halderman v. Pennhurst State School and Hospital*, involving the rights of and treatment provided for residents in a Pennsylvania institution for the severely retarded, under the federal Rehabilitation Act, the Developmentally Disabled Assistance Act, the Bill of Rights, and a state law.

White, Charles. "Beyond the Bill of Rights." *Update on Law-Related Education* 11 (Winter 1987): 19-22. EJ 351 630.

The article examines the history and thinking of the Federalists and Anti-Federalists in order to explain the formation of the ideas which allow the U.S. Constitution to provide for an effective government without sacrificing vital individual liberties.

Wiltse, John C. "The Road Not Taken: Control of Speech in Non-Public Forums, a Comparison of *Kuhlmeier* and *Sinn*." *Journal of Law and Education* 19 (Winter 1990): 51-76. EJ 405 175.

This article analyzes two court decisions that defined responsibilities and rights of student journalists. Both cases held that the newspapers involved were not "public forums." The article suggests that the Supreme Court may once again have to address questions that were left unresolved by the majority opinion in *Kuhlmeier*.

Yeaton, Connie and Karen Braeckel. "The Bill of Rights." *Update on Law-Related Education* 11 (Winter 1987): 12-14. EJ 351 627.

The article presents a lesson designed to introduce students to the Bill of Rights. Students learn that their rights are protected, but that they must act responsibly. The lesson uses several hypothetical situations and a 1983 U.S. Supreme Court case involving the use of vulgar language by a high school student during an assembly speech.

Young, D. Parker. "Legal Issues Regarding Academic Advising: An Update." *NACADA Journal* 4 (October 1984): 89-95. EJ 322 301.

The increasing number of court decisions dealing with classroom and academic matters attests to the growing judicial sensitivity to students' rights in academic affairs. The advisers' job falls within this academic affairs arena, and therefore he or she needs to understand these legal issues.

Part VIII
Bill of Rights Bookshelf for Teachers

VIII

Bill of Rights Bookshelf for Teachers

The books in this select annotated bibliography pertain to the origins, enactment, and development of the federal Bill of Rights. Each book includes ideas and information that teachers should know in preparation for curriculum planning and classroom instruction. The books in this list are merely a few of the many outstanding books in print on various aspects of the Bill of Rights. However, they represent some of the best works that are also related to the contents of the social studies curriculum and the objectives of history and civics/government teachers.

Abraham, Henry J. *Freedom and the Court: Civil Rights and Liberties in the United States*. New York: Oxford University Press, 1988.

This is a penetrating analysis of the role of the federal judiciary in protecting and shaping constitutional rights and liberties. There is an excellent discussion of issues associated with the incorporation of the Bill of Rights through the "due processes" clause of the Fourteenth Amendment to the Constitution.

Alley, Robert S., ed., *James Madison on Religious Liberty*. Buffalo, NY: Prometheus Books, 1985.

Alley and other writers, including A. E. Dick Howard, Ralph Ketchum, and Robert Rutland, examine Madison's contributions to the constitutional right of religious liberty. There is an excellent chapter on the religious freedom debate in Virginia, 1784-1786, which led to the enactment of Jefferson's Statute of Religious Liberty. Madison's role in the passage of Jefferson's statute is discussed in detail in relationship with key primary documents.

Baer, Judith A. *Equality Under the Constitution: Reclaiming the Fourteenth Amendment*. Ithaca, NY: Cornell University Press, 1983.

This explanation of the roots of equality in America raises issues and alternative viewpoints. Key federal court decisions of the twentieth century are discussed.

Barnett, Randy E., ed. *The Rights Retained by the People: The History and Meaning of the Ninth Amendment*. Fairfax, VA: George Mason University Press, 1989.

This work includes several chapters by experts on the theories and issues associated with the ambiguous Ninth Amendment to the U.S. Constitution.

Barth, Alan. *Prophets With Honor: Great Dissents and Great Dissenters on the Supreme Court*. New York: Alfred A. Knopf, 1974.

There are case studies on six crucial Supreme Court decisions on constitutional rights, in which the dissenting opinions, years later, became the basis for reversals.

Berman, Daniel M. *It Is So Ordered: The Supreme Court Rules on School Segregation*. New York: W. W. Norton, 1966.

This case study is an excellent treatment of the judicial process in the landmark Supreme Court decision in *Brown v. Board of Education of Topeka*.

Berns, Walter. *The First Amendment and the Future of American Democracy*. New York: Basic Books, 1976.

This eminent scholar examines the origins and development in American history of First Amendment freedoms. He defines and comments on continuing issues about the meaning and application of these constitutional rights, especially the right to religious liberty.

Cox, Archibald. *The Court and the Constitution*. Boston: Houghton Mifflin, 1987.

This is an excellent history of the federal Supreme Court and its part in constitutional development, especially the nationalization of the federal Bill of Rights in the twentieth century.

Curry, Thomas J. *The First Freedoms: Church and State in America to the Passage of the First Amendment*. New York: Oxford University Press, 1986.

The roots of religious liberty in America are examined. Curry treats the issues and alternative views about religious liberty during the American colonial era and the founding period of the United States.

Friendly, Fred W. *Minnesota Rag*: *The Dramatic Story of the Landmark Supreme Court Case that Gave New Meaning to Freedom of the Press*. New York: Random House, 1981.

This is a detailed case study of the landmark Supreme Court decision of *Near v. Minnesota*, which expanded the freedom of the press through the "no prior restraint" rule.

Friendly, Fred W., and Martha J. H. Elliot. *The Constitution*: *That Delicate Balance*. New York: Random House, 1984.

There are 16 chapters about critical constitutional issues and landmark decisions of the Supreme Court about these issues. Bill of Rights cases and issues are highlighted.

Garrity, John A., ed., *Quarrels that Have Shaped the Constitution*. New York: Harper & Row, 1987.

Twenty case studies about landmark Supreme Court decisions are presented as dramatic stories in American constitutional history. Most of these cases are about constitutional rights.

Hall, Kermit L. *The Magic Mirror*: *Law in American History*. New York: Oxford University Press, 1989.

This work treats the history of the American legal culture and the law in the lives of citizens. It includes discussions of key constitutional rights cases and issues.

Howard, A. E. Dick. *The Road from Runnymede*: *The Magna Carta and Constitutionalism in America*. Charlottesville: University of Virginia Press, 1963.

A distinguished constitutional lawyer and historian traces the development of limited government, the rule of law, and civil liberties from medieval England to the founding period of the United States and shows connections, similarities, and differences in the constitutional traditions of England and America.

Hyneman, Charles S., and George W. Carey, eds., *A Second Federalist*: *Congress Creates a Government*. Columbia: University of South Carolina Press, 1967.

This volume includes primary documents on debates in the First Federal Congress, including debates that led to the enactment of the federal Bill of Rights.

Irons, Peter, ed. *Justice at War*. New York: Oxford University Press, 1983.

This is the story of the internment cases of Americans of Japanese descent. It includes interviews with people involved in these cases.

Irons, Peter, ed., *The Courage of Their Convictions*: *Sixteen Americans Who Fought Their Way to the Supreme Court*. New York: The Free Press, 1988.

There are sixteen case studies about Bill of Rights issues, the people who raised them, and the Supreme Court decisions that resolved them.

Kaminski, John P., and Richard Leffler, eds., *Federalists and Antifederalists*: *The Debate Over the Ratification of the Constitution*. Madison, WI: Madison House, 1989.

This collection of primary documents illuminates the basic issues and ideas about the nature of a free government, which divided Federalists and Antifederalists during the founding period. There is a section on the Federalist-Antifederalist debate about a federal Bill of Rights.

Kammen, Michael. *A Machine that Would Go of Itself*: *The Constitution in American Culture*. New York: Alfred A. Knopf, 1986.

Kammen examines the cultural impact on the United States of America of its federal Constitution and Bill of Rights. There is a chapter on public opinion and knowledge about the Bill of Rights.

Kammen, Michael. *The Origins of the American Constitution*: *A Documentary History*. New York: Viking Penguin Books, 1986.

This collection of primary documents includes information about the origins and enactment of the federal Bill of Rights. Especially useful are reprints of letters exchanged between James Madison and Thomas Jefferson on the subject of constitutional rights.

Kammen, Michael. *Spheres of Liberty*: *Changing Perceptions of Liberty in American Culture*. Ithaca, NY: Cornell University Press, 1986.

Kammen analyzes the changing idea of liberty in American history, from the colonial period to the mid-twentieth century.

Kluger, Richard. *Simple Justice*: *The History of Brown v. Board of Education and Black America's Struggle for Equality*. New York: Alfred A. Knopf, 1976.

This book presents the story of the struggle against segregated schools, with emphasis on the landmark Supreme Court decision in the "Brown" case of 1954.

Kukla, Jon, ed. *The Bill of Rights: A Lively Heritage*. Richmond: Virginia State Library and Archives, 1987.

This volume is a collection of essays on the constitutional amendments that constitute the federal Bill of Rights. Issues about the meaning and application of these constitutional rights are highlighted. The essays are written for a general audience in terms that the non-specialist can readily understand.

Laqueur, Walter, and Barry Rubin, eds. *The Human Rights Reader*. New York: New American Library, 1989.

This collection of primary documents, with commentaries by the editors and other experts, traces the global development of constitutional rights from origins in Western civilization to incorporation into documents of the United Nations.

Levy, Leonard W. *Origins of the Fifth Amendment: The Right Against Self-Incrimination*. New York: Macmillan, 1969.

This volume treats the events and issues that led to the constitutional right against self-incrimination.

Levy, Leonard W. *Emergence of a Free Press*. New York: Oxford University Press, 1985.

Levy details the origins of a basic constitutional right, freedom of the press, in political theory and practice. There is an emphasis on antecedents to the freedom of the press in England and during the American colonial experience. There is a chapter on freedom of the press issues associated with the Sedition Act of 1798.

Levy, Leonard W. *The Establishment Clause: Religion and the First Amendment*. New York: Macmillan, 1986.

Levy examines continuing constitutional issues, in historical perspective, having to do with the "Establishment Clause" of the First Amendment right to religious liberty.

Levy, Leonard W., Kenneth L. Karst, and Dennis J. Mahoney, eds. *Encyclopedia of the American Constitution*, 4 volumes. New York: Macmillan Publishing Company, 1986.

This is an excellent comprehensive work on the origins, creation, and development of the Constitution of the United States. Each of the constitutional amendments that constitute the federal Bill of Rights is discussed by a renowned expert. Each article is followed by a brief bibliography.

Levy, Leonard W., and Dennis J. Mahoney, eds. *The Framing and Ratification of the Constitution*. New York: Macmillan, 1987.

This volume includes chapters by different experts on ideas and events associated with the making of the U.S. Constitution. There is a chapter on the Bill of Rights by Robert A. Rutland.

Lewis, Anthony. *Gideon's Trumpet*. New York: Random House, 1964.

This is the story of the landmark Supreme Court decision of *Gideon v. Wainwright*, which expanded the rights of a person accused of a crime.

Lockard, Duane, and Walter E. Murphy. *Basic Cases in Constitutional Law*. Washington, DC: Congressional Quarterly, 1987.

This book includes basic facts, issues, and decisions in 31 landmark cases of the U.S. Supreme Court. Most of these cases pertain to constitutional rights.

Lutz, Donald S. *The Origins of American Constitutionalism*. Baton Rouge: Louisiana State University Press, 1988.

Lutz examines fundamental primary documents in the development of the American concept of constitutionalism, which is a key to understanding the related concept of constitutional rights.

Morgan, Robert J. *James Madison on the Constitution and the Bill of Rights*. New York: Greenwood Press, 1988.

This work examines the political thought of James Madison, which greatly influenced the framing of the Constitution and the federal Bill of Rights.

Murphy, Paul L. *The Constitution in Crises Times, 1918-1969*. New York: Harper & Row, 1972.

This book is a history of constitutional rights during times of social conflict and change during the early and middle parts of the twentieth century.

Powe, Lucus A., Jr. *American Broadcasting and the First Amendment*. Berkeley: University of California Press, 1987.

Powe discusses how the development of broadcasting in the twentieth century led to new First Amendment freedom of expression issues. The regulations of the Federal Communications Commission are analyzed and appraised.

Project '87 of the American Historical Association and American Political Science Association. *This Constitution: From Ratification to the Bill of Rights*. Washington, DC: Congressional Quarterly, Inc., 1988.

This collection of articles, reprinted from the Project '87 magazine, includes several excellent pieces on the making of the federal Bill of Rights and the nationalization of the federal Bill of Rights.

Rutland, Robert Allen. *The Birth of the Bill of Rights, 1776-1791*. Boston: Northeastern University Press, 1983.

This work is a masterful account of the key events, persons, and ideas in the creation of the federal Bill of Rights.

Rutland, Robert Allen, and Charles F. Hobson, eds. *The Papers of James Madison*, volumes 10, 11, and 12. Charlottesville: University of Virginia Press, 1977.

These three volumes cover the ratification debate, including arguments for and against a federal bill of rights. These documents, annotated by Rutland and Hobson, also cover Madison's successful campaign for a seat in the first U.S. House of Representatives and his role in the enactment of the federal Bill of Rights.

Schechter, Stephen L., and Richard B. Bernstein, eds. *Contexts of the Bill of Rights*. Albany: New York State Commission on the Bicentennial of the United States Constitution, 1990.

This work includes articles by Donald S. Lutz, John P. Kaminski, and Gaspare J. Saladino on the origins, enactment, and development of the federal Bill of Rights.

Schwartz, Bernard. *The Great Rights of Mankind: A History of the American Bill of Rights*. New York: Oxford University Press, 1977.

This work surveys the ideas, issues, and events that led to the American Bill of Rights, and it examines ideas and issues on the development of constitutional rights.

Schwartz, Bernard, ed. *The Roots of the Bill of Rights: An Illustrated Source Book of American Freedom*. New York: Chelsea House Publishers, 1980.

This five-volume set documents the development of the ideas of constitutional rights from the Magna Carta in 1215 to the federal Bill of Rights in 1791. This set includes a rich collection of important primary documents that contributed significantly to the contents and enactment of the federal Bill of Rights.

Sexton, John, and Nat Brandt. *How Free Are We? What the Constitution Says We Can and Cannot Do*. New York: M. Evans and Company, 1986.

This book raises and answers questions about the constitutional rights of citizens.

Urofsky, Melvin I. *A March of Liberty: A Constitutional History of the United States*. New York: Alfred A. Knopf, 1988.

This is a solid treatment of U.S. constitutional history. The author includes detailed discussions of important Bill of Rights issues.

Witt, Elder. *The Supreme Court and Individual Rights*. Washington, DC: Congressional Quarterly, 1988.

This volume provides a detailed treatment of principles and issues about constitutional rights. There is a discussion and comprehensive listing of Supreme Court cases on civil liberties and rights.

Part IX
Directory of Key Organizations and Persons

IX

Directory of Key Organizations and Persons

Included in this part are three major sections. Section One lists important national organizations involved in the study of the Constitution and Bill of Rights and law-related education. These national organizations develop curriculum materials and sponsor civic education workshops and institutes that foster the understanding of our constitutional form of government. A brief synopsis of each organization's mission is included.

Section Two lists by state key law-related education contact persons. A (S) next to a person's name designates the state coordinator for the Office of Juvenile Justice and Delinquency Prevention (OJJDP). This contact person is very important, in that he or she coordinates the involvement of national projects in local areas and is often a valuable resource for teachers looking for excellent curriculum materials. The national organizations affiliated with OJJDP are the American Bar Association (ABA), the Center for Civic Education (CCE), the Constitutional Rights Foundation (CRF), the National Institute for Citizenship Education in the Law (NICEL), and Phi Alpha Delta (PAD).

A (N) next to a person's name designates the state coordinator for We the People . . . Bicentennial Program on the Constitution and Bill of Rights co-sponsored by the Commission on the Bicentennial of the United States Constitution and the Center for Civic Education. This contact person is important because he or she coordinates the National Bicentennial Competition, its companion program, We the People, Congress and the Constitution, and the National Historical Pictorial Map Contest.

A (C) next to a person's name designates involvement with the Center for Research and Development in Law-Related Education (CRADLE). This contact person works with local teachers, administrators, and scholars to develop exciting teacher-tested K-12 lessons on law, the Constitution, and Bill of Rights. Educators are encouraged to submit original lessons to the CRADLE National Repository funded by the Commission on the Bicentennial of the United States Constitution.

Contacting state Law-Related Education persons can be helpful in discovering local LRE programs and national projects working within the state.

Section Three highlights addresses and key people in state Bicentennial Commissions. These organizations coordinate local efforts that celebrate the Bicentennial of the U.S. Constitution and Bill of Rights.

Section One: National Organizations Involved in Education on the Constitution and Bill of Rights and Law-Related Education

American Bar Association Special Committee on Youth Education for Citizenship (YEFC)
541 N. Fairbanks
Chicago, IL 60611-3314
(312) 988-5735
Director: Mabel McKinney-Browning
   Since 1971, YEFC has supported state and local development of inter-disciplinary programs in law-related citizenship education for K-12 grade students. YEFC acts as a national clearinghouse for LRE programs across the country. YEFC also sponsors the annual LRE Leadership Conference.

American Historical Association
400 A Street, SE
Washington, DC 20003
(202) 544-2422
Director: Samuel Gammon
Associate Director: James Gordon
   Founded in 1884, the association promotes historical studies, the collection and presentation of historical manuscripts, and the dissemination of historical research. The oldest and largest historical society in the United States, its membership includes over 14,000 historians, professors, teachers, and administrators.

American Political Science Association

1527 New Hampshire Avenue, NW
Washington, DC 20036
(202) 483-2512
Director: Catherine Rudder
Director, Division of Education: Sheilah Mann

The association sponsors educators in their efforts in research, teaching, and professional development. The organization, founded in 1903, is associated with a number of civic education publications and projects.

Anti-Defamation League of B'nai B'rith

823 United Nations Plaza
New York, NY 10017
(212) 490-2525
Director: Abraham Foxman

For more than three-quarters of a century, the ADL has dedicated itself to translating the ideals of America into reality. The ADL has attempted to secure "justice and fair treatment for all citizens alike," and has worked to improve intercultural understanding in America. The ADL funds a number of civic education programs and produces numerous curriculum materials, many of which focus on the Bill of Rights.

Center for Civic Education/Law in a Free Society (CCE/LFS)

5146 Douglas Fir Road
Calabasas, CA 91302
(818) 340-9320
Director: Charles N. Quigley

The Center, founded in 1969, develops curriculum that helps students increase their understanding of American legal institutions and develop effective citizenship skills. The Center prepares classroom materials, teacher training materials, and services for school systems wishing to develop civic education programs. The Center also coordinates the National Bicentennial Competition on the U.S. Constitution and Bill of Rights and the National Historical Pictorial Map Contest.

Center for Research and Development in Law-Related Education (CRADLE)

Wake Forest University School of Law
Box 7206, Reynolda Station
Winston-Salem, NC 27109
(919) 761-5872
Director: Julia Hardin

CRADLE was established in 1983 for the purpose of encouraging individuals who wish to research or develop civic education programs. It has received federal funding to develop a national clearinghouse for materials relating to the Bicentennial of the U.S. Constitution and Bill of Rights and other law-related curriculum. CRADLE also sponsors yearly summer institutes.

Close Up Foundation

44 Canal Center Plaza
Alexandria, VA 22314
(703) 706-3300
President: Stephen A. Janger

The organization encourages responsible participation in the democratic process through educational programs in government and citizenship. The Foundation is committed to developing new and better ways for young people, teachers, and citizens of all ages to gain a practical understanding of how public policy affects their lives and how individual and collective efforts affect public policy. By increasing civic involvement, promoting civic achievement, and developing civic awareness, Close Up's diverse programs help strengthen a nation's most valuable resource, its citizens.

Commission on the Bicentennial of the U.S. Constitution

808 Seventeenth Street, NW
Washington, D.C. 20006
(202) 872-1787
Chairman: Former U.S. Supreme Court Chief Justice Warren E. Burger
Director: Herbert M. Atherton

The Commission was established by Congress to direct and encourage constitutional awareness activities during the five-year bicentennial commemorative period, 1987-1991. The Commission sponsors many national programs including the National Bicentennial Competition on the Constitution and the Bill of Rights and the National Historical Pictorial Map Contest. Many state programs have developed local projects funded through the Commission.

Constitutional Rights Foundation (CRF)

601 S. Kingsley Drive
Los Angeles, CA 90005
(213) 487-5590
Director: Todd Clark

Chicago Office of the CRF

Suite 1700, 407 South Dearborn
Chicago, IL 60605
(312) 663-9057
Director: Carolyn Pereira

This private, non-profit organization has been developing programs on a broad range of civic education topics for more than twenty-five years. Curriculum materials are available for elementary and secondary students for government, U.S. history, international affairs, geography, law courses, and English as a second language (ESL).

Council for the Advancement of Citizenship (CAC)

1200 18th Street NW, Suite 302
Washington, D.C. 20009
(202) 857-0580
Director: John H. Buchanan, Jr.

An umbrella for seventy citizenship programs throughout the country, CAC was founded in 1981 to foster and increase public awareness about citizenship education and to encourage the study of citizenship. Current projects include the Bicentennial Leadership Project, a series of teacher workshops on developing ways to teach the Constitution, and the Civitas Project, a citizenship program for elementary and secondary students.

ERIC/ChESS
2805 East Tenth Street
Suite 120
Bloomington, Indiana 47408
(812) 855-3838
Director: John J. Patrick

ERIC/ChESS is a clearinghouse for Social Studies/Social Science educational materials. ERIC provides ready access to educational documents through its information and retrieval system. Among these materials are curriculum guides, teaching units, descriptions of innovative programs, bibliographies, articles, and research reprints. Customized searches of the ERIC database are conducted for a small fee. Contact the ERIC/ChESS User Services Coordinator, Vickie Schlene.

The Institute of Bill of Rights Law
Marshall-Wythe School of Law
The College of William and Mary
Williamsburg, VA 23185
(804) 221-3810
Director: Rodney Smolla

The institute was established at William and Mary in 1982 to support research and education on the Constitution and Bill of Rights. One of the principal missions of the Institute is to facilitate interaction between the professions of law and journalism. Today the Institute is a dynamic center for mediating the past and the future, making debate over the meaning of the Bill of Rights relevant to policy conflicts in the modern world.

The Jefferson Foundation
1529 18th St., N.W.
Washington, D.C. 20036
(202) 234-3688
Director: Mary Kennedy

The Foundation is a private, non-profit organization dedicated to bringing alive the Constitution. It has designed the "Jefferson Meeting" on the Constitution, a discussion for students and adults on various aspects of the Constitution.

National Archives and Records Administration
7th and Pennsylvania Avenue, NW
Washington, DC 20408
(202) 501-5215
Archivest of the United States: Don W. Wilson

The Archives produces a variety of educational packets related to the Constitution and Bill of Rights designed for high school classroom use.

National Association for Mediation in Education (NAME)
525 Amity Street
Amherst, MA 01002
(413) 545-2462
Director: Annette Townley

NAME is an organization of school officials, teachers, community mediation project staff, university and law professors, law-related education specialists, and staff of educational organizations from across the country interested in working with conflict resolution programs in schools and universities. The goals of NAME are to provide a central clearinghouse on mediation in education and to disseminate information on mediation in the schools. NAME sponsors a bi-monthly newsletter, development of resource materials, and national conferences.

National Council for the Social Studies (NCSS)
301 Newark Street, N.W.
Washington, D.C. 20016
(202) 966-7840
Director: Frances Haley

NCSS is a national organization for social studies teachers. Its annual conference and *Social Education* magazine for teachers often include civic education topics.

Note: Teachers are encouraged to contact state councils for the Social Studies.

National Institute for Citizen Education in the Law (NICEL)
711 G Street, S.E.
Washington, D.C. 20003
(202) 546-6644
FAX: (202) 546-6649
Directors: Jason Newman, Edward L. O'Brien

NICEL is a non-profit organization dedicated to fostering widespread understanding of the law and the legal system. NICEL staff offers teacher workshops, coordinates a course for law students to teach in secondary schools entitled "Street Law", educates teens on crime prevention, and develops a variety of civic education classroom materials.

National Training and Dissemination Program (NTDP)
711 G Street, SE
Washington, D.C. 20003
(202) 546-6644
Director: Lee Arbetman

NTDP coordinates delinquency prevention training for teachers, administrators, and law enforcement officers provided by five national civic education programs with funding from the national Office of Juvenile Justice and Delinquency Prevention (OJJDP).

Office of Juvenile Justice and Delinquency Prevention (OJJDP)
633 Indiana Avenue, NW
Washington, D.C. 20531
(202) 307-5940
Director: Robert W. Sweet, Jr.
   OJJDP funds a variety of Law-Related Education programs aimed at delinquency prevention, most recently in the area of drug-focused education.

Phi Alpha Delta (PAD) Public Service Center
7315 Wisconsin Avenue, Suite 325E
Bethesda, MD 20814
(301) 986-9406
Director: Robert C. Redding
   The Center is an affiliate of the PAD fraternity and administers PAD's law-related education program. It publishes civic education and delinquency prevention material and supports school and community LRE projects, with a focus on community resources.

Social Science Education Consortium (SSEC)
3300 Mitchell Lane
Boulder, CO 80301-2272
(303) 492-8154
FAX: (303) 449-3925
Director: James Giese
   SSEC is a private, non-profit educational foundation devoted to research on all aspects of social studies, including law-related education. The Consortium also acts as a clearinghouse for a variety of civic education curricula.

Social Studies Development Center (SSDC)
Indiana University
2805 East Tenth Street, Suite 120
Bloomington, IN 47408
(812) 855-3838
Director: John J. Patrick
   SSDC conducts programs and projects in the social studies and houses the ERIC Clearinghouse for Social Studies/Social Science Education. The center also develops curriculum materials that foster a better understanding and appreciation of our constitutional heritage. The Center includes the Indiana Program for Law-Related Education, which is directed by Robert S. Leming.

Section Two: Law-Related Education Contacts

Alabama
   Thelma Brazewell
   Administrative Office of the Courts
   817 South Court Street
   Montgomery, AL 36130
   (205) 834-7990

   Jan Loomis (S)
   Executive Director
   Alabama Center for Law and Civic Education
   Cumberland School of Law
   800 Lakeshore Drive
   Birmingham, AL 35229
   (205) 870-2701

   David W. Sink, Professor (N)
   University of Alabama at Birmingham
   Political Science and Public Affairs
   UAB Station
   Birmingham, AL 35294
   (205) 934-9679

Alaska
   Marjorie Gorsuch (S) (N)
   Curriculum Specialist Social Studies
   Alaska Dept. of Education
   P.O. Box F
   801 W. 10th Street
   Juneau, AK 99811
   (907) 465-2841

   Deborah O'Regan
   Alaska Bar Association
   P.O. Box 100279
   Anchorage, AK 99510
   (907) 272-7469

American Samoa
   Teresa Stanley, Specialist, (N)
   Division of Curriculum & Instruction
   Department of Education
   American Samoan Government
   Pago Pago, AS 96799
   (684) 633-1246

Arizona
   Diana Iglesias,
   Arizona Center for Law-Related Education
   Arizona Bar Foundation;
   South Regional Office
   177 N. Church Ave.
   #101
   Tucson, AZ 85701
   (602) 623-8258

   Don Nordlund, Program Consultant (N)
   8433 E. Angus Drive
   Scottsdale, AZ 85251
   (602) 946-8026

Linda Rando (S)
Arizona Center for Law-Related Education
Arizona Bar Foundation
363 North First Avenue
Phoenix, AZ 85003
(602) 252-4804

Arkansas

Judy Butler (N)
Social Studies & International
Education Specialist
Arkansas Dept. of Education
State Education Bldgs
Rm 405-B
4 State Capital Mall
Little Rock, AR 72201-1071
(501) 682-4395

Becky Thompson, Director
Criminal Law Education for Schools
400 Tower Bldg.
4th & Center Street
Little Rock, AR 72201
(501) 682-2007

Eric Weiland (S)
Executive Director
Learning Law in Arkansas, Inc.
Box 521
209 West Capitol, Suite #316
Little Rock, AR 72201
(501) 372-0571

California

Margaret Branson
Superintendent of Curriculum Services
Kern County Superintendent of School
Offices
5801 Sundale Avenue
Bakersfield, California 93309
(805) 398-3600

Roy Erickson
Program Specialist
San Juan Unified Schools
3738 Walnut Avenue
Carmichael, CA 95608
(916) 971-7139

Jack Hoar
Long Beach Unified School District
701 Locust Avenue
Long Beach, California 90813
(213) 436-9931, Ext. 1288

Joy Maskin
Joe Maloney (S) (N)
Citizenship and LRE Center
9738 Lincoln Village Drive, #20
Sacramento, CA 95827
(916) 366-4389

Lou Rosen
Center for Civic Education
5146 Douglas Fir Road
Calabasas, California 91302
(818) 340-9320

Colorado

Ginny Jones (N)
Social Studies Specialist
Colorado Dept. of Education
201 E. Colfax
Denver, CO 80203
(303) 866-6762

Barbara Miller (S)
Colorado Civic Legal Education Program
3300 Mitchell Lane, Suite 240
Boulder, CO 80301-2272
(303) 492-8154

Connecticut

Joani Byer (N)
Connecticut Law-Related Education
Project
Office of the Attorney General
110 Sherman Street
Hartford, CT 06105
(203) 233-1983 (H)
(203) 566-5374 (W)

Denise Wright Merrill, Coordinator (S)
Law-Related Program
State Dept. of Education
25 Industrial Park Road
Middletown, CT 06457
(203) 638-4217

Delaware

Lewis Huffman, Social Studies (N)
Supervisor
Dept. of Public Instruction
Townsend Bldg., P.O. Box 1402
Dover, DE 19903
(302) 736-4885

Kenneth A. Sprang (S)
Assistant Professor of Law
Widemer University School of Law
P.O. Box 7474, 4601 Concord Pike
Wilmington, DE 19803-0474
(302) 477-2133

Duane Werb, Director
Street Law Project
Delaware Law School
300 Delaware Avenue
P.O. Box 25046
Wilmington, DE 19899
(302) 652-1133

District of Columbia

Jim Buchanan, Program Consultant (N)
D.C. Center for Citizen Education
25 E Street, N.W., Suite 400
Washington, DC 20001
(202) 662-9621

Richard L. Roe
Program Director
D.C. Street Law Project
25 E Street, N.W., Suite 400
Washington, DC 20001
(202) 662-9615

Judy Zimmer (S)
Program Director
D.C. Center for Citizen Education
in the Law
711 G Street, SE
Washington, D.C. 20003
(202) 546-6644

Florida

Ron Cold, Coordinator
LEGAL Project
School Board Administration
Dade County Public Schools
1450 Northeast Second Avenue
Miami, FL 33132
(305) 376-1951

Karen Kelly
Public Interest Programs and Services/
The Florida Bar
600 Apalachee Pkwy
Tallahassee, FL 32301
(904) 222-5286

Annette Boyd Pitts (S)(N)
Executive Director
The Florida Law-Related Education Assn.
325 John Knox Rd., Ste. 104, Bldg. E
Tallahassee, FL 31303
(904) 386-8223

Maria Cedeno (C)
CRADLE Region 4 Coordinator
Curriculum Coordinator, Social Studies
Dade County Public Schools
2201 SW 4th Street
Miami, FL 33135
(305) 642-7555
(305) 444-2723

Georgia

Ann Blum (S)
Law Education Coordinator
Carl Vinson Institute of Government
University of Georgia
Terrell Hall
Athens, GA 30602
(404) 542-2736

Michelle Collins, Program Consultant (N)
412 John Hand Road
Cedartown, GA 30125
(404) 291-9660

Guam

James Szafranski, Specialist (S)(N)
Dept. of Education
P.O. Box 84
Agana, GU 96910
(671) 472-2383

Hawaii

Ray Conrad
Executive Director HCLEY
643 Kanaha Street
Kailua, HI 96734
(808) 262-0278

Jane Kinoshita (S)
Department of Education
189 Lunalilo Home Road
2nd Floor
Honolulu, HI 96825
(808) 396-2543

To Be Selected, Coordinator (N)
Dept. of Education
Office of Instructional Services
189 Lunalilo Home Road, 2nd Floor
Honolulu, HI 96825
(808) 396-2543

Idaho

George Gates, Assoc. Professor of
Education (N)
Idaho State University
Dept. of Education
Campus Box #8059
Pocatello, ID 83209-0009
(208) 236-2645

Patricia J. Mooney, LRE Coordinator
Idaho Law Foundation
P.O. Box 895
Boise, ID 83701
(208) 342-8958

Dana Weatherby (S)
LRE Coordinator
Idaho Law Foundation
P.O. Box 895
Boise, ID 83701
(208) 342-8958

Illinois

Denee Corbin, Director (N)
Social Studies Development Center
National Louis University
1 South 331 Grace Street
Lombard, IL 60148
(708) 691-9390

Diana Hess
Constitutional Rights Foundation
Suite 1700
407 South Dearborn
Chicago, IL 60605
(312) 663-9057

Steve Klein (S)
Constitutional Rights Foundation
Suite 1700
407 South Dearborn
Chicago, IL 60605
(312) 663-9057

Donna Schechter, Assistant Staff Liaison
Committee on Law-Related Education for
the Public
Illinois State Bar Association
Illinois Bar Association
424 South Second Street
Springfield, IL 62701
(217) 525-1760

Marsha Turner, Coordinator
Loyola Street Law Project
Loyola University Law School
One East Pearson Street
Chicago, IL 60611
(312) 372-7901

Indiana

William G. Baker, Attorney
Chairperson, Committee on Law-Related
Education of the Indiana State Bar
Association
1722 Memorial Drive
New Castle, Indiana 47362
(317) 529-9620

Robert S. Leming, Director (S)(N)(C)
Indiana Program for LRE
Social Studies Development Center
Indiana University
2805 E. 10th Street, Suite 120
Bloomington, IN 47408
(812) 855-0467

Iowa

Tim Buzzell (S)(N)
Center for LRE
Drake University
Des Moines, Iowa 50311
(515) 277-2124

Kansas

Mary Lou Davis (S)
Kansas State Department of Education
120 West 10th Street
Topeka, KS 66612-1103
(913) 296-7159 or 296-6659

Richard D. Leighty (N)
Education Program Specialist
Social Studies
Kansas State Dept. of Education
120 E. 10th Street
Topeka, KS 66612
(913) 296-4946

Kentucky

Bruce Bonar, Director (S)
Model Laboratories School
Eastern Kentucky University
Richmond, KY 40475
(606) 622-3766

Tami Dowler, Staff Associate (N)
Kentucky Education Assn.
1124 Hopi Trail
Frankfort, KY 40601
(606) 277-6934

Louisiana

William Miller (N)
State of Louisiana
Department of Education
P.O. Box 94064
626 North 4th Street
Baton Rouge, LA 70804-9064
(504) 342-1136

Wanda Anderson-Tate (S)
1 Galleria Blvd.
Suite 1704
Metairie, LA 70001
(504) 836-6666

Maine

Kay Evans (S)
246 Deering Avenue
University of Maine
School of Law
Portland, ME 04102
(207) 780-4159

Virginia Wilder Cross
Public Affairs Director
Maine State Bar Association
124 State Street
Augusta, ME 04332
(207) 622-7523

Rusty Willette, Program Consultant (N)
P.O. Box 155
Dover-Foxcroft, ME 04426
(207) 564-8351

Maryland
James Adomanis (N)
Social Studies Specialist for Gifted and
Talented
Anne Arundel County Schools
2644 Rida Road
Annapolis, MD 21401
(301) 224-5434

Bill Golden (C)
CRADLE Region 3 Coordinator
Morgenthaler High School
3500 Hillen Road
Baltimore, MD 21218
(301) 396-6496
(301) 265-6628

Beth Lindeman (S)
Citizenship/LRE Program for Maryland
Schools
UMBC/MP 007
5401 Wilkens Avenue
Baltimore, MD 21228
(301) 455-3239

Massachusetts
Nancy J. Kaufer, LRE Director
Massachusetts Bar Association
20 West Street
Boston, MA 02111
(617) 542-3602

Marj Montgomery (C)
CRADLE Region 1 Coordinator
12 Waban Street
Newton, MA 02158
(617) 552-7379
(617) 527-7055

Jean Sanders, Program Consultant (N)
Merrimack Education Center
101 Mill Road
Chelmsford, MA 01824
(508) 256-3985

Nancy Waggner (S)
Massachusetts Supreme Court
Public Information Office
218 Old Courthouse
Pemberton Square
Boston, MA 02108
(617) 725-8524

Michigan
Linda Start (S)(N)(C)
Michigan Law-Related Education Project
2100 Pontiac Lake Road
Waterford, MI 48328
(313) 858-1947

Minnesota
Jennifer Bloom (S)(C)
Center for Community Legal Education
Hamline University
School of Law
1536 Hewitt Avenue
St. Paul, MN 55104
(612) 641-2411

Roger K. Wangen (N)
International Education Specialist
Minnesota Dept. of Education
635 Capitol Square Building
550 Cedar Street
St. Paul, MN 55101
(612) 296-4076

Mississippi
Lynette McBreyor (S)
LRE Coordinator
Mississippi Center for LRE
Mississippi Bar Center
P.O. Box 2168
Jackson, MS 39225
(601) 948-4471

Melanie Henry
Mississippi Bar Center
P.O. Box 2168
Jackson, MS 39225
(601) 948-4471

Linda Kay
Social Studies Specialist
Mississippi State Dept. of Education
605 Walter Sillers Bldg.
550 High Street
Jackson, MS 39205-0771
(601) 359-3791

Charles Washington, Director (N)
John C. Stennis Institute of Government
P.O. Drawer LV
Mississippi State University
Mississippi State, MS 39759
(601) 325-3328

Missouri
Christopher C. Janku
LRE Field Director
The Missouri Bar
326 Monroe Street
Jefferson City, MO 65102
(401) 769-2347

Linda Riekes, Director (S)
Law and Education Project
St. Louis Public Schools
5138 Raymond
St. Louis, MO 63113
(314) 361-5500

Terry Taylor, Program Consultant (N)
415 East Washington
Kirksville, MO 63501
(816) 665-2727

Montana

Michael Hall (S)
Montana Law-Related Education Program
Office of Public Instruction
State Capitol, Rm 106
Helena, MT 59620
(406) 444-4422

Linda Vrooman Peterson (N)
Social Studies Specialist
Office of Public Instruction
State Capitol
Helena, MT 59620
(406) 444-3693

Nebraska

Janet Hammer
Administrative Assistant to the Court
Administrator
1220 State Capitol, #1214
Lincoln, NE 68508
(402) 471-3205

Tom Keefe, Director (S)(C)
CRADLE Region 6 Coordinator
Law-Related Education Program
Nebraska State Bar Association
635 S. 14th Street
P.O. Box 81809
Lincoln, NE 68501
(402) 475-7091

Dennis Lichty, Specialist (N)
State Dept. of Education
301 Centennial Mall South
P.O. Box 94987
Lincoln, NE 68509
(402) 471-2446

Nevada

Phyllis Darling (S)(N)
Curriculum Services
600 N. 9th Street
Las Vegas, NV 89101
(702) 799-8468

New Hampshire

Pat Barss
New Hampshire Bar
112 Pleasant Street
Concord, NH 03301
(603) 224-6942

Carter Hart, Jr., Consultant (N)
State of New Hampshire
Dept. of Education
101 Pleasant Street
Concord, NH 03301
(603) 271-2632

Sally Jensen Ricciotti (S)(C)
RFD 3, Box 197C
Old Route 175
Plymouth, NH 03264
(603) 536-4241

New Jersey

Sheila Boro
Director of Communications
New Jersey State Bar Foundation
1 Constitution Square
New Brunswick, NJ 08901-1500
(201) 249-5000

Arlene Gardner (S)
Director, NJ Center for LRE
634 Carleton Road
Westfield, NJ 07090
(201) 789-8578

Robert Flood (N)
Social Studies Supervisor/Media
Smith Administrative Center
East Brunswick Public Schools
1 Bonner Road
East Brunswick, NJ 08816
(908) 613-6762

Rebecca McDonnel
Institute for Political and Legal
Education
Education Information and Resource
Center
700 Hollydell Court
Sewell, NJ 08080
(609) 582-7000

New Mexico

Linda Hueter Bass
Executive Director
New Mexico Bar Foundation
P.O. Box 27439
Albuquerque, NM 87125
(505) 764-9417

Debi Johnson (N)
Project Director
New Mexico Law-Related Education
P.O. Box # 27439
Albuquerque, NM 87125
(505) 764-9417

Linda Rhodes (C)
CRADLE Region 9 Coordinator
9424 Avenida De La Luna
Albuquerque, NM 87111
(505) 475-7091
(505) 474-2434

Judith Stoughton (S)
Project/Program Director
New Mexico Law-Related Education
P.O. Box 27439
Albuquerque, NM 87125
(505) 764-9417

New York
James J. Carroll, Director
Project LEGAL
Syracuse University
712 Ostrom Avenue
Syracuse, NY 13244
(315) 443-4720

Michael Fischer, Associate (N)
Bureau of Social Studies Education
New York State Education Dept.
Washington Avenue, Room 312 EB
Albany, NY 12234
(518) 474-5978

Eric Mondschein, Director (S)
Wayne Kunz, Asst. Dir.
Law, Youth and Citizenship Project
New York State Bar Association
One Elk Street
Albany, NY 12207
(518) 474-1460

Thomas J. O'Donnell, Director
Project P.A.T.C.H.
Northport-East Northport UFSD
110 Elwood Road
Northport, NY 11768
(516) 261-9000, Ext. 284

North Carolina
Don Bohlen (N)
Social Studies Director
Greensboro City Schools
PO Drawer V
Greensboro, NC 27402

Julia Hardin, Executive Director (C)
Center for Research and Development of
LRE (CRADLE)
Wake Forest University School of Law
Reynolda Station, PO Box 7206
Winston-Salem, NC 27109
(919) 759-5872

Doug Robertson (S)
Division of Social Studies
North Carolina Department of Public
Instruction
116 W. Edenton Street
Raleigh, NC 27603-1712
(919) 733-3829

North Dakota
Phil Harmeson, Associate Director (N)
Bureau of Governmental Affairs
University of North Dakota
P.O. Box 7167
University Station
Grand Forks, ND 58201
(701) 777-3041

Deborah Knuth, Exec. Dir. (S)
State Bar Association of North Dakota
P.O. Box 2136
Bismarck, ND 58502
(701) 255-1404

Ohio
Beverly Stokes Clark (C)
Elementary Law-Related Education Program
Office of Social Studies
Cleveland City School District
6900 Harvard Avenue
Cleveland, OH 44105
(216) 475-6408

Patti L. Denney, Faculty Assoc. (N)
Mershon Center
Ohio State University
1387 Portage Drive
Columbus, OH 43235
(614) 457-8260

Elizabeth T. Dreyfuss
Street Law Program
Cleveland-Marshall College of Law
Cleveland State University
Eighteenth and Euclid
Cleveland, OH 44115
(216) 687-2352

Phillip A. Mattingly
Social Studies Supervisor
Secondary Social Studies
LRE Project
Dayton City Schools
4280 North Western Avenue
Dayton, OH 45427
(513) 262-3786

David Naylor, Executive Director
Center for LRE
608 Teachers College
University of Cincinnati
Cincinnati, OH 45221
(513) 556-3563

Deborah Hallock Phillips (S)
Executive Director
Ohio Center for LRE
33 West 11th Avenue
Columbus, OH 43201
(614) 421-2121

Oklahoma
Rita Geiger (N)
Social Studies Specialist
State Dept. of Education
Oliver Hodge Education Bldg.
2500 North Lincoln, Room 3-15
Oklahoma City, OK 73105
(405) 521-3361

Michael H. Reggio (S)(C)
CRADLE Region 8 Coordinator
Oklahoma Bar Association
1901 North Lincoln Blvd.
Oklahoma City, OK 73105 or
P.O. Box 53036
Oklahoma City, OK 73152
(405) 524-2365

Oregon
Marilyn R. Cover, Director (S)(N)(C)
Oregon Law-Related Education Project
Lewis & Clark Law School
10015 SW Terwilliger Blvd.
Portland, OR 97219
(503) 244-1181

Pennsylvania
Robert G. Crist, Professor (N)
Pennsylvania State University
1915 Walnut
Camp Hill, PA 17011
(717) 737-1896

Beth E. Farnbach (S)
Executive Director
Law, Education and Participation (LEAP)
Temple University School of Law
1719 North Broad Street
Philadelphia, PA 19122
(215) 787-8948

David Keller Trevaskis (C)
CRADLE Region 2 Coordinator
Law, Education and Participation (LEAP)
Temple University School of Law
1719 North Broad Street
Philadelpha, PA 19122
(215) 787-8949

Puerto Rico
Israel Irizarry, President (N)
Bayamon Community Private School
Box 8006
Bayamon, PR 00621
(809) 799-0580

Rhode Island
Henry F. Cote, Director (N)
Chapter I and Chapter II
Pawtucket School Dept.
Administration Building
Park Place
Pawtucket, RI 02860
(401) 728-2120

Robin Haskell McBee (S)
Rhode Island Legal Educational
Partnership
22 Hayes Street
Providence, RI 02908
(401) 277-6831 or 456-9259

Joyce L. Stevos
Social Studies Area Supervisor
Providence School Department
211 Veazie Street
Providence, RI 02904
(401) 456-9259

Theresa Watson, Associate Director
University of Rhode Island
Ocean State Center for Law and
Citizenship Education
22 Hayes Street
Providence, RI 02908
(401) 861-5737 or 277-3982

South Carolina
Jack C. Hanna (S)(N)(C)
Pro Bono Director
Law-Related Education Consultant
South Carolina Bar
950 Taylor Street
P.O. Box 608
Columbia, SC 29202
(803) 799-6653 or 799-4015

South Dakota
Marilyn Hadley, Professor (N)
School of Education
University of South Dakota
Vermillion, SD 57069
(605) 677-5681

Marvin Scholten (S)
South Dakota LRE Project
State Bar of South Dakota
112 14th Ave. South
Brookings, SD 57006
(605) 692-4498

Tennessee
Dr. Dorothy Hendricks (S)
Professor of Education
University of Tennessee
205 Claxton Building
Knoxville, TN 37916
(615) 974-2541

Bruce Opie
Tennessee Department of Education,
CI-103
Central Services Building
Nashville, TN 37219
(615) 741-7856

Dorothy J. Skeel (N)
Economics and Social Education Center
Peabody College
Vanderbilt University
Nashville, TN 37203
(615) 322-2871 or 322-8090

Texas
Hope Lochridge (S)(N)
Law-Focused Education, Inc.
State Bar of Texas
P.O. Box 12487
Austin, TX 78711
(512) 463-1388

Utah
Rulon Garfield (N)
Professor of Educational Leadership
Brigham Young University
Box 1, McKay Building
Provo, UT 84602
(801) 378-5076

Nancy N. Mathews (S)
Project Director
Utah Law-Related Education Project
250 East Fifth South
Salt Lake City, UT 84111
(801) 538-7742

Vermont
David L. Deen (S)
LRE Consultant
Vermont Bar Association
RFD 3, Box 800
Putney, VT 05346
(802) 869-3316

John C. Holme, Jr.
Vermont Bar Association
P.O. Box 100
Montpelier, VT 05602
(802) 223-2020

Kathleen DeSilvey (N)
Program Consultant
R.D. #2, Journey's End
Mendon, VT 05701
(802) 773-4177

Virgin Islands
Roderick Moorehead, Chairman (N)
Bicentennial Commission
RR2
10,000 Kingshill Road
St. Croix, VI 00850
(809) 778-1620 Ext. 123

Virginia
Helen Coalter, Program Consultant (N)
1313 Nottoway Avenue
Richmond, VA 23227
(804) 262-7579

Joseph O'Brien, Director (C)
Virginia Institute for Law and
Citizenship Studies
School of Education
Virginia Commonwealth University
VCU Box 2020
Richmond, VA 23284-2020
(804) 367-1322

Washington
Margaret Armancas-Fisher (S)
Univ. of Puget Sound
Institute for Citizenship Education in
the Law
950 Broadway Plaza
Tacoma, WA 98402-4470
(206) 591-2215 Direct
(206) 591-2201 Switchboard

Kathy Hand, Program Coordinator (N)
560 South 158th Street
Seattle, WA 98148
(206) 244-3463

Richard G. Moulden (C)
CRADLE, President
Chinook Middle School
2001 98th Avenue, NE
Bellevue, WA 98004
(206) 455-6218

West Virginia

Barbara Jones (N)
Social Studies Coordinator
West Virginia State Dept. of Education
B-330 Capitol Complex
Charleston, WV 25305
(304) 348-7805

F. Witcher McCullough
West Virginia Bar Association
P.O. Box 346
Charleston, WV 25322
(304) 342-1474

Thomas R. Tinder (S)
Executive Director
West Virginia State Bar
E-400 State Capitol
Charleston, WV 25305
(304) 348-9126

Wisconsin

Michael Hartoonian
Wisconsin Department of Public
Instruction
125 S. Webster St.
Box 7841
Madison, WI 53707
(608) 267-9273

Karen McNett (S)
Associate Executive Director
Wisconsin Bar Foundation
402 W. Wilson Street
Madison, WI 53703
(608) 257-9569

Tom Rondeau (N)
Program Consultant
Wauwatosa East High School
7500 Milwaukee
Wauwatosa, WI 53213
(414) 786-6438

Wyoming

Richard Kean (C)(N)
Cheyenne East High School
2800 East Pershing Blvd.
Cheyenne, WY 82001
(307) 635-2481

Robert C. Points
Wyoming LRE Project
College of Education
University of Wyoming
Laramie, WY 82071
(307) 766-5279

Jerome F. Statkus, Executive Director
Wyoming State Bar
P.O. Box 109
Cheyenne, WY 82003
(307) 632-9061

Section Three: State Bicentennial Commissions*

Alabama   Alabama Bicentennial Task Force, Governor's Office, State Capitol, Montgomery, AL 36130 (205/261-7182). Chairman: Honorable C.C. "Bo" Torbert, Jr. Contact: Dr. Anita Buckley, Executive Director.

Alaska   Alaska Commission to Celebrate the United States Constitution, State Department of Education, Public Information Office, P.O. Box F, Juneau, AK 99811 (907/465-2821). Chairman: John E. Havelock. Contact: Harry Gamble, Executive Director.

Arizona   Arizona Commission on the Bicentennial of the United States Constitution, Arizona Bar Association, 363 North 1st Avenue, Phoenix, AZ 85003 (602/252-4804). Chairman: Honorable Frank X. Gordon, Jr.

Arkansas   Arkansas Constitution Bicentennial Commission, Lieutenant Governor's Office, State Capitol, Little Rock, AR 72201 (501/682-2144). Chairman: Honorable Winston Bryant (Lt. Gov.) Contact: Charles Miller.

California   State of California Commission on the Bicentennial of the United States Constitution, 316 Alta Vista Avenue, South Pasadena, CA 91030 (213/256-7350). Chairman: Jane A. Crosby.

Connecticut   United States Constitution Bicentennial Commission for the State of Connecticut, c/o Old State House, 800 Main Street, Hartford, CT 06103 (203/522-6766 or 203/522-1216). Chairman: Ralph G. Elliot, Esq. Contact: Wilson (Bill) Faude, Executive Director.

Delaware   Delaware Heritage Commission, Carvel State Office Building, 4th Floor, 820 North French Street, Wilmington, DE 19801 (302/652-6662). Chairman: James R. Soles, Ph.D. Contact: Dr. Deborah P. Haskell, Executive Director.

District of Columbia   District of Columbia Bicentennial Commission, 1511 K Street, NW, Suite 738, Washington, DC 20005 (202/727-5753). Chairman: Ms. Teri Y. Dokes. Contact: Peter Share, Executive Director.

Florida   Florida Bicentennial Commission, Supreme Court Building, Tallahassee, FL 32399-1925 (904/488-2028). Chairman: Honorable Ben F. Overton. Contact: Jeffrey Jonasen, Executive Director.

Georgia   Georgia Commission on the Bicentennial of the United States Constitution, 4290 West Club Lane, NE, Atlanta, GA 30319 (404/262-2797). Contact: Helen Dougherty, Executive Director.

Hawaii   Hawaii Bicentennial Commission, Suite 1500, Pauahi Tower, 1001 Bishop Street, Honolulu, HI 96813 (808/522-5133). Chairman: Vernon F. L. Chair, Esq.

Idaho   No active Commission.

Illinois   Committee on Law-Related Education, Illinois State Bar Association, 633 North East Avenue, Oak Park, IL 60302 (708/383-9724). Chairman: Cheryl Niro. For Education Materials: Committee on Law-Related Education, Illinois State Bar Association, 424 S. Second Street, Springfield, IL 62701 (217/525-1760). Contact: Donna Schechter.

Indiana   Indiana Commission on the Bicentennial of the United States Constitution, Indiana State Library, 140 North Senate, Room 108, Indianapolis, IN 46204 (317/232-2506). Chairman: Honorable Randall T. Shepard. Contact: Pamela Bennett, Executive Director.

Iowa   Iowa State Commission on the Bicentennial of the United States Constitution, c/o State Historical Society of Iowa, 402 Iowa Avenue, Iowa City, IA 52240 (319/335-3917). Chairmain: Dr. Joseph Walt. Contact: Loren N. Horton, Coordinator, Bicentennial Projects.

Kansas   Kansas Commission on the Bicentennial of the United States Constitution, c/o Kansas State Historical Society, 120 West 10th Street, Topeka, KS 66612 (913/235-1787). Chairman: Honorable Frank Theis. Contact: Marjorie Schnacke, Executive Director.

Kentucky   United States Constitution Bicentennial Commission of Kentucky, Kentucky Academy of Trial Attorneys, 12700 Shelbyville Road, The Cumberland Building, Louisville, KY 40243 (502/244-1320). Chairman: Penny P. Gold.

Louisiana	Louisiana Commission on the Bicentennial of the United States Constitution, LSU Law Center, Baton Rouge, LA 70803 (504/388-8846 or 504/568-5707). Chairman: James L. Dennis. Vice Chairman: Michael M. Davis. Contact: Paul Baier, Executive Director.
Maine	Maine Commission to Commemorate the Bicentennial of the United States Constitution, The Maine Law-Related Program, University of Maine Law School, 246 Deering Avenue, Portland, ME 04102 (207/564-3466 or 207/780-4159). Chairman: Hugh Calkins, Esq. Contact: Kay Evans, Esq., Executive Director.
Maryland	Maryland Office for the Bicentennial of the Constitution of the United States, c/o Maryland State Archives, 350 Rowe Boulevard, Annapolis, MD 21401 (301/974-3914). Chairman: Dr. Edward C. Papenfuse. Contact: Dr. Gregory A. Stiverson, Executive Director.
Massachusetts	*Constitution Bicentennial Committee of Stoneham, 2 Harrison Street, Stoneham, MA 02180 (617/662-2059). Chairman: Mr. Paul E. McDonald.
Michigan	Michigan Commission on the Bicentennial of the United States Constitution, P.O. Box 30026, Lansing, MI 48909 (517/335-4460). Chairman: Morley Winograd. Contact: Dr. James McConnell, Executive Director.
Minnesota	Minnesota Commission on the Bicentennial of the United States Constitution, Vets Service Building, 4th Floor, 20 West 12th Street, St. Paul, MN 55155 (612/297-4217). Chairperson: Dorothy Molstad. Contact: Todd Lefko, Executive Director.
Mississippi	United States Constitution Bicentennial Commission of Mississippi, 2309 Parkway Drive, Tupelo, MS 38801 (601/842-7913). Contact: Margaret DeMoville, Executive Director.
Missouri	United States Constitution Bicentennial Commission of Missouri, States Capitol Building, Room 116-3, Jefferson City, MO 65101 (314/751-5938). Chairman: Honorable Albert L. Rendlen. Contact: Joanne M. Hibdon, Executive Director.
Montana	Montana Constitutional Connections Committee, Statehood Centennial Office, P.O. Box 1989, Capitol Station, Helena, MT 59620-1989 (406/444-1989). Chairman: Honorable Frank Haswell. Contact: Carolyn Linden.
Nebraska	United States Constitution Bicentennial Commission of Nebraska, 351 Jeffrey Drive, Lincoln, NE 68583 (402/466-4720). Chairman: Jack Schuetz. Contact: Lois Noble, Executive Director.
Nevada	Nevada Commission on the Bicentennial of the United States Constitution, 2501 East Sahara, Las Vegas, NV 89158 (702/486-4506). Chairman: Honorable John Mowbray.
New Hampshire	State of New Hampshire Bicentennial Commission on the United States Constitution, 10 Emerald Avenue, Hampton, NH 03842 (603/271-2169 or 603/926-3853). Chairman: Honorable Ednapearl F. Parr.
New Jersey	New Jersey Historical Commission, Department of State, 4 North Broad Street, Trenton, NJ 08625 (609/292-6062). Contact: Mary Alice Quigley, Director, Public Programs & Field Services. For Education Materials: Smith Administration Center, One Bonner Road, East Brunswick, NJ 08816 (908/613-6766). Contact: Mr. Robert J. Flood, Supervisor for Social Studies/Media.
New Mexico	For Clearinghouse Information Only: P.O. Box AA, Albuquerque, NM 87103 (505/842-6262). Contact: Michael L. Keleher, Esq.
New York	Council for Citizenship Education, "The Legacy Project of the New York State Commission," Russell Sage College, Troy, NY 12180 (518/270-2363). Contact: Dr. Stephen L. Schechter, Director.
North Carolina	North Carolina Commission on the Bicentennial of the United States Constitution, c/o FOCUS (Friends of the Constitution of the United States), 202 East Park Drive, Raleigh, NC 27605 (919/821-5206). Contact: Marianne Wason, Executive Director. Bob Geary, Assistant.
North Dakota	North Dakota Constitution Celebration Commission, Supreme Court of North Dakota, State Capitol Building, Bismarck, ND 58505 (701/224-2689). Chairman: Honorable Herbert L. Meschke. Contact: Lawrence D. Spears, Executive Director.

Ohio	Ohio Historical Society, 1982 Velma Avenue, Columbus, OH 43211 (614/ 297-2350 or 614/297-2354). Contact: Gary Ness, Director. Steve George, Assistant Director.
Oklahoma	Constitution 200, Tulsa Junior College, 909 South Boston, Tulsa, OK 74119 (918/587-6561 Ext. 172.) Co-Chairman: Joseph A. Blackman.
Oregon	Oregon Governor's Commission on the Bicentennial of the United States Constitution, Multnomah County Courthouse, 1021 Southwest 4th Avenue, Room 206, Portland, OR 97204 (503/ 248-3198). Chairman: Honorable Charles S. Crookham.
Pennsylvania	Commonwealth of Pennsylvania Commission on the Bicentennial of the United States Constitution, c/o Pennsylvania Department of Education, Arts and Sciences Building, 8th Floor, 333 Market Street, Harrisburg, PA 17126-0333 (717/783-1832). Contact: Dr. James J. Wetzler.
Rhode Island	Rhode Island Bicentennial Foundation, 77 Plain Street, Providence, RI 02903 (401/273-1787). Chairman: Dr. Patrick T. Conley.
South Carolina	United States Constitution Bicentennial Commission of South Carolina, Department of Archives and History, 1430 Senate Street, P.O. Box 11669, Columbia, SC 29211-1669 (803/734-8591). Contact: Mrs. Alexia J. Helsley, Director and Ben F. Hornsby, Jr., Assistant Director.
South Dakota	South Dakota Centennial Commission, State Capitol, Pierre, SD 57501 (605/ 773-4036). Chairman: Shelly Stingley. Contact: James Larson, Executive Director.
Tennessee	*Constitution Bicentennial Committee (Knoxville/Knox County), University of Tennessee, Room 3, Hoskins Library, Knoxville, TN 37996-4010 (615/974-2806). Chairman: Dr. Milton M. Klein.
Texas	*Texas State Bar Association, P.O. Box 12487, 1414 Colorado Street, Austin, TX 78711 (512/463-1388). Contact: Hope Lockridge.
Utah	No active Commission.
Vermont	Vermont Statehood Bicentennial Commission, 6 Church Street, Rutland, VT 05701 (802/775-0800). Chairman: William B. Gray, Esq. Contact: Carolyn Meub, Executive Director.
Virginia	Virginia Commission on the Bicentennial of the United States Constitution, Center for Public Service, Room 309, 2015 Ivy Road, Charlottesville, VA 22903-1795 (804/924-0948). Chairmain: Dr. A. E. Dick Howard. Contact: Dr. Timothy G. O'Rourke, Executive Director.
Virgin Islands	United States Constitution Bicentennial Commission of the Virgin Islands, University of the Virgin Islands, RR 02, 10,000, St. Croix, VI 00850 (809/778-1620). Chairman: Dr. Roderick E. Moorehead.
Washington	Secretary of State, Legislative Building, Stop Code AS-22, Olympia, WA 98504 (206/753-7121). Contact: John Dziedzic.
West Virginia	United States Constitution Bicentennial Commission of West Virginia, Cultural Center, Capitol Complex, Charleston, WV 25305 (403/348-0220). Contact: Ken Sullivan, Executive Director.
Wisconsin	Wisconsin Bicentennial Committee on the Constitution, Wisconsin Bar Center, Post Office Box 7158, Madison, WI 53707-7158 (608/257-3838). Chairman: Honorable Roland B. Day. Contact: George Brown, Executive Director.
Wyoming	Wyoming Bar Association, 500 Randall Avenue, P.O. Box 109, Cheyenne, WY 82001 (307/632-9061). Contact: Tony Lewis.

---

*Indicates no official State Bicentennial Commission in existence. Local Designated Bicentennial Community serves as an alternate "unofficial" contact.